❰❰ THE OX-BOW MAN ❱❱

WESTERN LITERATURE SERIES

Books by Jackson J. Benson

Hemingway: The Writer's Art of Self-Defense (1969)

The True Adventures of John Steinbeck, Writer:
A Biography (1984)

Looking for Steinbeck's Ghost (1989)

Wallace Stegner: His Life and Work (1996)

Wallace Stegner: A Study of the Short Fiction (1998)

Down by the Lemonade Springs: Essays on Wallace Stegner (2001)

The Ox-Bow Man: A Biography of Walter Van Tilburg Clark

THE OX-

❬❘❭❘❬❘❭❘❬❘❭❘❬❘❭❘❬❘❭❘❬❘❭❘❬❘❭❘❬❘❭❘❬❘❭❘❬❘❭

UNIVERSITY OF NEVADA PRESS

RENO & LAS VEGAS

BOW MAN

A Biography of
Walter Van Tilburg Clark

▶|⟨|⟩|⟨|⟩ JACKSON J. BENSON

Winner of the Wilbur S. Shepperson Humanities Book Award for 2004

*This book is the recipient of the Wilbur S. Shepperson Humanities Book Award,
which is given annually in his memory by the Nevada Humanities and the
University of Nevada Press. One of Nevada's most distinguished historians,
Wilbur S. Shepperson was a founding member and long-time supporter of both organizations.*

This publication is made possible in part by a grant from Nevada Humanities,
the state program of the National Endowment for the Humanities.

Western Literature Series
University of Nevada Press, Reno, Nevada 89557 USA
Copyright © 2004 by Jackson J. Benson
All rights reserved
Manufactured in the United States of America
Design and composition by Tag Savage
of Wilsted & Taylor Publishing Services

LIBRARY OF CONGRESS CATALOGING-IN-PUBLICATION DATA
Benson, Jackson J.
The Ox-Bow man : a biography of Walter Van Tilburg Clark /
Jackson J. Benson.
p. cm. — (Western literature series)
Includes bibliographical references (p.   ) and index.
ISBN 0-87417-589-5 (alk. paper)
1. Clark, Walter Van Tilburg, 1909–1971. 2. Authors, American — 20th century —
Biography. 3. Western stories — Authorship. I. Title. II. Series.
PS3505.L376Z56 2004
813'.52 — dc22   2004001834

The paper used in this book meets the requirements of American National Standard
for Information Sciences — Permanence of Paper for Printed Library Materials,
ANSI Z.48-1984. Binding materials were selected for strength and durability.
First Printing
13 12 11 10 09 08 07 06 05 04
5 4 3 2 1

For Julia Grace Michaels

❰❰ CONTENTS ❱❱

CONTENTS

≪ ILLUSTRATIONS ≫

ILLUSTRATIONS

❮❮ PREFACE ❯❯

WHATEVER HAPPENED TO Walter Van Tilburg Clark? The author of *The Ox-Bow Incident* and *The Track of the Cat*? For several decades he was one of our most famous authors — in demand as writer, speaker, and teacher of creative writing. More than this, he was probably the most celebrated of our writers about the West, if not starting, at least contributing mightily to the tradition of viewing the West realistically. He turned the "gun and gallop" popular Western on its head.

But something happened — something that stopped his writing career cold in its tracks at a time when he should have been at the height of his powers. What happened to the writer? And behind that, what, indeed, had happened to the man? His friends were mystified, his colleagues baffled, and most of all, the editors at his publishing house were not only puzzled but, as time went by, frustrated. He had been a writer of first rank, of great promise, and his editors at Random House had looked forward to publishing much more of his work.

There are many theories as to why Clark stopped publishing. One proposes that he gradually found more satisfaction in teaching than in writing, and since he cared little for fame, he preferred to stay in the trenches rather than climb onto the stage. He had taught in high school, college, and graduate school, and was, according to his students, one of the most gifted and devoted teachers of his time. Many students who had him as a teacher fifty or more years ago remember him with fondness and gratitude. Clark was particularly proud of his teaching, more often identifying himself as a teacher than as a writer, and he thought of the hundreds of students he taught over the years as his legacy. At least four hundred of his creative writing students had their works published.

But as I interviewed relatives and friends, I began to realize that there was one thing that defined him above all: he was a westerner. He was a westerner in dress, in his choice of liquor, in his devotion to western history and landscape, and in the stories he told. He might tell them to friends at a bar in a local saloon, to the classes he taught, to his family around the dinner table, or to the rest of us in the books that he wrote and published. He was an inveterate storyteller, a teller of western tales. When invited to speak at a literary conference, rather than talking abstractly about theory, he would tell the story of a colorful madame in Virginia City or a miner trapped by a cave-in hundreds of feet underground. He was fascinated by the lives of real cowboys and prospectors (versus the myths and movies), by old western towns, and was most alive breathing, moving, and looking in the outdoors. He loved the mountains of the eastern Sierra Nevada but was even more at home in the desert, and when teaching duties took him to one place or another around the country, he missed it terribly.

But he didn't start out in the West. He was born on August 3, 1909, in a log cabin, not on the slopes of the Sierra Nevada but in the woods on the shore of Toddy Pond, outside the small farming community of West Orland, Maine. Just about as far east as you could get. He spent his first few years in the New York area while his father worked in New York City. But it was as if the writer's life really started with the family's move to Reno when he was eight. In Clark's autobiographical novel, *The City of Trembling Leaves*, the story begins with the young boy, his counterpart, in Reno; there is no mention of New York. With the boy born in the East moving to the West, I am reminded of the reverse being true of Robert Frost, who was born and lived his first years in San Francisco before moving to New Hampshire. No poet's work became more representative of New England than that of Robert Frost, and no prose writer's fiction more representative of the Far West than that of Walter Clark.

《 ACKNOWLEDGMENTS 》

I AM IN DEBT TO THE MANY PEOPLE who gave of their time to talk or write to me about Walter Clark — his relatives, colleagues, students, and friends. I have listed and thanked them individually as sources in my documentation at the end of the book. The person above all to whom I am grateful is Walter Clark's son, Robert Morse Clark, who gave his permission for this biography and who provided much invaluable information and over a period of years was always willing to help. My thanks also to other members of the family, Barbara Clark Salmon, David Chism, and George E. Lowe.

Several libraries provided help. I owe an enormous debt of gratitude to the librarians at the Special Collections department at the Mackay Library, University of Nevada, Reno. Most of Walter Clark's letters and manuscripts are deposited there, and the librarians at Special Collections, Susan Searcy and Jacquelyn K. Sundstrand, spent much time guiding me through the extensive collection. I was able to consult other Clark letters through the

ACKNOWLEDGMENTS

generosity of the libraries at Utah State University, Columbia University, and Brown University. Special Collections at the Library of the University of Vermont provided Clark's M.A. thesis on Robinson Jeffers.

Over several years Katherine Shumate provided research help, digging up materials that proved invaluable during the course of writing the manuscript. Fiona Becker took on the difficult job of transcribing both my interview tapes and typing many of Clark's handwritten letters. James H. Maguire deserves my thanks for getting me started on the biography and providing some preliminary materials to get me on track. And during the writing of the biography, I depended a great deal on pioneering discussions of Clark, his life and work, by Charlton Laird, Robert Gorrell, and Max Westbrook.

《 THE OX-BOW MAN 》

CHAPTER ONE

FROM MAINE TO NEVADA

YES, THE WRITER WHO DEARLY LOVED the West, its land-scape and history, and who wrote one of its signature novels, was born in the East. He is the writer who is remembered by many as the one who made the western novel real. Walter Van Tilburg Clark did not talk much about his childhood in the East to either family or friends, and no one who witnessed it is still alive. So, most of the information about his early years comes from Clark himself in a short autobiographical sketch he wrote to send out in response to numerous requests from students for information about the author.

In that sketch he writes that he spent his first three years in a small upstairs apartment on Amsterdam Avenue in New York City. Reflecting on that period, he writes that "[I] hated the city — I still hate cities, too many people elbowing other people in too little space, with nothing else alive except in a zoo or on a leash (which is not really being alive)." The only things that made the

Interior of Clark house in West Nyack, New York.
Courtesy of Robert M. Clark

city tolerable were walks in the park, Christmas displays in the department stores, and the fire engines going by at night. He remembers that

> they were still horse-drawn engines, three big dapple-grays abreast, sparks flying from the hooves and the tires on the cobblestones, and from the chimney of the pumper, and a spotted Dalmatian running under the rear axle. Magnificent.

Clark's children and his nephew have been able to reconstruct the family history and describe the characters of the writer's father and mother. The father, Walter Ernest Clark, was born in Ohio, the son of a Methodist minister. The minister died of yellow fever, leaving the family destitute. Nevertheless, Clark's father, in an act of will that was typical of him, put himself through school, earning a B.A. and M.A. from Ohio Wesleyan and then his Ph.D. from Columbia. He went on to a very successful career, first as a pro-

Clark house, West Nyack, New York.
Courtesy of David Chism

fessor of economics at the City College of New York, then as head of its Political Science Department, and finally as a university president.

Clark's father had a talent for investment and began to accumulate a substantial amount of money. In 1912 he purchased a large former farmhouse in West Nyack, New York, that an old photograph shows to have looked less like a farmhouse than a southern plantation mansion. Clark's father had a reputation for being rather severe and reserved. Although he was a loving father, he had a formidable presence. It is said by his descendents that he refused to have much to do with his children when they were infants, saying, only partly in jest, that he would socialize with them "only when they could carry on an intelligent conversation."

Clark's mother, on the other hand, following the Victorian pattern, was gentle and indulgent. She was born Euphemia Murray Abrams, daughter of a well-to-do Hartford, Connecticut, physician. She graduated from Cornell University and studied piano and composition at Columbia. With graduate work on the part of both parents, it is almost an understatement to say that the family was intellectual. And both parents had social consciences. Clark's mother gave up a possible career in music to do settlement-house work at Greenwich House in New York City, and Clark's father devoted himself to educating the young.

Walter Ernest Clark and Euphemia Murray Abrams were married in June of 1908 and Walter Van Tilburg Clark was born on August 9, 1909, the first of four children. The only two stories from his early childhood that the young Clark told his own children were about his struggle to release himself from his mother in order to gain some masculine independence. According to the practice of the time (reflecting the immense influence of *Little Lord Fauntleroy,* the perfect little gentleman), his mother allowed his dark, curly hair to grow to his shoulders and wanted it to remain at that length. At school age, Clark rebelled against this and was able to enlist his father in his behalf. The same pattern was repeated when the youngster wanted to graduate to long pants.

On the other hand, his mother was probably the greatest influence on Clark's early life. She had gentle consideration for all live things and was strongly connected to the fine arts, music, drawing, and literature. We might surmise that this was a culturally fertile household, giving an artistically diverse foundation to the eldest son. We do know that for a certain number of years, Clark was educated at home by his mother. We know that he started to learn to play a musical instrument, the violin, and learned to draw, as well as beginning early a reading program of serious literature. He would bring together all of this — his education in the arts, his reading, and his parents' social consciences — to his own writing. He came to look at the world around him as a painter or musician would, thinking of the processes of living not as events so much as a series of sensory experiences.

Walter Clark with his mother, Euphemia Clark, and his sister,
Euphemia Clark, on the porch at Clark camp, East Orland,
Maine, summer 1911. Courtesy of David Chism

V. T. Clark hated the city but, as one might suspect, loved his summers at the cabin in Maine, near the seashore and called "the farm." He found "lots of space and sky and weather, all sorts of things growing, wild and in gardens ... and fields, and all sorts of living things, domestic and wild, from tadpoles in the cow-pond to a huge, red bull." From the time he was five, he even had a little vegetable garden of his own. Clark went on to write in a brief autobiographical essay that "the deep interest in all kinds of life which I developed then [on the farm in Maine] has never left me."

From early in life he developed what today we would call an ecological sensibility — man was simply one animal among many, just part of a whole, not to be valued any more or any less. Each life

David Clark (Walter's brother), Walter V. T. Clark, and
Euphemia Clark (his sister) in West Nyack, New York.
Courtesy of David Chism

was to be considered sacred. Later as an adult, while teaching at the University of Montana, he would argue from this point of view with a colleague, Walter Brown. Brown thought that Clark didn't value humanity highly enough, and specifically, they disagreed about a story Clark had written called "The Indian Well."

In this story an old prospector comes to the well to rest and recover after a season of looking for gold in the hills of the Nevada desert. The well is a stone basin under a spring, and there is a small abandoned cabin nearby. The prospector comes with his donkey, Jenny, his only friend and companion, and takes up temporary residence. During one night, a mountain lion attacks and kills the donkey. Distraught, Jim Suttler, the prospector, sets up an ambush for the cat, night after night, until he is able to shoot and kill it.

It is not clear from the surface of the story that Clark, according to Walter Brown, thought that the killing of the cat was a terrible act. Brown argued that it was only natural: the story, in his view, was a love story — love between Jim Settler and his Jenny — and from a human point of view, the revenge could be seen as perfectly justified. One can read the story that way and be glad that the prospector gets satisfaction for his loss. However, if one looks carefully at what Clark does in the story, a different interpretation comes to the fore.

First, Clark adopts a flat tone and objective, distant approach to the telling of the story so that we are removed from the prospector and less likely to identify with him. Second, the author spends a good deal of space on setting up a natural environment at the well, which, although in the middle of the desert, is rife with animal and plant life. It is, in short, a complete, miniature ecosystem, and as the story states, one that has persisted for thousands of years. Man, the prospector, is the intruder, the unnatural ingredient. This is underlined in the story by the names of other temporary inhabitants scratched on the walls of the cabin. As allegory, the story suggests that it is man alone, of the animals, who kills out of emotion rather than the need for food. And humanity itself is but a temporary visitor on this earth. From this, Clark's point of view, the shooting was shameful and outrageous. Reflecting back on his life, Clark has written that as a teenager he did a lot of hunting and fishing, but he gave them up before he was twenty: "Learned then, and still believe, that living creatures are a great deal more beautiful than dead ones, and that only real physical need, as among the animals themselves, justifies killing."

But how natural for the human reader to join in with the prospector's emotions, no matter how objectively they are presented, and to justify mentally the prospector in his vengeance, and how easy for the reader to miss Clark's point. The question, as Brown would state it, is where are your sympathies, with humanity or with natural processes? Brown felt that Clark failed philosophically by his lack of allegiance to humanity.

Clark's point of view, as alien as it may seem to the sensibilities of many of us, is key to understanding his perspective on the world and humanity's place in it, as well as key to understanding his writings. Nearly everything he wrote shows humanity in a diminished role in respect to its high opinion of itself. And nearly everything he wrote places the emphasis on the environment and sensory appreciation of that environment. Writing for him was an art, an art intimately connected to the other arts, and his art was an appreciation of all life rather than a declaration of human primacy. And Clark even thought of what we normally call "inanimate objects" as part of that life, part of the whole that is governed by a unifying principle bringing harmony and wholeness to what we sense.

Commenting on his early education in the arts, Clark wrote,

> On farm, too, by way of my mother's piano, my father's fine
> story-telling and reading aloud to us, King Arthur, Robin
> Hood, Indian and frontier tales, Greek, Roman and Nordic
> gods and heroes, the Bible, much else, and the kind interest
> of a neighbor who was a painter, developed the love of read-
> ing and writing, music and art which have also continued.

The tales of King Arthur and the Greek, Roman, and Nordic gods and heroes that he speaks of here clearly had a profound effect on him, for he refers to them frequently in his writings. Tim Hazard, in Clark's autobiographical novel, *The City of Trembling Leaves,* often thinks in terms of Arthurian legend and Tristram and Isolde. (Clark's M.A. thesis at the University of Nevada was entitled "Sword Singer: The Tale of Tristram Retold—With an Introductory Essay Concerning Sources of the Tristram Legend.") The twelve-year-old in the novelette "The Watchful Gods" is, like Tim Hazard in *The City*, almost constantly aware of benevolent or angry gods and spirits around him in nature. It is this boy's way of thinking, obviously influenced by *his* father's storytelling and his reading (as Clark surely was by his father's storytelling and his reading). But this use of legend, gods, and heroes is also a way for Clark to invest the environment, indeed the universe, with a dimension beyond appearances and to connect everyday reality with the unconscious mind.

This investment, or seeing through appearances, is according to Clark precisely what the painter must do and the writer, as artist, must do. He quotes his close, lifelong friend, the artist Robert Caples, who wrote, "To be aware. To look with awareness. How long it takes to find that out. To look *with*, to look *for*, to look *through*, not to look *at*. To look every way except *at*." A key concept in Clark's life and work was that of experience — to experience places and people and in his writing to get the reader to experience the story. At a literary conference where he read his story "Hook," Clark commented that in order to write the story about a hawk, he had to get beyond just a description of the bird and begin to think like a hawk — and he wanted to persuade the reader to think like a hawk as well.

One must reach down and make a connection below the surface, in a process similar to what John Steinbeck's marine biologist friend, Ed Ricketts, called "deep participation." Clark did not even like cameras — as a writer he wanted to experience from within and remember from within. Critic Max Westbrook, in his book on Clark, has summed up the author's literary efforts as "quests in search of the long and ancient memory, efforts to restore the capacity of the unconscious to hear the archetypal voices of primordial reality."

V. T. Clark's efforts at art came early, and significantly, they were spread across several disciplines — and we are not talking here about a kindergarten child coloring in apples and beating on a tom-tom. Under a painter neighbor's tutelage, Clark worked with watercolors. He remembered his very first one, "a very wet and mingled water-color of the first football game I ever saw, which had excited me very much." He didn't remember his first poem, but his parents told him later that it was a quatrain about a pair of galoshes. During these early years in West Nyack, he wrote many

> very adventurous and very short short-stories, even serials of a distinctly cliff-hanging variety, all of which were "published" in a very local weekly paper, THE CLARK NEWS, to which I also contributed poems and illustrations.

When Clark was eight, his father was offered the job of president at the University of Nevada, Reno. He had a reputation as a good administrator and, of even more interest to the regents of the university, he was good at raising and managing money. Clark's father put this skill into practice almost immediately by insisting that in order for him to accept the job, he would have to get an eighteen-thousand-dollar-a-year salary (a very large amount in 1917, more than the governor of the state was making) and the university would have to build a home suitable to house the president and his family. Both conditions were met, and the family moved to Reno. Clark's father found a campus with only two buildings and a university that was unaccredited. He then went on to get the university accredited and put it on a sound financial basis, obtaining endowment money from several prominent Nevada families. The Mackay family had made its money from Virginia City mining and had retired to Long Island. Clark's father traveled many times to visit the family, and the university ended up with the Mackay Stadium and the well-considered Mackay School of Mines.

Clark's mother, in the meantime, organized a faculty wives group and arranged dinners for faculty from each department, and

*Walter on couch with cat, his sister, Euphemia, and his brother,
David, in president's house on the University of Nevada campus,
February 1920. Courtesy of Robert M. Clark*

there was at least one such dinner every month. The children, Clark's sister Miriam recalls, looked forward to these dinners because they received portions of the dessert, which were sent up to them in the dumbwaiter.

Walter E. Clark's children were not made to go to church or Sunday school. Instead, on Sundays the whole family would play tennis or basketball. Sometimes on weekends the family would go to Pyramid Lake with Colonel Ryan, of the university's Military Science Department, and his family. Miriam remembers waking in the night at Pyramid Lake to see a light in the next tent, smoke coming out of it, and the silhouettes of her father and Colonel Ryan playing chess.

In those days Reno was a railroad and college town, one that had not yet welcomed divorcées or high rollers (although there was a good deal of illegal gambling). "The Biggest Little City in the World," as it called itself, did have some tourist trade by its proximity to Lake Tahoe and the Sierra Nevada. The city had its rough district of saloons and bordellos and a bustling banking and commercial area, but for most residents it was a sleepy large town that housed the state's university. Except for the trains that came through on the transcontinental railroad at all times of the day and night, it was quiet and relatively pastoral and, surrounded by ranches and mining towns, had something of a frontier atmosphere.

Clark's autobiographical novel begins by describing Reno as a city of trees. "Such a city," the narrator tells us, "is drawing out of its alliance with the eternal, with the Jurassic Swamps and the Green Mansions." He goes on to say,

> In Reno, however, this universal importance of trees is intensified, for Reno is in the Great Basin of America, between the Rockies and the Sierras, where the vigor of the sun and the height of the mountains, to say nothing of the denuding activi-

ties of mining booms, have created a latter-day race of tree
worshippers . . . and Tim Hazard [the novel's protagonist]
is high in the cult.

Clark came to love Reno, which for him was a city of trees, and was
very upset when, in the 1950s, the First National Bank built its
building in the middle of the city at First and Virginia Streets, de-
stroying the view from the west looking down on the city.

For Clark the move to Reno was an opening out of his experience, both externally and internally. Although in a city, he nevertheless found himself surrounded by the wide, open spaces of the
Far West, and Reno was nothing like crowded New York City.
Life around him was more informal, more basic and relaxed. It was
a place where a young boy could get around to almost any place on
a bicycle. Clark began to attend elementary school, the Orvis Ring
School, named after a pioneer Nevada educator.

His eighth-grade teacher and the principal at Orvis Ring was a
woman named Libby C. Booth. Clark described her as "an eagle-
eyed, durable, devoted, strict and knowing old lady." He, in turn,
became devoted to her when he found out that she had come across
the plains in a covered wagon when she was only sixteen and had
fought off Indians beside the body of her new young husband,
whom they had killed. She made a lasting impression on Clark, although sometimes he suffered from her strictness. He remembered
he had to spend two hours doing algebra on the blackboard every
afternoon while the rest of the team was practicing football—and
he was, at eighty-nine pounds, first team left halfback.

He went on to play some football but mainly basketball in high
school, and basketball and tennis in college. Athletics would play
an important part in his life. He would coach high-school teams in
basketball and tennis, and he played pickup basketball until he
reached middle age and tennis until near the end of his life. As an
adult in a group, his conversation was usually on sports. He was an

enthusiast. He could lean against the refrigerator in the kitchen during a party, with glass in hand, and go on for hours about basketball, to the point that friends would gradually drift away. Heart and soul were important to him, but the physical dimension of life had an importance for him as well.

In high school, in addition to sports, he participated in dramatics, publications, and debating. In later years he would be the high-school teacher who put on and directed the school plays. As far as academics were concerned, he recalled that by his junior year of high school, he "even began to make good grades in subjects other than English and art, where everything just naturally went happily." In addition to his studies and all of his extracurricular activities, he spent two hours every afternoon practicing finger exercises on his violin—a chore he loved but found difficult, since the rest of the gang would be playing baseball or football on the lawn outside. He had incredible energy even for a youngster. But though he spent a lot of time on his studies and school activities indoors, he became an outdoor person as well, spending weekends and vacations hiking and camping in the Sierras or the region east of Reno. Walking, if he was trapped in town, or hiking, if he had access to the outdoors, became constant activities throughout his life, even up to a few months before his death. During his high-school years, he was an active hunter and fisherman.

Walter Clark was a handsome teenager who would become a handsomer adult. Nevertheless, while he claimed to have fallen in love at least two dozen times during these school years, only a couple of the objects of his adoration knew about it, and "the knowledge did not seem to make them happy." To fall in love within the Courtly Love tradition, to suffer and adore from afar, is a persistent pattern in the behavior of Tim Hazard in *The City of Trembling Leaves*; indeed, this autobiographical novel might well be called a love story, or a series of love stories.

It was during Clark's high-school years that he met the person who would become his closest friend, Robert Caples. And to understand Clark, you have to know something about Caples and the relationship between the two men, a relationship that developed and continued throughout their lifetimes. The two had much in common. We don't know how they met, but in Clark's autobiographical novel, we see the meeting between Tim Hazard and the counterpart of Caples, Lawrence Black. The described meeting may be a true account, but if not, it still says a great deal about the state of mind and heart of both Clark and Caples. Black is depicted as quiet, thoughtful, and precociously artistic. By contrast with Hazard, who is open, voluble, and often blundering, Black is deep, and although friendly, almost mysterious in the way he keeps his own counsel.

In the novel Tim and Lawrence meet on the beach at Pyramid Lake, northeast of Reno. In life this location would have special meaning for Clark and Caples. The two would frequently camp there, not to hunt or fish, but to hike, swim, and meditate — and above all, to play chess. It became a magical place for them, haunted and haunting, a place that gave off a sense of timelessness, a place that had been much the same since prehistory. Later in life, Caples was mistakenly referred to as a "Paiute Indian artist" (probably because Indians were favorite subjects for his art). He responded in a letter:

> Well, maybe the next life 'round — with the waters of Pyramid
> where they were when I was an awestruck teenager. Lord, but
> that first view of that blue water was an event. Such unexpected
> beauty really hurt. It was like being struck with the sky.

We see this special meaning developed in the novel.

The fictional counterparts of Clark and Caples are somewhat younger than the two boys could have been in life. Tim is walking along the edge of the lake and decides to go up from the beach to a sun shelter built by the Indians out of tree boughs. Several things have happened that have upset him, and he decides that he will sit under the shelter and pray and then take a swim to wash away his unhappiness. (Clark's fictional children have rich spiritual lives and often perform rituals.)

As he approaches the shelter, he encounters a boy sitting under it cross-legged on the ground. He thinks at first that the boy is an Indian but then sees that he is a white boy

> probably about his own age, but even thinner, so that all his ribs showed distinctly, and burned even darker. He had black hair, like an Indian, but his eyes were larger and rounder than Indians' eyes, and a strip of white skin showed on the thigh where his shorts were pulled up. The shorts were all he had on. The boy sat there and returned Timmy's stare seriously and calmly.

Tim sees that the boy is looking at a large desert tortoise in front of him. There is a bucket near the boy's right elbow, and on two old boards there is a mound of partially modeled clay. Lawrence, as his name turns out to be, is in the process of sculpting a turtle, using the tortoise as a model. He tells Tim, who has been singing something he has made up at the top of his voice as he walks along the beach, that he likes Tim's singing. At this point we have the pairing which is a reflection of the pairing in real life — Tim, the singer who becomes a composer, and Lawrence, the sculptor who becomes a painter. These artistic occupations are similar to Clark's starting out as a poet and becoming a fiction writer and Caples's starting out as a sculptor and ending up a painter.

Lawrence invites Tim to join him and use some of the clay he has gathered to make his own turtle. Tim feels "very clumsy, as he watched [Lawrence] dexterously reproducing the malformed flipper, leaning over the tortoise to look closely at the part he was working on." Tim decides to retreat and make some little turtles, babies, and they decide to put them together in a family. " 'Maybe we can fool the real turtle,' Tim said, laughing.... 'Maybe,' [the boy] said, 'but I don't believe so. He must know nearly everything.' "

When they are through modeling, they decide not to take the turtles home with them but to put them "where we are the only ones that know." They carry the turtles on the two boards between them along the beach until they find a sort of ceremonial stage, a circular arena with a floor of black sand, an arena defined by an escarpment of tufa two or three feet high. They carefully place the turtles so that they are in formation, with the large turtle in the middle, marching toward the lake. With that, the boys go to the edge of the lake to wash the clay and sand from their hands. They feel at that point that "the affair of the turtles was ceremoniously completed." The whole encounter is loaded with a sense of the mystical, with overtones of the primitive.

The modeling of the turtles is reminiscent of several Indian myths of the Creation, as well, of course, of Genesis. As dual creators, the two boys are joined together spiritually, more than they realize consciously at the time. And as incipient artists, they will be joined as creators throughout their lives as well. Caples wrote one book that was published in 1971, the same year that Clark died, which was called *The Potter and His Children: A Stone Age Fable.* It is remarkably like the turtle episode in Clark's book and, like it, based on Indian myths of the Creation:

The Potter is an ageless craftsman who spins the Great
Wheel in the ancient land of Eon, a place where the Animals
live together in peace and complete harmony with Nature. One
day the Potter decides to create four Children-helpers out of
dough [representing the four races of humankind]. [However,]

unlike the Animals, the children have no desire to share the good things which the Potter bestows on all the Creatures. They feel superior to the animals, and eventually have to be taught a lesson in love.

There could be no better statement of Walter Van Tilburg Clark's philosophy than this summary of Caples's book. To overcome divisions—of race, class, or religion—through love and understanding was fundamental to Clark's creed. And like Wallace Stegner, Clark did not write just to tell a story, just to entertain, but wrote out of belief and wanted to get his reader to experience something that would lead him to share his beliefs.

TWO MAJOR INFLUENCES— ROBERT COLE CAPLES AND ROBINSON JEFFERS

Like clark, robert caples was born in the East and spent his childhood in New York City. His parents divorced early in his life—his father, a doctor, had gone to Reno for a divorce and decided to stay. Living with his mother alone, Robert became a withdrawn, troubled child. He would not do his lessons in school and isolated himself from his classmates. Noting his artistic sensibility, his mother tried to save him by sending him to the National Academy of Design to take daily lessons in drawing. However, the teacher rejected him as too young, at twelve, to profit from his instruction. Finally, giving up when Robert was sixteen, his mother "shipped [him] to his father [in Reno] to be straightened out." Always sensitive to light and shadow, to strange landscapes and people, he was at first, in Reno, overcome by the "unbelievable, even frightening world of naked landscapes, tremendous spaces, geological rather than historical time and, above all, intent [*sic*] light."

In regard to this sudden immersion in the West, Clark has noted that Caples had to make a different kind of connection to his environment. Clark goes on to say,

> The desire to possess as a means of knowing, almost inescap-
> able in a city world made up entirely of buildings, objects and
> people — even fish in an aquarium are not quite truly fish —
> diminished in the constant presence of the manifestly unpos-
> sessable. [And he quotes Caples as saying,] "What mattered
> most, at all times, everywhere? Pyramid Lake country, and the
> hills around Reno." Yet, it never crossed Caples's mind that he
> could draw or paint them.

Again quoting Caples, Clark says, "I thought painters did portraits or still lifes." Caples went on to more art school, this time at
Santa Barbara Community Arts. But this rigidly academic schooling, Clark notes, did not "close the gap between what the heart, or
the whole self, was learning and what the head still believed."

In his twenties Caples began to work on his own, under artificial light, in the large, gloomy basement of his father's house in
Reno. To escape the basement, he began the practice, which he
would continue for nearly three decades, of going out into the
desert to search for subjects. In 1928 he moved into a real studio of
his own in the Masonic Temple Building, which had, he recalled,
"a view of the Truckee [river], a rubber plant in the southwest corner, a model stand and a linen smock hanging on a hook." After a
couple of years at this location, he went back to Santa Barbara
Community Arts for another year of study. Then, after returning to Reno, he rented a space on the top floor of the Clay-Peters
Building and began to do charcoal portraits by appointment.

Caples was all too successful with these portraits. One thing he
did not want to be was popular, but he began to get more and more
customers as notice of his work spread. His work even traveled to

New York, and he got several offers to go there to do portraits. His object was to look and understand, to learn, to advance his own consciousness, so that his portrait-by-appointment business became uncomfortable for him. For relief, he turned to drawing faces of Nevada Indians, but he also continued with the portraits. For both Caples and Clark, commercial success would seem to have been an anathema; it was indication of a lack of artistic success. After a time, according to Clark, Caples became very depressed: "A seeing *into* of a sort that RC didn't like began in spite of him, and it showed in his portraits. . . . He had no wish to be a satirist."

Strugging to find his direction, he found some freedom in sketching buildings and landscapes in and around Virginia City. He strove to remember the lights, shadows, and shapes, and then returning to his studio, he would rearrange them to suit his needs, and the rearranging gave him a blessed freedom from the literal.

It was about this time, while still depressed, still searching for some direction, that Caples took off from the art colony at Indian Springs without telling anyone, once again going into the desert on a walking tour. Actually, he would hike or hitch rides from one small settlement to another, paying for his stay at a tourist court or for a beer by doing charcoal landscapes or portraits. This journey or one like it is the basis for the extended, climactic episode in *The City*. In the novel Lawrence Black leaves his wife in Southern California, a wife whom he feels is stifling him, trying to possess him with her wealth. (She is a conflation of Caples's first two wives.) She is hurt and doesn't understand his reluctance to accept her gifts. She has Tim Hazard come down from Reno to help her find her husband. She tells Tim,

Oh, this isn't the first time. You know that as well as I do. And it is running away, Tim, it really is. And always some place like Austin, always. There's something unhealthy about the way he loves those old, dead mining camps, Tim. He feels at home in them. He loves to sit around in those old bars and talk for hours with any kind of bum who wanders in.

In life, Caples would often go to Austin, a small mining town halfway across the state, east of Reno, or to Indian Springs, north of Las Vegas. This description of loving old mining towns, sitting around in old bars, and talking for hours "with any kind of bum" is precisely how Clark himself has been described by those who knew him and applies equally to Caples. Black sends a letter to his wife, a letter which speaks just as Caples would in life: "I wander and I look, but as yet I see nothing clearly. I tell myself aloud where I am. I am in a cabin in a tourist camp. I have forgotten for the moment where the camp is, but it doesn't matter."

Black has headed northeast to cross the Mojave Desert, and Tim suspects he will go on into Death Valley in the middle of summer: "In Death Valley the little things were shed, and great, simple and ancient shapes emerged in the spirit. Lawrence loved Death Valley because of this." Worried about his friend, who can be very impractical, Tim tries to track him down. After several stops at diners, auto courts, and bars along the way where he picks up the trail, Tim finds Lawrence, near death, in Death Valley, rescues him, and they spend several days in an auto-court cabin while Lawrence recovers.

As a fitting sequel to their ordeal in the desert, they go to the mountain, on to Tonopah, about halfway between Las Vegas and Reno. Clark's description of Tonopah is worth noting, since it shows his skill in the use of metaphor and his ability to combine the physical with the metaphysical in his fiction:

There in the middle of a plain which is almost as white in September as it is when snow has fallen, rears up a solitary mountain, like an old volcano, and its topmost creases hide Tonopah, which is very old for its years, having more memories than hopes. To the wanderer coming in there, whether by the south

road or the north, or the east, it reveals itself only at the last
moment, and if he has been long in that land, and is feeling
very small after its uninterrupted instruction concerning astral
time, geological architecture, and the insignificant history of
mankind, it will open its gates between rusty dumps and old
mine tailings, the splendor of ancient Nineveh or Tyre.

It is as if Tim and Lawrence have arrived at a western American Shangri-La, a place that might well provide a spiritual, life-
changing experience—and yet, of course, in reality, if one insists
on reality, it is a run-down, half-abandoned old mining town.

One evening at Luigi's saloon in Tonopah, Tim and Lawrence
have a bad experience, involving a very unhappy young lady, and
a longer, very good experience, involving everyone in the bar.
Lawrence draws it, the singing and the dancing, and Tim plays the
piano. Their art elevates the occasion to a celebration of life. One
of the women who is in Lawrence's drawing feels insulted, but
Lawrence tells her that "I never make anybody look the way he really looks." He buys her a drink and explains "how intent and composition were superior to mere reproduction."

Years later, after he had read of *The City of Trembling Leaves,*
Caples accused Clark of romanticizing these episodes in the novel.
Insulted, Clark hotly insisted to his friend that the account was a
totally accurate representation of what happened. This argument
displays an odd contradiction in Clark's attitude toward his novel,
since to others he insisted that it was essentially fictional and only
vaguely autobiographical. In any event, the accounts of Clark
searching for his friend in the desert and the later scene in the saloon did, according to friends, have a basis in life, describing a visit
Clark made to Nevada during 1937.

———

Robert Caples's portraits became fewer and fewer and in 1932
stopped altogether. Whatever he had finished or was in progress

went into the trash. His desire to draw Indians took over, and he went out to sketch them in their own places, and they became less and less portraits. "They sought Indian," Clark has written, "not single Indians. They were the simplified, strong faces of an outdoor people, of connectors, bridgers."

Throwing away what he was dissatisfied with became a ritual not only for Caples, but for Clark as well. They were both perfectionists. On several occasions, Clark took page after page from a manuscript, crumpled it up, and threw it into the fireplace. When he did this in front of witnesses, they were dumfounded, and he would smile, amused by their astonishment. Many people thought that Caples had become a recluse toward the end of his life, but his wife testified after his death that her husband "never offered his latter day works publicly because he became insistent upon perfection, which he never believed he achieved." This sentiment would seem to have been the same for Clark and might at least partially explain his turning away from writing fiction in his last decade. Teaching was for Clark his most important occupation, for it had nothing to do with fame and fortune and a lot to do with caring and serving. It was an expression of the heart, rather than the head.

In the early 1930s, after the depression hit Reno, Caples's Indian drawings won him an appointment with the Federal Arts Project. It was with this appointment that he did the two series of charcoal drawings of Indians that made him, at least locally, famous. About these drawings, a Reno art critic wrote,

> There is a quiet humanity about them, which belies their stylistic familiarity. Simply put, they are beautiful, but in the way a man keeps records of the things he loves. Caples seemed to be more involved in the subjects of his work than in the work itself.

In the meantime, Caples and Clark went together frequently to the mountains and to Pyramid Lake, usually camping out for two days and nights. Aside from drinking bourbon and playing chess,

Caples would sketch while Clark would write. At this point in his life, Clark was writing a long narrative poem for his M.A. thesis (1931) and then was student teaching and taking courses for his secondary-teaching credential at the University of Nevada. He took these courses at the urging of his father, who was concerned that his son have something to offer in the job market, a means to make his way while writing poetry. Clark's writing at this time was almost always with a stubby pencil on a yellow, unlined legal pad and was therefore completely portable (and usually, for others, unreadable).

During this period, Clark had an unpleasant experience at Pyramid Lake—uncomfortable for him, humorous to others. He was there picnicking with friends. Always proud of his swimming prowess, he allowed to his friends as how it didn't look like a bad swim across the lake to the Pyramid. When none of his friends took him up on the swim, he decided to do it himself. The distance was further than he had estimated, and by the time he got to the rock, he was totally exhausted and cramping badly. He didn't dare start back across. So there he was, alone and stranded on the roadless side of the lake. It would have been a long hike out, and an uncomfortable one too, because skinny-dipping had been the order of the day, and he was not wearing a stitch of clothing. After some time, he spotted a speedboat out on the lake—the only one he had seen all day. It was getting late, so he swallowed his pride and hailed it. Unfortunately, the boat was filled with a group of young women. He got into the boat—no word of how the women reacted—but it must have been, for him anyway, one of life's most embarrassing moments.

From the mid-thirties until 1945, Clark was getting a second M.A. degree, getting married, teaching in the East, and writing his most important works. When World War II broke out, he tried to activate the commission that he thought he had from taking ROTC in high school and college. But he was turned down because of bad knees, whereas Caples enlisted in the navy. Caples put down his occupation on his navy application as "painter" and of course was directed to paint latrines and stairwells until, finally, he was assigned more appropriately to mapmaking. During these years before and during the war, Clark and Caples got together only infrequently, until Clark moved back to the West in the mid-1940s, living first in Taos, New Mexico, then in a former ranch house in the Washoe Valley (outside of Carson City) and then renting a house in Virginia City. At this point Caples had a gallery in Virginia City and was living in nearby Dayton, out in the desert.

During the early 1950s, Caples spent several months in the desert at Indian Springs, north of Las Vegas. Clark was off as a visiting professor at the University of Montana and received this letter from Caples, who was at Indian Springs:

> Biggest adventure of all. Had terrific times making paints, building own studio, rough-firing pottery, built etching press out of an old-fashioned washing wringer, made dyes out of boiled fruits and vegetables, scraped soot from studio chimney to make rich black. Ground up colored clays, ran leaves and flowers through washing wringer.

And then typically of Caples, he added, "The yield from all this wonderful liberation and discovery was virtually zero—own work changed almost not all." Commenting on this, Clark says,

> True, perhaps, in the sense in which he means it. But the distance between such experimental works ... and the earlier charcoals is not altogether an external one, either.... [But] the *looking at,* at least, was certainly importantly changed. (My emphasis)

Caples had been married and divorced four times when he met his fifth wife, Rosemary, who had come to Reno for a divorce. She had no plans to meet another man, just the opposite, but they fell

Robert Caples, 1969, in Connecticut. Courtesy of Barbara Clark Salmon

in love, and in 1955 Caples decided to give up his beloved desert to go east to Connecticut, where Rosemary had a farmhouse and two children to raise. Thereafter, Robert and Rosemary only saw the Clarks on a couple of trips west. As mentioned earlier, Caples continued working on his painting until the end of his life, walking out every day to the barn he had converted to a studio. However, during the last few years of his life, as a result of his search for perfection, he refused to sell any of his paintings and people thought that he had either died or become a complete recluse. In addition to his painting, he also wrote and published his fable, *The Potter and His Children.* But then he missed his desert so much during his last years in Connecticut, he had several loads of sand trucked onto the farm in order to create his own small version of Nevada.

———

One thing should be added to the story of Walter Clark's growing up. If it is not clear by now, it must be said that his was a childhood of privilege. His nephew recalled that during the Depression, the

Clarks's great concession to hard times was that they got rid of their butler—but kept the housekeeper and cook. Several of the surviving family members have suggested that Clark's liberalism, both politically and in his personal generosity, came as a response to his early privilege, either as a rebellion or out of a sense of guilt. No writer was more a champion of the common man. As privileged as he may have been growing up, their family life, according to Clark's sister Miriam, seemed to them perfectly normal. She recalled "lively conversations at the dinner table on all sorts of subjects and [remembered] waking every morning to the sound of her mother playing the piano." Then promptly at seven every morning, her father would go off to work as president of the university.

Although Walter was privileged, his father insisted that he work for his spending money. During his high-school years, V. T. Clark worked as a student janitor and also, as he has recalled, "helped out (the amount of help is questionable) driving horses and cutting cattle on some of the ranches in the region." He loved to associate with and talk to the ranch hands and cowboys and got from them another kind of education.

Clark's father insisted that his son take a year off between high school and college on the theory that such a year of working and hard knocks would be good for him and help him value his education all the more. Clark worked in Southern California, in the Imperial Valley, for his Uncle Warren and Aunt Jesse. His uncle owned a hardware store, and Walter worked as a truck driver and warehouseman. Then, since his father was president of the University of Nevada, it was expected that he would go to college there. During his entire time at the university, he lived with his family in the president's residence. During his summers he continued to take a variety of jobs in order to pay for part of his college expenses. The jobs included gardening, feeding the fish in an

President's house on the University of Nevada campus, Reno, ca. 1920.
Courtesy of Robert M. Clark

aquarium (at the Scripps Institution of Oceanography in La Jolla), driving a truck, laying linoleum, and painting houses. This latter job gave him lead poisoning, and he was on a diet of bread, milk, and pills for six months afterward. His experience led him to avoid house painting whenever possible.

He earned a B.A. and M.A. in English but took almost as much philosophy and psychology. He held an "A-" average throughout his college career. Again, as in high school, he was involved in a variety of activities. Because his knees gave out, he was unable to play basketball after his freshman year, but he was ranked fifth in the state in tennis. He took part, once again, in dramatics and wrote prose and poetry for the university humor magazine and the yearbook. At the same time he was writing on his own, mostly poetry, and had his first semiprofessional publications with a few poems (in 1930, 1932, and 1933, mainly in the journal *Troubadour*).

Clark's interest in poetry was stimulated by his admiration for the poems of Robinson Jeffers and Jeffers's professed philosophy.

*Walter Clark, portrait upon graduation from
the University of Nevada, Reno, May 1931.
Courtesy of David Chism*

In 1932, while he was on vacation with his family in Carmel, Clark went to Tor House and was able to meet and talk for some time with the reclusive Jeffers. He reported the scene and the occasion of their meeting in a letter to Barbara Morse, the woman he would marry the following year:

> I have been here since the middle of May and find it a stirringly beautiful place, though somewhat overinclined to fog from my desert point of view. I have tramped about quite a bit, on Point Lobos, and Cypress Point, and down the clean cut vastness of the coast south. Lobos especially is fascinating with its low, wind flattened cypress trees, and great granite rifts where the surge comes in. On sea separated rocks beyond the point the

seals and sea lions roll and hunch themselves, and bark and roar all day, a sound which comes in only intermittently, like fog horns, through the sound of the surf in the rocks. The gulls are flying there about always, and at sunset, those rare sunsets when the fog is so far west that there is a sun blood rim on the world, the great dark pelicans fly in undulating processions, single file against the darkening sky. . . .

I have been playing a little tennis, reading quite a bit, having finished everything that Robinson Jeffers has published. (I met that really great man by the way, and was even more immediately impressed by the man than by the work.) (7/20/32)

Later, Clark stated that he was attracted "most profoundly by Jeffers's love of nature, his 'contact with earth and air.'" Clark later described his meeting place in Tor House:

[I] had the additional pleasure, after knowing his work for two years, of meeting the poet himself, in that stone-paved, raftered, lower room of Thor House [sic], with its big fireplace, its heavy oak table, the shelves of bright orange breakfast dishes and shining copper.

He described the poet himself as tall,

broad shouldered, proportioned for power, and spare of flesh. His hands are large, well shaped, hardened with working earth, and his face avoids handsomeness only in favor of strangely contained masculine strength and intensity. His hair, dark and coarse and thin over the crown of his head, flares back in brief white wings at the temples. His gray, almost emotionless eyes, examine one with grave directness from within their deep setting. His bodily movements are so slow and even as to pass almost unnoticed, the movements of a man accustomed to watching birds and animals for hours at a time without

Robinson Jeffers

Walter Clark's sketch of Robinson Jeffers, which was included
in his master's thesis, 1934. Courtesy of Special Collections,
Bailey-Howe Library, University of Vermont

startling even their tense alertness. He speaks little, and that little in a very low and almost uninflected voice, though each word is exactly enunciated. A sense of great will and considered restraint dominates his presence.

What one sees behind this description is a man who has been very observant and who is, even quite young, an accomplished writer of prose. The same year that Clark met Jeffers, he published a book of poems, a publication financed by his father. Also in 1932, he got a teaching fellowship at the University of Vermont, where he spent the next two years. While at the university, he wrote another thesis for a second M.A., this time on Robinson Jeffers's poetry.

Like Caples, Jeffers had a great influence on Clark, by his personality as we see above, but primarily through his poetry. Still, with justification, the critic Max Westbrook in his book on Clark has cautioned,

> It is quite possible that Jeffers exercised much less influence on Clark than is commonly supposed, for Clark came to Jeffers as one comes in an unexpected place to a sudden friend. There may have been more recognition than influence.

In any case, Clark's study of Jeffers is important, whether it validated previously held ideas or instructed him and led him to expand his vision. As someone aiming toward becoming a poet (while teaching in order to make a living), Clark would seem to have adopted Jeffers as his ideal.

In the letter quoted above to Barbara Morse, Clark recounts his recent literary activity, indicating—at least at this point in his life—a preference for poetry:

> My "literary" endeavors have been confined to ten or a dozen short poems, two short stories which I completed, and threw away, and one one act play, a satirical harlequinade in verse. The short stories came out fairly well, but I was so

irked by them, and strained by their building that I have finally abandoned the idea of ever having any money and settled myself to poetry, where I can feel a growth, and can stretch with every trial. (7/20/32)

At the end of his letter, he included three of his poems for Barbara, one of which follows:

THE WHITE PELICANS (PYRAMID DESERT)

In a slow ascending turning they
Go up and round, and up into the blue,
As each half circle sweeping out anew
As the east sun opens a sudden play
Upon the slowly plying, cloud white wings.
Then imperceptibly gone in the sky
A moment, they flash bright again, gone high,
And higher. The swinging, silver spiral sings.

They are an intermittent light in the
Domed heaven over all the burning hills
And the heat blackened butte slumbering there;
A half-attentive, brief ascendency
Of spring dreaming which sudden spills
Into the virgin column of a prayer.

In his thesis about Jeffers, Clark explains what values the reader should find in the poet's work:

Jeffers postulates inherent force, call it what you please, God, Power, Will, Electricity, Entelechy. It is this scientific pantheism which, more than anything else, lends the repute of mysticism to much of his work. And truly, in any ultimate sense, there is little to distinguish between the informing force of science and the God-in-all of the pantheists. Only Jeffers must not be conceived as going beyond this conception of God in any belief in mystic unity of the individual with the central source, any unity, that is, beyond like physical basis.

Clark, too, has at times been classified as a mystic, since he talks about a unity of all or a unifying force in the universe. But it is important to note that he agreed with Jeffers in declining to endorse any unity of the individual with the whole except on a physical basis.

Since there was such a correspondence between Clark's and Jeffers's philosophies, it is interesting to note that there were rough parallels between Jeffers's parents and his circumstances while growing up and those of Clark. John Robinson Jeffers was born on January 10, 1887, a generation before Clark, into a family that like Clark's had culture and some wealth. Jeffers's father, like Clark's, was patriarch of the family, and like Clark's father was highly educated and a college professor. Jeffers's father, however, was much more austere and authoritarian than his Clark counterpart. He was also more guided by religion, since he was Professor of Old Testament Literature and Exegesis and of Biblical and Ecclesiastical History at Western Theological Seminary near Pittsburgh.

His wife and Jeffers's mother, Annie Robinson, was twenty years younger than her husband, with whom she fell in love when he was a visiting curate. She was lively, beautiful, and charming, and — like Clark's mother — well-educated, sociable, and a talented musician. Jeffers critic Robert Brophy sees the differences between the father and mother as a key to the course of Jeffers's life and career:

> Robinson, their first of two sons, was clearly caught throughout his early life between two extremes — the distant, older, stern, taskmaster father and the emotional, youthful, vivacious, unfulfilled mother — the basis for later psychological angst and lifelong creative tensions.

One major difference in the young lives of Clark and Jeffers was that much of the latter's education came, starting at age four, in various schools in Europe. His peers thought of him as solitary and stoic, traits that may have developed in response to a succession of stern teachers and his father's constant dissatisfaction with his son's progress and habit of relocating him in one school after another. As disturbing emotionally as his experiences abroad were, he nevertheless got a very good education in diverse subjects. And by the age of twelve he was, like his father, fluent in several languages.

Upon his father's retirement to California, Jeffers matriculated at Occidental College at age sixteen as a junior and graduated two years later. At Occidental (in Eagle Rock, part of Los Angeles) he was able to make lasting friendships for the first time, to participate in athletics, and to write verse that was published in the school literary magazine. His education was no doubt deeper than Clark's. While Clark was taking English, philosophy, and psychology at Nevada, Jeffers was taking courses in biblical literature, geology, history, Greek, rhetoric, and astronomy—nearly all of which would be reflected in his poetry. But both men can be seen as extremely bright and having a wide scope of interests and activities, and both had a relatively early publication of their poetry. It should be added that Jeffers and Clark were both very handsome young men, tall and well built (Clark was six feet tall—tall for that time), with penetrating eyes. They both gave off a sense of self-assurance without arrogance, a presence that impressed others.

Jeffers went on to a series of graduate schools, first studying literature at the University of Southern California, then at the University of Zurich, where he took a variety of literature, history, and philosophy courses. Back at U.S.C. he attended medical school and taught physiology at the dental college, and when his family moved to Seattle, he enrolled in the forestry school at the University of Washington. In the meantime, he had met his future wife,

Una, while he was taking literature at u.s.c. She was already married, and after a series of events during these years that critic Brophy describes as sounding like "a soap opera scenario," during which there were breakups and clandestine meetings, Una got a divorce. She and Jeffers were married in August of 1913.

Of the ingredients that consciously formed Jeffers's philosophy and poetic sensibility, perhaps the earliest and strongest was his exposure to the poetry of Dante Gabriel Rossetti at age fourteen. In a little essay for an anthology, he recalled that

> no lines of print will ever intoxicate as Rossetti's rather florid
> verses did, from *The Blessed Damozel* to the least last son-
> net.... And now, if I should ever wonder about the uses of
> poetry, I have only to remember that year's experience.

He went on to Swinburne, Shelley, and the whole catalog of major Romantic and Pre-Raphaelite poets. It is probable that Rossetti and the poetry of the Romantics freed him from the conventional and Victorian, leading to what might be called a wildness, a strong individual will, in the young man's imagination. What some called the savagery of Jeffers's verse made it as shocking for his time as Rossetti's eroticism was for his. The romanticism that was planted so early in Jeffers's consciousness would seem also to have contributed to his limited mysticism and pantheism, beliefs that Clark shared with him.

But there is a hard edge to Jeffers's wildness, an edge that would seem to have come to him less than consciously out of influences in his early experience. His father's sternness, the constant dislocations from one place and one school to another, the harshness of much of his schooling without friends or emotional support no doubt contributed to a harshness, an unforgiving toughness in his view of life. There is a hard edge to Clark's fiction as well, but the unforgiving nature of it is less overt than it is in Jeffers's writing. Both men were influenced also by the Old Testament and Greek tragedy, which brought the further dimension to their works of inexplicable suffering at the hand of God or the gods. While both men thought of God as including the universe as a whole, indifferent to man's needs and desires, Jeffers puts more emphasis on the cruelty implicit in that indifference. He even objected to the use of the pronoun *He* in referring to God.

As one might expect, Jeffers's first two books of poetry were strongly imitative of Keats, Shelley, Wordsworth, Swinburne, and Coleridge—melodramatic and melancholic. But according to Jeffers's wife, at the end of this first period he had a conversion experience, shedding rhyme and the romantic modes of expression and emotion. As Brophy has put it, Jeffers now created verse that was "thematically turbulent, ritualistic, mythical, and philosophically integrated under a kind of stoic, celebratory, devout pantheism." In a much-quoted passage from "The Answer," Jeffers states an anthem for himself, and one that would be wholeheartedly endorsed in Clark's fiction:

> Integrity is wholeness, the greatest
> beauty is
> Organic wholeness, the wholeness of life and things, the divine
> beauty of the universe. Love that, not man
> Apart from that, or else you will share man's pitiful confusions, or
> drown in despair when his days darken.

After Robinson and Una were married, the couple moved, on a friend's suggestion, to the area near Carmel, California, in 1914. There, they lived for several years in a log cabin in the woods, and then in 1919 they bought a piece of property on a knoll that overlooked Carmel Bay. It was on this property that Jeffers helped a stonemason build Tor House and went on himself to build the now famous forty-foot stone tower from which he could gaze up at the stars and look out over the coastal landscape as it ran down toward

Big Sur. It was a rugged country and a rugged life. A visit to an outhouse at night in such a cold and windy climate is not pleasant, and although one of the couple's main occupations was reading, long reading sessions under a dim kerosene lantern can be wearisome and difficult. It would seem that the Jeffers were determined to lead hard and primitive lives, perhaps as a reminder of human fragility in the face of a harsh and indifferent nature. In this regard, it is interesting to note a part of Jeffers's *Roan Stallion, Tamar* as quoted by Clark in his thesis and especially the parts that Clark has underlined:

> .... also I heard my masters
> Speak of Pelorum head and the Attic rocks of Sunium, or
> that Nymphaean
> Promontory under the holy mountain Athos, a warren of monks
> Walled in with prayer-cells of old stone, perpetual incense
> and religion
> Smoke from it up to *him who is greater than they guess,*
> through what huge emptiness
> And chasms above the stars *seeking out one who is here*
> *already, and neither*
> *Ahunting nor asleep nor in love;*

Many of those who have written about Robinson Jeffers have pointed to the influence that Tor House, its location, and the surrounding landscape had on Jeffers and his poetry. Wild and untamed the surroundings certainly were — the rugged canyons, the steep bluffs, and, below, the pounding surf. Wild animals — deer, rabbits, mountain lions, and rattlesnakes — abounded. The climate, for anyone who spent considerable time outside, as Jeffers certainly did, could be very unpleasant. The area is frequently shrouded in fog, a cold fog in summer, and in winter low clouds can produce a constant drizzle. One could think of the situation as

Thor House and the Hawk Tower

Walter Clark's sketch of Jeffers's Tor House and the Hawk Tower.
Courtesy of Special Collections, Bailey-Howe Library, University of Vermont

very romantic, or one could, after months of exposure to such weather, simply be depressed. Rather than the surroundings influencing Jeffers, it might be more accurate to say that Jeffers chose surroundings that matched his emotional needs — those of a highly civilized man who chose to live in primitive conditions in a wild and melancholy place in order to be inspired to wild, or at least unconventional, melancholy verse.

While agreeing for the most part with Jeffers's philosophy, his sense of the unity of all and the insignificance of humankind, Walter Clark's emotional needs, as reflected by the surroundings he preferred, were somewhat different — although place and one's relationship to place were as important to him as to Jeffers. Instead of the rugged coast between Carmel and Big Sur, Clark had three places that inspired him or gave him comfort. One was certainly

Reno, the city of trees with leaves that trembled in the sunlight. Over time Reno changed, in his view, for the worse, but it had been the comforting surroundings where he grew up. Another dear place was the desert country around Pyramid Lake—a place that he emotionally attached to his close friendship with Robert Caples and later to his love for his wife, but which also reminded him of human mutability in the face of the age-old rock formations. And finally, were the old mining towns—Austin, Tonopah, and, particularly, Virginia City, where he chose to live for much of the later part of his life. What did old mining towns mean to Clark? Unlike Jeffers, Clark loved company. He has said,

> My favorite diversion, by long odds, socializing, just sitting around with a beer or more in all kinds of places talking to all kinds of people about all kinds of things. (It's a professional necessity for a writer too, but it's no good to him if he takes it that way, watching people and listening to them, making mental notes and saying to himself, "This I must remember." He'll never get to know people in the ways that matter most if he treats them as specimens. . . . The thing is to be really a part of whatever is going on, without a thought about "using" it. The memory will keep what matters.)

Old towns like Virginia City meant companionship, conversation, and conviviality—all within the atmosphere of what Clark believed to be the genuine Old West, or at least the Old West recovered as best one could in the mid-twentieth century. To be in those towns was to live western. Jeffers wrote about and within a western landscape, but it was Clark who was the regionalist, defining the meaning of the West in terms of his philosophy of life.

Clark finished his thesis on Jeffers in 1934 and received his M.A., with honors, from the University of Vermont. In addition to his thesis, he was writing poetry and published numerous poems in the college literary magazine. Although he gradually became convinced that prose was his best medium, he continued to write poetry for many years and even at one point considered financing—this time himself—the publication of a collection of his poems. While he was still enrolled at Vermont, he spent the summer of 1933 with his mother and the other Clark children in Maine at the same cabin in which he had been born. In November of that year, he had his first national publication, with two poems in *Poetry* magazine.

CHAPTER THREE

MARRIAGE, CHILDREN, AND CAZENOVIA CENTRAL SCHOOL

WHILE HE WAS IN GRADUATE SCHOOL at Nevada, Walter Clark met Barbara Frances Morse, the attractive and very bright daughter of a retired Presbyterian minister. Barbara, who suffered from serious sinus problems, had come to Reno for her health after three years at Oberlin. A key to her somewhat eccentric personality might be seen in the fact that she was a music major at Oberlin although she was tone deaf. Their son Robert has reflected on the match between his father and mother:

> I suspect that it was her liveliness, her intelligence, and perhaps her relative worldliness that was the initial attraction — plus being attractive enough physically — she had the long, bent nose she called the Morse nose. [In] that early photo of her, when she was about the age she was when they met, she is looking something like a flapper, and she was close to three years older than dad. . . . I wouldn't be surprised if she didn't more or less vamp the relatively innocent Walter.

Relatively innocent? Such a description puts Clark in a somewhat different light. Nevertheless, this would seem to be an appraisal that Clark, in looking back, made of himself. One has to think of his fictional self-portrait, Tim Hazard, in *The City of Trembling Leaves*—a dreamy, sensitive, artistic, young man inspired by romantic legends.

In October of 1933, while Walter was still in graduate school at the University of Vermont, the couple was married by Barbara's father in his home in Elmira, New York. After a brief honeymoon at a borrowed cabin in the Adirondack Mountains, Barbara went back to Elmira while her husband returned to his rented room in a professor's house in Burlington to finish his work at the university.

Walter and Barbara were well matched. Both loved conversation and convivial companionship. They would stay together throughout their lives—he the breadwinner and sometime star of the family and she the supporter in everything he did. As their son has said,

> She certainly belongs with those wives who take over more of
> the burdens of everyday and family to help the husband with
> his art. Later in the marriage, however much the fun-loving,
> high spirited and more experienced one she might have been
> early, she saw herself as the practical one. And she was. She did
> all the bill-paying, did the taxes (and had frequent skirmishes
> with local IRS offices over deducting things related to the writ-
> ing as business expenses.) . . . She certainly was the housewife,
> and the main raiser of us children, and protecting Dad from us
> so he could write, although she said Dad would play with us as
> she didn't, when he came home from teaching school.

When Barbara and Walter met, she had an ambition to become a writer of mystery stories, and she continued to work at her writing throughout much of her life. Her imagined hero was a

Anne Jenette (Barbara's sister) and Barbara Frances Morse at Morse summer house in Essex, New York, ca. 1927. Courtesy of Robert M. Clark

Walter and Barbara Clark, probably near Missoula, Montana, on automotive tour by Walter and a friend around the country, 1929. Barbara was taking summer school at the University of Montana. Courtesy of Robert M. Clark

Studio portrait, Barbara Frances Morse, summer 1929, when she was twenty-two years old, in Missoula, Montana. Courtesy of Robert M. Clark

Pennsylvania state trooper. At one point, with her husband's help, she finally submitted a manuscript to a publisher. The rejection letter became a family story, repeated by mother and father with some amusement. The letter said, as son Robert recalls, that "the writing was very good, as was the basic plot (which was hers), but the long descriptions of people and places slowed down the action too much." So according her husband's wishes and her agreement, Barbara, for the most part, settled on playing the conventional role of wife and mother as prescribed in the first part of the twentieth century. Nevertheless, she was in many ways her own person. She could be sharp, critical, and outspoken, although no one ever heard her complain or express anger with her husband. Several friends have mentioned that they thought she had a more logical, or at least a more down-to-earth mind-set than Walter, the idealist who tended to emphasize feeling and emotion over intellect. And she was somewhat unconventional in becoming the repair person for the family, the one who tacked screens back together or fixed the faucet.

Barbara's nephew, David Chism, remembers her as "brilliant":

And she was a fun character because we used to accuse her of having an Einstein hairdo. She always had, and as kids, one of the things we were really impressed with Barbara was that she played correspondence chess. We thought that was pretty interesting. She would have those postcards coming from all over the world—bishop, knight.

Of course Walter was addicted to chess as well, but according to Chism, "She was far better than he was. He loved it, but it drove him nuts that he could never beat her. The intellect was what sort of attracted the two of them, I am sure."

Clark's son remembers these things differently. He doesn't recall his mother playing correspondence chess, and he has said,

My sense is certainly that Dad was the stronger player, and certainly the most devoted and enthusiastic about the game. . . .
For much if not all the time I was growing up . . . he did chess exercises at breakfast, before beginning to write. He did them from chess books, of which he had a goodly number. Greatest games of some Russian master, etc., openings, closing, all that. Worked out the problems offered in the newspaper. Mom might sometimes have done those, too. Family lore has Mom as the better defensive player, preferring black, and Dad the attacker, preferring white when they played each other. And . . . sometimes Mom would defeat him, or force a draw.

After the marriage and back at the University of Vermont in 1933, Clark took further graduate classes in American literature and Greek classical drama, poetry, and philosophy. In addition to writing his thesis and a great deal of poetry, he was also doing part-time teaching as part of his teaching fellowship obligations. It was during this period, however, that, in his words, "[I] found the subjects I most wanted to write about drawing me out of poetry and into fiction." Or, as he put it in another personal essay,

A long story I was trying to tell in verse [which eventually became *The Track of the Cat*] gradually taught me that I should be trying to tell it in prose. Only one other person, Barbara Morse, whom I had met at Nevada, seemed to care what I wrote it in, so I married her.

After finishing at Vermont in 1934, Walter and Barbara lived for a year in an old farmhouse, which was the Morse family summer home, outside of Essex, New York. They had it rent free, but it had no electricity or running water (shades of Robinson and Una Jeffers in their Carmel cabin). Walter and Barbara spent their time "shoveling snow, drawing water, splitting wood, and [and in Walter's case] writing." They were following a rather romantic plan to give Walter a year to write, and he did, writing constantly and for long hours. In an interview several years later, Clark recalled this year:

> "We weren't too well heeled," he [recalled], but they were determined to give his chance for writing success a thorough trial. "I do the first draft entirely in long hand," said Mr. Clark, "using the typewriter for revisions. Usually, when once I get started, a story rolls along rapidly, but I remember one day in the farmhouse when I ran into some pretty tough knots."
>
> That day Clark began writing at 8 a.m. and didn't stop until 11 p.m. " 'I guess I've turned it out today, all right,' I said, when I had finished, but I had completed exactly three paragraphs."

He did not achieve his goal of starting to make a living from his writing, again publishing only a few poems. He continued to work on the first version of *The Track of the Cat* as a narrative poem, but after finishing it, he set it aside, coming back to the story fifteen years later and telling it as a novel.

It was the depth of the depression and they had very little money, but, as Clark recalled, nothing cost very much either. Essex, where the house was, is very far north, on the shore of Lake Champlain. It was cold and humid during the winter, and they had only a wood cookstove and fireplace with which to keep warm. They stored away a whole side of beef, which cost them only seven cents a pound, but since they had little heat in the house, the beef froze and was difficult to thaw and use. Yet, he recalled, they had "a fine life, nevertheless." It was a good thing that Walter and Barbara were both young and in good health.

During the summers the whole Morse clan would gather for several weeks at the farmhouse. Then Clark would write in the little room in the "tower" on the third floor; in the winter, he worked at the kitchen table. The Morse clan was a large one — Barbara was

Morse summer home, Essex, New York, ca. 1927.
Courtesy of Robert M. Clark

one of six children—and they and their own children, wives, and husbands would gather annually, sometimes putting up tents in the yard. The kids and at times the adults played deck tennis, badminton, and cow-pasture golf. Nearly every day there was swimming, the kids with several attending adults hiking the two miles to the lake. On special occasions, the family would take a picnic and swim in the nearby Bouquet River.

Clark's nephew, George Lowe, remembers visiting the Clarks at the Morse vacation home during one summer and seeing his uncle

> go out and dive in Lake Champlain, which tourists think is very cold. He would swim for miles—he was a long distance swimmer. He would use the Australian crawl and swim across to Vermont, which is a mile and half, two miles away, then swim back.

The nephew remembers his uncle telling stories: "He would just tell anecdotes . . . the story of one-eyed Joe, for instance, or something like that." His uncle, he recalls, was a "great conversationalist. I can remember he and my father would talk at great lengths. [Also I can] remember him as a clever artist. He could sketch things out.... I was impressed as a kid. I remember thinking, "Hey man, that looks like a whatever it is, a parrot, a cowboy."

At the end of their year at the farmhouse, in order to get some money, Clark taught summer school at City College of New York, where his father had taught. Then in the fall of 1935, they moved to the lovely old village of Cazenovia in the Finger Lakes region of New York. Barbara's brother-in-law, Wayne Lowe, had become the superintendent of an experimental grammar–high school, and he offered Walter a half-time job teaching English. Clark became full-time soon after he was hired and stayed at Cazenovia Central School until 1945, with a year off to write from 1941 to 1942. We normally think of someone who, like Clark, became a prominent writer as teaching creative writing in college. He did that, but he spent almost as many years teaching high school. At first he did so because he was prepared with the credential his father insisted he get and because the position was offered to him. But he taught in high school even later, when he didn't have to, which is unusual and is testimony to his dedication to the profession and to young people. If there was more status in teaching in college, that didn't seem to mean anything to him.

He had begun his teaching career in Reno, student teaching in the high school and taking on several freshman composition classes at the university. On his introduction to teaching, Clark commented that he was "scared green at first, of course, but so happy when things went right, which they did once in a while, that I was hooked for life." He noted also that it had been "my chief means to bread and butter ever since." He added, with a slight note of regret, that teaching is

an occupation I respect so much and am so fond of that it's kept
me from doing anything like as much writing as I should have.
Who's Who lists me as a teacher first and writer second, as I
should have.

Cazenovia was a small town of about two thousand residents in
those days, with a rich history going back to the late eighteenth
century and the early Dutch settlers in New York. (However, the
town got its name from a Swiss land agent, Theophilus de Caze-
nove, who never saw the area that took his name.) Located in the
central New York State uplands, Cazenovia is nestled in rolling
hills and bordered on the west by a beautiful lake. From the beginning, the attraction was Cazenovia Lake, and many of the inhabitants over the decades have been drawn to the town as a vacation spot. Coming largely from Boston and New York City,
they brought wealth with them, and during the last part of the
nineteenth and early twentieth centuries, they built vast vacation
homes that were really mansions, some of them occupied year
around. Stability was provided by the prosperous farm community that surrounded the town and later also by some faculty and
staff from Syracuse University who built homes in the area and
commuted the twenty miles to work.

Homes in the town today, many of them quite old but beautifully maintained, display a mixture of styles — Federalist, Greek
Revival, Colonial Revival, Italianate, and Gothic Revival. These
are surrounded by green lawns and well-tended gardens, and here
and there throughout the village are several open public spaces
with expansive lawns. Throughout the village and beyond, there
is a virtual umbrella of tall, mature trees, mostly sugar maples.
The main street has a variety of small shops, with no neon signs or
plastic facades. Early in the last century some large estates were
created near the village; others, later, were created stretching out
along East Lake Drive, bordering the lake. Some of the estates still

exist, a few have become bed-and-breakfast establishments, while others have been broken up by developers.

A few blocks from the center of the village stand the solid red-brown brick buildings of Cazenovia Central School. There is something grand and solid about these old school buildings when they have been well taken care of. They seem to insist that this community thinks education is important, very important. In the center of the front of the main, original building is an imposing broad stairway leading up to three double-entry doors under arches. Facing the school, to the right of the entry doors, one can see the windows of the spacious English Room, where Clark taught his classes. Across the street from the school is a wide median strip of grass, and across from that are the houses, side by side, that had been the superintendent's house and the house the Clarks occupied. Sister lived next door to sister. (After Walter's leave in 1941–42, the Clarks lived in a house on Fenner Street.)

When Clark arrived in the mid-1930s, there were about eight hundred students, kindergarten through high school. The atmosphere was friendly and relaxed but at the same time academically sound. One of Clark's former students recalls that the school was a firm part of the community: "Everyone was really part of a big family [there]. We had a faculty that was fabulous. There were a lot of things that went on outside of school, [and] the faculty and kids were all involved in it." If there were a dance,

> the community would be there too. If you had a night where
> they did some square dancing, you would find the janitor
> and his family joining in—they were all intermixed.... There
> wasn't this sharp division [between people] that you seem to
> have today. Everybody [in Cazenovia] knew everybody else.

At the Central School, Clark taught high-school English, coached the basketball and tennis teams, and was faculty advisor to the drama club. This latter duty involved producing and direct-

Cazenovia Central School, 1938. Photo by Carlton M. Straub

ing at least two plays a year; among them he put on *The Journey's End*, *Our Town*, *The Importance of Being Ernest*, *Mr. Pym Passes By*, and *Something In Spite of Himself*. He often had his classes write plays and then present them on stage to school assemblies. According to the testimony of dozens of his ex-students at Cazenovia, he was a superb teacher. Ex-student John Bennett recalled that Clark was

> an extremely innovative and imaginative teacher. He liked
> kids. He was not an extrovert—he was almost a shy person in
> many ways. But in class he would relate stories, and he would
> get us involved in discussions. They were very unique.... He
> would get into a discussion mode and he would take either side
> of an argument and make you defend whatever your feeling
> was.

He worked very hard at his job, planning projects and writing extensive commentaries on written assignments. He had a mellifluous, baritone speaking voice and a gift for reading other people's

First Clark house, in Cazenovia on Eastlake Road.
Courtesy of Barbara Clark Salmon

writing aloud expressively. Although he did not teach in an age when students called their teachers by their first names, he was very close to his students. Several of his former students have said that he was practically "one of us" — "one of us" even though in the custom of the time he wore brown pants, tweed sport jacket with elbow patches, white shirt, and tie every day to work. Tall, dark, and handsome (he was six foot, tall for his time), the girls were crazy about him, and his reserve may have been in part a reaction to this adoration. Although he had the common touch and never gave the impression that he thought too well of himself, still he had, as one of his former male students recalled, "a presence."

When the school opened in 1932, it brought together youngsters who had formerly been in several small schools spread around the district. To accommodate the students, the school brought them in by buses, and to make sure that they had the opportunity to participate in extracurricular activities, the school established a double bus schedule, one group that left just after school at three P.M. and another that left later at five P.M. When he

Senior Room—English Room at Cazenovia Central School.
Photo by Carlton M. Straub

Teaching staff at Cazenovia Central School, ca. 1939.
The English Department consisted of Walter Clark, third from left,
first row; Walter Moon, seventh from left, first row; Kenneth Webber,
ninth from left, first row. Courtesy of Barclay Webber

had a basketball game out of town or late practice for a play, Clark would take students home in his car, even those who might live far out of town on a farm. And since this was during the war, gas was rationed.

Glen Slack, one of Clark's students who had him for English and as a drama coach, recalls,

> Everyone liked him immensely, and actually the rehearsals tended to run late, and so the late school bus had already gone, so he would personally drive all the cast around the countryside to their homes:
>
> I lived about six miles out in the country. He used to sing us cowboy songs [while he was driving]. I remember one of them was about "the handsome young cowboy all covered with gore. He won't be a-riding his pinto no more. There was blood on the saddle, there was blood on the ground, great big puddles of blood all around." We would all join in the chorus.

Clark's son, Robert, remembers that his dad

> did sometimes say that he was going to be remembered as the man who wrote *The Ox-Bow Incident* and sang "Blood on the Saddle." When I was growing up, the family had a 78-rpm rendition of that by Tex Ritter, and it was sort of a party specialty of Dad's, making a real plosive on the "B" of bloods in the chorus.

As an English teacher his forte was creativity. He was not interested in teaching grammar and punctuation on their own, only on a teacher-to-an-individual-student basis and only in the context of writing. Fortunately, his students had a firm foundation in writing mechanics from elementary and junior high school. Clark had his classes, during various semesters, write poetry, plays, and stories as well as the more traditional essays. A former student recalled, "We did short stories in class and he was very big on writing the proper lead in terms of creating an immediate interest and getting the reader involved in what the story was about and was going to be. And that helped me." It was as if he were teaching college creative writing to his high-school students. Another student recalled that "he had us read newspapers, and he had us reading to keep up with current events, and he wanted us to know about art history." He often had his students write poetry, something few of them had done before, and while most of them responded to the challenge, others were baffled by it. One student remembers,

> Sometimes he would do poetry. Oh, God, poetry and me didn't mix. I didn't care much for poetry, and we were supposed to write, the whole class. . . . He gave us three weeks to do it, and well, at the end of three weeks nobody had anything. He gave us another three weeks. We finally all came up with at least part of the assignment.

He had his classes read plays aloud, students taking various parts, and they read many plays, both Shakespeare and modern. "We all took turns," John Bennett recalled, "and then we would play off each other too. Different people would take different parts and that made for fun and it stimulates the interest that people had in whatever it is they are reading." Clark was particularly attracted to drama—the emotion and interaction. He was experimental. One semester he had his students play chess and then write about their experiences—their strategy and their opponent's and the progress of the game. According to a former student,

> He taught us chess for a reason. It was logical and sequential, and it was thought—made you think. . . . He taught us the opening game, the middle game, the closing gambit, and then he tied the chess movements to life and writing. He was really philosophical in many ways—probably one of the most innovative, imaginative teachers I have ever had.

Another experiment which was not very successful had to do with his role as senior class advisor. Along with the principal and the other English teachers, he decided to have the students make their own yearbooks. Each of them would create a yearbook by filling a scrapbook with journal entries from the year, clippings from the local paper, notes written by fellow students, and photos taken or borrowed and copied. Creative perhaps, but several of his former students have still not forgiven him for depriving them of the traditional yearbook they had expected for their graduation.

One of his most experimental and successful projects was a motion picture. The main impetus for the picture was one of his students who was entranced by the processes of photography, both still and motion. Carlton Straub found a love of photography as a teenager and, after graduating from nearby Syracuse University, spent his whole career working at Kodak in Rochester, New York. In high school Straub became friendly with the projectionist at the local movie theater. At the same time, he was active in the drama club as part of the stage crew, and although he was mainly interested in production, he also occasionally filled in by taking small acting parts.

These experiences led Straub to propose the movie project to the club advisor, Clark. It was just the kind of educational, creative departure that Clark reveled in. So enthusiastic was he, that he talked the school into purchasing a professional movie camera. (We are used to small, relatively inexpensive video cameras. This camera was very large and cost hundreds of dollars.) Straub wrote a script and filmed, while Clark directed. The script was based on a two-reel silent melodrama of the 1920s, an episode of the "Hairbreadth Harry" serial called "Sawdust Tragedy." The climax of the original was a scene of a young woman, tied and helpless, on a belt moving toward a large circular saw. Since they had no sawmill in Cazenovia, Clark and his crew used a train. Near to the town a train track came out of a quarter-mile tunnel. The student playing

On location for the filming of Love Conquers All, *outside Cazenovia.*
Photo by Carlton M. Straub

the victim was tied and actually lay on the tracks. (Straub recalled that he was surprised to find out that Clark knew the train schedule.) They used dialogue panels (subtitles), and the movie was self-contained — that is, one wouldn't have to be already familiar with the continuing characters of the original series. The finished product was a triumph. Everyone had a lot of fun, and Straub had a great sense of accomplishment. Who knows what might have happened if instead of Rochester, he had gone to Hollywood? Clark himself had a cameo as the clerk in the local grocery store.

Clark became the basketball coach a year or so after his arrival at Cazenovia. Before him, the football coach had also coached basketball but hadn't taken the latter seriously. For him the basketball season was an opportunity to keep his football players in shape dur-

Student Carlton Straub in the auditorium projection room preparing to project the senior film, Love Conquers All. *Photo by Carlton M. Straub*

ing the off-season. When the coach left to go with the u.s.o., Clark took over basketball, and since the sport was one of his passions, he worked hard at it. And it was difficult. There was a significant lack of talent. But the chess player loved strategy and knew the sport — one of his former players called him "innovative" — and Cazenovia won its share of games. As one former Cazenovia student recalls, "Clark did more to really get into basketball the way we sort of see it today, a little faster." He was a calm but enthusiastic coach who practiced with his squad and enjoyed pickup games and one-on-one with his players in the off-season. He had a number of playground moves — behind-the-back passes, over-the-head blind shots, and air dribbling (throwing the ball in the air as you go down court and catching it, then throwing it up again — not legal).

Clark as coach at Cazenovia High School. Courtesy of Robert M. Clark

When Long Island University, a big power in basketball in those days, came to Syracuse, Clark took his players over to watch them, hoping they would be inspired. But he was as concerned about the morale of his players as about winning—although he was a very competitive man. It was often hard for him to stay calm.

But at work, whether in the classroom or on the basketball court, Clark was almost always even tempered, at times reserved and at times, in the company of his peers, voluble. However, occasionally the safety valve would blow off at home after a bad day. He did have a temper. As part of his routine at Cazenovia, one aspect of his life that wore him down was the long hours—many extra hours that were often voluntary. He commonly got home long after school hours in the evening. As young and energetic as he was, he found that it was difficult to find time to write, and during the school year, his writing was primarily at night after the children were in bed. Writing at the kitchen table late at night, he was sustained, he has said, "by too many cigarettes and too much coffee." He made as much use as he could of weekends and vacation periods, pushing himself so hard that eventually he would have a physical breakdown.

As part of his routine, he would play with his children after he got home from school—his daughter, Barbara, was born in 1937 and his son, Robert, in 1939. It was a ritual too that the entire family would sit down to dinner and there would be much conversation. Often Clark would hold forth with stories. Daughter Barbara (he called his wife "Bub" and his daughter "Babs") recalled a continuing story at dinnertime that he began after they left Cazenovia about a Hispano boy who, in his journey through the Southwest, would encounter one obstacle after another—high mountains, heavy snow, dangerous strangers. Because of time and money constraints, recreation for the Clarks was somewhat limited, but one thing they were able to do was listen to music. Elizabeth Finke, a colleague and friend at Cazenovia who taught physical education, remembered,

> We used to listen for hours. He had a lot of records and listened to symphonic music. When I left to go into the Army, they had a party for me, and they gave me gift of some records. He picked them out. He knew some of them that I liked particularly.

Clark's competitiveness came when he was playing chess or tennis; for some reason, as a writer he didn't feel competitive—except, perhaps, with himself. His son has commented that his father

> just thought about being a good writer and a published one. But I do think that, as soon as he was published, something like competitiveness began to be felt, though perhaps it can be called self-consciousness, and that is a little different.

For the most part, however, his art was a private struggle, a struggle to get it right in his own mind. He seemed to have no need to please an audience or to convince the critics that he should be somehow rated as better than another author—he was his own toughest critic. Tennis, on the other hand, was another matter. Carl Straub recalled,

> I did play tennis with Mr. Clark, quite frequently. There were two or three of us that I recall that played with him, a lot in the summer. We were no match for him. Now that I look back on it, which was reasonable. We were kids, just developing. He was a seasoned player. He would serve the ball, and you wouldn't see it go by you. He seemed to revel in that. He loved that.... We never really won many games from him. In the long run, it was probably good for us, for somehow we never got discouraged. We became more determined than anything else. You would win a game once in awhile. He didn't give it to us—we would win it.

Robert Moon, son of the other English teacher at Cazenovia, recalled that he read in one of Clark's introductions to *Oxbow* that "it says that he doesn't have any use for cover girls, on the cover or in person.... Let me tell you, the girls he played tennis with, he wasn't particularly democratic there. They were all good looking."

One of these girls that played tennis with him was Betty (Shaw) Heffernan. She also had Clark as a teacher and advisor, and babysat for the family on numerous occasions. The first time she played tennis with Clark, after school one day, Betty had the experience other opponents have testified to. Clark's first serve was so fast and hard, Betty dropped to the ground to avoid being hit. She recalled, "After that, he asked if I wanted to play tennis, and I said to him, 'Only if you play senior high school tennis.' He just laughed, and we had a good game."

Betty Shaw became close to Clark and to his family. He gave her special attention, not only because she was bright and promising but because of the circumstances of her life. Her father had died early in her life, and her mother remarried. Unfortunately, two years later her stepfather died, leaving two sons from his previous marriage. So Mrs. Shaw brought up Betty and her stepbrothers through the depression years, and as Betty recalled,

> She worked very hard to do that.... I would go home after school, and I would clean the house and cook the dinner. My stepbrother would come home and do the outside chores and make sure everything was fine. That way when my mother came home, she could rest and relax. Then, there was always homework and sometimes I would baby-sit for someone in the evening.

Despite her full schedule, Clark on several occasions challenged Betty to do still more. This was typical of him—he continually challenged his students to go beyond, to tackle the difficult. He approached life and encouraged others to approach life the way he played tennis. One day he said to her, "You know, Betty, you write beautifully. Do you write anybody in the service?" When she said "No," he said,

> Why don't you start a newsletter? Look at all the people from the school that you know that are in the service. I bet you could find information that they'd be interested in, that their parents don't know about. I think you ought to start a newsletter. There are seven or eight boys that you went to school with that year before they went in the service that you know. Why don't you do that?

So she did. She started writing seven or eight boys, one letter a week. Then these boys wrote her saying that there were other servicemen in their outfits who never got any mail, so by the end of three months, she was writing thirty-five letters a week—five letters a night, seven nights a week. She recalled, "Mr. Clark was very proud of me, and I'd have to admit, I was proud of myself."

On another occasion, Clark asked her what she did after school and in the evening. She told him, "Well, I go home. My mother works all the time." He said, "But there must be some hours in your week that you could devote to some community service." She had never heard of community service and asked what he thought she should do. "Why don't you be an air raid warden?" She went to the town authorities to volunteer, but they told her that since she was only seventeen and a woman, she couldn't be a warden. Betty recalls that neither she nor Clark could understand what difference either of those items would make. But Clark went on to suggest that the town needed aircraft spotters, and after investigating, Betty found that they needed volunteers in the nighttime. She was given plans that provided the configurations of aircraft that might fly over and then took and passed a test on recognition. Three nights a week she would get up at two-thirty A.M., go up three flights of stairs to the roof of the school where there was an aircraft spotter's shack, and watch for planes until school started. "I had a marvelous time," she recalled.

Betty babysat for the Clarks. One afternoon, Barbara had gone to Syracuse to take a class at the university and Walter, who usually went with her, was painting a house to earn extra money (he hated to paint because of his earlier lead poisoning, so he must have been desperate). As the little girl, Babs, went out the backdoor, she was bitten several times by a neighbor's dog that was usually tied up. Horrified, Betty chased the dog away, gathered up the bleeding girl, and put her in the bathtub, washing her off to find out how serious the wounds were. Another neighbor called Walter, who came home immediately, exclaimed "Oh, my God," and took his daughter to the doctor. Although the little girl was all right, only requiring a couple of stitches, Betty felt bad—responsible and worried that she would never be called on to babysit again. However, the Clarks did not blame her and hired her many times afterward. "Babysitting for Mr. Clark," she has said, "was a badge of honor."

When her stepbrother was killed in the war, Betty went to Clark as the one person she could talk to about her feelings. He invited her into his office — he had already heard what had happened. She recalled, "We talked about my stepbrother and the fact that I should be very proud of him, and that he, among thousands of others, were doing for their country what needed to be done. That helped a lot. Up until then, the fact of his death had consumed me."

She has summed up her two years with Clark as her teacher:

> [He] was always looking for a way to encourage his students
> to expand their horizons, give them another avenue to travel,
> make them think about things, and talk about things and
> explore.... I can never remember that he ever had a judgmen-
> tal thought in his head about any student. He took them at face
> value. He understood that everybody has problems. He tried to
> be there for everybody, to help them think the battle through
> to its finality.

"He still influences my life," she added. She said this fifty-five years later.

CHAPTER FOUR

THE OX-BOW INCIDENT
AND THE WESTERN NOVEL

ONE DAY WALTER CLARK TOLD Betty Shaw something that he asked her to remember: "Live every day, no matter what happens. Live every day. Feel everything. Let every thought that comes to your brain follow itself to the end, even if it is a dead end." She wrote it down. Clark was a thoughtful man with a rich inner life, an inner life that was seldom apparent to those around him. In class he would throw out a topic or question and then sit back in his chair, fold his hands behind his head, put his feet up on his desk, and listen. Many students thought of him as quiet and a bit reserved, even contemplative. Although he wrote almost constantly throughout the 1930s, 1940s, and early 1950s and was engaged periodically thereafter, particularly during vacations, he published little throughout his career. It may be that his art was more an extension of his thoughtfulness than a sustained effort to reach out to others through publication.

He was concerned "to live every day," keenly observing and mentally registering the places, people, and animals around him and then thinking about what had been stored up. Often he was prompted to write in response to this thinking, writing quickly in longhand with dashes instead of normal punctuation. Frequently, he would cast aside what he had written, burning it or filing it away to be forgotten. In 1965 Clark wrote to his son, Robert: "I regret having *had* to throw away so much of what I have written, I don't regret having written it. I learned much while I wrote even the worst of it." But what he learned was not so much about the processes of writing as about what he found out once he put his thoughts into words on the page. Putting his thoughts into artistic form was for him part of his process of living fully.

Writing rapidly in response to an idea, he found, was his best mode of expression, and once expressed, the process was often, to his mind, completed. Writing was complementary to thinking, and thinking was complementary to experience. According to friend and colleague at the University of Nevada Charlton Laird, Clark would begin with an idea, "which was probably no more than a specific quirk for handling one of the themes that were always with him." And then he would

> plot the incident, considering technical matters such as point of view, straight narrative, or a compressed scene with throwbacks, and the like. If the piece was to be long he might leave himself notes, write sketches of principal characters, and something about them. When he felt ready, when he trusted that the story was about to "come," he would write, scribbling very fast in that beautiful but almost illegible calligraphy that was his handwriting. He would hope to keep going, trusting that his memory would supply without hesitation or question anything he needed.

He seldom revised, and only a few of his works went through several drafts—most notably the novels he published. And the drafts were often discrete. If he did revise, he went through a manuscript word by word, sentence by sentence to make minor changes or corrections prior to submission. He seldom took a draft and reworked it, but occasionally he might leave a manuscript with notes for a future attempt, or he might, after burning it, go back the very next day and try a different approach.

The decades of the 1930s and 1940s were his most productive, both in terms of what was written and what was published. Thus, in Cazenovia from 1935 to 1945, he produced much of his writing while teaching high school, including two of his three published novels. One of those was his best-known novel, *The Ox-Bow Incident,* which he began during Christmas vacation in 1937. This first draft, he said later, was an attempt to do for the popular Western with its myths and clichés what Cervantes did in burlesquing the chivalric romances of seventeenth-century Spain in *Don Quixote.* Professor Laird attended a class question-and-answer session in which Clark was asked why he had picked the subject for *Ox-Bow* that he did. Laird recalled his answer:

> I had become irked at the way the West was treated in popular fiction and the moving pictures, with two-gun cowboys stuffed with Sunday-school virtues, and heroines who could go through a knock-down without getting a curl misplaced.... I decided to write a Quixotesque "western" that I hoped in my youthful enthusiasm would make the whole thing look so silly that people would stop writing or reading such junk.
>
> About the same thing happened to me that happened to Cervantes. My satire was pretty trivial, and I probably knew deep down it wouldn't make much difference, anyhow. And I was disturbed about what had happened in Italy with fascism there, and was growing in Germany with the Nazi horror, and I thought that was the great threat to the modern world, and specifically to American democracy. I saw the seeds of Nazism in our country, and maybe especially in the Old West—or if

not, then in a simple dramatic incident in the West you could get a sort of test-tube sample, the local version of what had been standard treatment of the Indians and many free-thinking white men all the way west from the Pequod War. So I dumped the stuff I had written into the wastebasket and started over.

A number of friends have suggested that one of the "seeds" of fascism Clark speaks about here was a youth group in Cazenovia that upset him—but there has been no way to confirm that any such group existed.

The first draft of Clark's novel in the manner of Cervantes was completed over Easter vacation of 1938. We don't know how many subsequent drafts there were before publication of the novel in October of 1940, but Clark did complete a draft over Christmas vacation, 1938–39. The chronology of composition is not made any clearer by a comment Clark made to an interviewer when he told him, "The first draft of 'The Oxbow Incident' was completed in a month but revisions consumed two years. It isn't the writing . . . it's the rewriting." Notice he doesn't say "revision" but "rewriting." Robert, Clark's son, has said that his father spoke of the drafts altogether as "finger exercises." This suggests that he had no pressing need to seek publication of the manuscript. What happened is that Clark did submit a manuscript entitled "Water" to a contest, where it won second prize. But it failed to find a publisher. However, it did attract the attention of an agent who asked if Clark had anything else that he thought might be publishable. According to Robert Clark, his father told him he had bundled up and tossed the "Ox-Bow" manuscript into a corner, and then—when he got the request from the agent—retrieved it, dusted it off, and sent it to the agent. It would seem almost accidental that *The Ox-Bow Incident,* Clark's masterpiece, was published at all. We will never know how close Clark came to burning the manuscript as he had burned many another.

The novel got universally good reviews and many raves in the national media. Part of the reason for this was the exposure and promotion it was given by Bennett Cerf, who not only was the head of Clark's publishing house, Random House, but was a very influential spokesman on literary matters. Cerf loved the book and thought that it was one of the best published by his house in recent memory. (Cerf had a relationship with Clark that lasted many years, and while Clark did not travel to New York—which he hated—Cerf did travel to Nevada to see Clark. Cerf spent a lot of time and effort encouraging Clark to write more novels.)

The theme echoed by many reviews was struck by Fred T. Marsh in *The Saturday Review of Literature* when he wrote that this was "a first novel of maturity and virtuosity." Marsh also interpreted the novel pretty much as other reviewers did, primarily as a psychological study: "It is a novelist's study of simple universals with respect to men of very different kinds, both individually and under mass pressure, during a crisis," the crisis being the lynching and its aftermath, which the critic calls "a ghastly fiasco." But perhaps the most influential reviewer was Clifton Fadiman, writing in *The New Yorker,* who said,

> There's a kind of cabinet-worker precision about "The Ox-Bow Incident;" everything—characters, plot, style, rhythm, even the title, so cool and complete—falls into place not mechanically but organically, as if the final effect had been calculated shrewdly and patiently, with nothing left to improvisation.

Fadiman called the book a "masterpiece," so perfectly done that "it seems to deny the possibility of growth on the part of the author." Clark couldn't get any better. With two such champions as Bennett Cerf and Clifton Fadiman, Clark could not have asked for more, and he was on his way to fame, if not fortune.

Although *The Ox-Bow Incident,* largely because of the shocking mistaken lynching at the center of the novel, attracted attention as a new twist on an old genre, it is actually part of a counter-tradition of its own. There are two kinds of opposing Western stories involving typical and sometimes stereotypical Western figures in western landscapes—one kind that could loosely be called romantic, the other realistic. The focus of these two opposing traditions has extended from the 1880s, the Wild West period, into more modern western environments. *The Ox-Bow Incident* is firmly within the latter, realistic tradition.

In his introduction to Ben Vorpahl's *My Dear Wister: The Frederic Remington–Owen Wister Letters,* Wallace Stegner explores the creation of the cowboy myth that is at the heart of the popular, romantic Western:

> In [these] pages we watch the complete, triumphant ontogeny
> of the cowboy hero, the most imagination catching and durable
> of our mythic figures. Owen Wister and Frederic Remington,
> whose collaboration is the subject of Ben Vorpahl's study, cre-
> ate him before our eyes. They begin to mold him out of the
> observed realities of the brief, furious, passing empire of the
> cattlemen. They shape him by imitation and trial and error
> into the hero of a romantic fiction, and in the process they are
> themselves shaped, as the cowboy image is, by the torque of
> an anonymous public, everywhere and nowhere myth-making
> impulse. Believing they record reality, they helplessly remake
> it larger than life, until when they are done their creation rides
> off the page into the sunset of a thousand horse operas, the
> free, lonely, self-reliant, skilled, eternally ambiguous embodi-
> ment of a national, indeed a human, fantasy.

Clark's attack on the popular Western, particularly the cir-cumstances of a charismatic leader leading a mob to conscienceless violence, could be read as a political statement. But the fantasy Stegner speaks of as coming out of the myth has had wide and deep implications. The Marlboro Man, who has largely disappeared from the American scene because of legislation, is still present throughout much of the world, suggesting how far the fantasy has spread its wide appeal. Political messages extend from the myths behind the popular Western. As signaled by the hats and boots of the last three Republican presidents, images have been projected that certify a philosophy of rugged individualism.

Owen Wister's *The Virginian* is usually granted to be the first Western. The Virginian is a southerner, an ex-Confederate officer, who brings to the West southern rituals, including a corrupted sense of chivalry inherited from medieval Europe. Mark Twain said, in regard to the Confederacy and the spirit that led the Confederacy into the Civil War, that the South had read too much Sir Walter Scott. Twain added,

> A curious exemplification of the power of a single book for good or harm is shown in the effects wrought by *Don Quixote* and those wrought by *Ivanhoe*. The first swept the world's admiration for the medieval chivalry silliness out of existence; and the other restored it. As far as our South is concerned, the good work done by Cervantes is pretty nearly a dead letter, so effectually has Scott's pernicious work undermined it.

Descended from the Virginian, a southern gentleman, the cowboy hero took on some of the characteristics of the knight (remember the TV program *Have Gun, Will Travel*) — the loner who is gentlemanly in response to women, heroic, stoic, and self-reliant and who brings extralegal justice to whatever injustice, in his view, he finds in his travels. The duel, an inheritance from medieval Europe, was transferred to the Old South and transmogrified to the Western walk-down, and the extralegal justice of the knight-errant was transformed into mob justice in the South, spreading from there to the Midwest and West. It is therefore no accident, in-terms of the final form of his novel, that Clark began with a satire in the manner of *Don Quixote,* that his ringleader is an ex-Confederate officer, Tetley, and that the central incident is an extra-legal search for justice with a lynching. He strikes at the very roots of the myth. His novel can be said to be as much a parody of *The Virginian* as a satire of a genre in the manner of Cervantes.

It should be noted that in *The Virginian* one of the respected figures in the novel, Judge Henry, defends Western lynch law by comparing it to lynchings in the South. In the South, he claims, the "Negro" is taken away from the law, but in the West, which is without formal law, "your ordinary citizen ... must take justice back into his own hands," so that "far from being a *defiance* of the law, it is an *assertion* of it." But there is formal law in Bridger's Wells, the town in *The Ox-Bow Incident*—law that is competent but ignored in a rush to judgment.

The Virginian was followed by many imitations and changed the course of the "dime novel" Western, which had first appeared about the time of the Civil War, by certifying the cowboy hero and his code. Stegner has pointed out that in later years these dime novels were often avidly read for inspiration and comfort by real cowboys behind the bunkhouse, "reading their own myth." More serious, but still essentially romantic Westerns were produced by such writers as Zane Grey, Luke Short, and Louis L'Amour. Nevertheless, there were realistic elements in these and similar popular writers: the landscape descriptions in Grey and Short, for example, and the scrupulous attention to details regarding Indian lore and weaponry in L'Amour. What the novels had in common was the "code," largely adopted from *The Virginian*—stoic self-reliance on the part of the protagonist and a chivalric sense of honor and duty.

The problem with the popular Western, as Stegner has pointed out, is that it falsified history by spreading the contention that the

West was won by the lone horseman; whereas, in fact, the Wild West was a relatively brief period and the West was won by the less glamorized "clod busters," the farm and ranch families who worked in conjunction with each other to build their homes and communities. In opposition to the popular, more or less romantic Westerns have been the literary Western novels that have been realistic, antimyth, and antistereotype in their depiction of character and situation. Critic Thomas J. Lyon calls them "revisionist" writing, the classic examples of which he traces back to Robinson Jeffers, Harvey Fergusson, Vardis Fisher, A. B. Guthrie Jr., and Frank Waters. These writers, Lyon states,

> did not view the West as an endless frontier; they did not make one-dimensional heroes of explorers, trappers, cowboys, gunfighters, and so forth, and they did not share the arrogance of Manifest Destiny. In short, their works are not simple-minded. Their writings' complexity anticipates by several decades the analytic position of the current "New Historicism." In some cases — particularly in the philosophies of Robinson Jeffers and Frank Waters — these classic writers have mapped territory that remains untraveled by most contemporary critics of the West.

In light of the impact that Robinson Jeffers had on Walter Clark, it is interesting that he is at the head of Lyon's list. There are so many romantic elements in Jeffers — his extremism in image and theme, his attachment to nature, his emotionalism, and his looking back to Greek myth (in the manner of Shelley) — that it is hard to think of him as a realist. And Jeffers would seem to fit M. H. Abrams's definition as applied to the major poets of the Romantic period: "The important romantic poems are in fact poems of feelingful meditation about central human problems."

And yet, as Lyon points out, what is "revisionist" about Jeffers is that "he attempted to go beyond the standpoint of anthropocentric thought. His paradigm, as we would say, was not set solely by speciesist rules. 'Something utterly wild had crept into his mind.' " Lyon adds that Jeffers

> was on a kind of frontier, where what he termed the "perma-
> nent life" of non-modern culture could be observed and where
> the sheer magnificence and vastness of the coastal environ-
> ment—an epitome of the true wildness of this world—stood
> as a reminder that all human life is a mere flicker within some-
> thing unimaginably greater.... Jeffers's western wilderness
> was a key to perceiving the essential wildness of the universe
> as a whole, in which human personality is only something like
> a lichen on a rock. No tall heroics for Jeffers.

This philosophy, as we have seen, is largely shared by Clark and is demonstrated in *Ox-Bow* (as well as in all of his Western fiction) by the smallness, even the pettiness of the people in their mistaken violence within the larger, more enduring landscape. Behind Clark's novel is the search for community, the constructive oppo-site of the destructive mob.

To Lyon's list of revisionists we might certainly add others who are "classic" or have continued the tradition: Willa Cather, Wal-lace Stegner, Walter Van Tilburg Clark, Ivan Doig, and William Kittredge. They, for the most part, have followed the example of A. B. Guthrie Jr. in novels such as *Big Sky* by showing the cowboy, the mountain man, or the sheriff as flawed and guilty of despoil-ing the environment and engaged in violence—often senseless—against animals, other whites, and certainly Native Americans. Aside from Cather, who shows the pioneers building and helping one another, the history of the West in these writers is a sad one. Jeffers was able to stand on the last frontier on the edge of the Pacific and declare the smallness of man in respect to the wild; oth-ers would grant the smallness of man within a relatively wild land-scape but also see him as destructive and shortsighted.

The difference between the popular and the literary novel is succinctly put in Lyon's description of the main theme of Harvey Fergusson. Whereas Jeffers concerned himself cosmically with the polarity of humanity and nature, Fergusson deals with the opposition of romance and realism: "The struggle between nostalgia and static allegiances on the one hand, and realistic adaptation on the other." Wallace Stegner was once asked by an interviewer what the difference was between what he wrote and what Louis L'Amour wrote: "The difference between L'Amour and me is that he's made two or three million dollars more than I have by writing the kind of western books he writes. . . . writing western myths, not writing western realities." Much of the American public wants desperately to preserve its myths and tends to resent those who seek to dispel them. It is amazing, then, that *Ox-Bow* was as popular as it was, and one suspects that many readers read it simply because it *was* a Western, although with a difference (and readers do enjoy a surprise ending, no matter how gruesome). Clark would seem to have gradually realized that his novel was popular for the wrong reasons, and that became a matter of discouragement for him.

Good and just people must say and do what they know is right in order to create a good and just community. In the novel Clark presents a variety of character responses to the lynching process. Some good men object but are too weak to sway the crowd; others are strong enough but do nothing. A major theme in *Ox-Bow* is what happens when good men fail to act against evil. Mark Twain, over a hundred years ago, talked about this problem in "The United States of Lyncherdom":

> Why does a crowd of the same kind of people in Texas, Colorado, Indiana, stand by, smitten to the heart and miserable, and by ostentatious outward signs pretend to enjoy a lynching? Why does it lift no hand or voice in protest? Only because it

would be unpopular to do it, I think, each man is afraid of his neighbor's disapproval, a thing which, to the general run of the race, is more dreaded than wounds and death.

The problem is human, but it has a particular western flavor here — the preservation of an image of manhood. We are back to the Marlboro Man. The two cowboys in *Ox-Bow,* Art Croft and Gil Carter, who carry the story as the novel's narrator and his sidekick, are shown to be tough and resilient. Yet, as Max Westbrook points out, "Repeatedly Art and Gil show themselves ready to fight with fists or with guns in order to show their allegiance to a cause in which they do not believe." Clark's point against the popular Western is further clinched by his presentation of two cowboys who are hardly heroic. These men are definitely not your Lone Ranger and Tonto. According to Westbrook, free will, or what I would call the western code of rugged individualism, leads to greed and "an exaggerated evaluation of the male ego."

Intellect, which in the novel is associated with the weakest characters, is thus associated with a degraded version of the feminine, and "the lynch mob in *The Ox-Bow Incident* misappropriates for itself a monopoly on virtuous masculinity." What we see throughout the novel is a failure of personality integration — the feminine is separated from the masculine, the intellectual from the emotional, and the mythic or archetypal from apparent reality. In Westbrook's terms, both Art and Gil participate in the murder while knowing it is wrong, because "they fear an inner reality," giving in to social pressure. This fear is placed by Carl Jung in "the realm of the unconscious. . . . People [Jung explains] are 'afraid of becoming conscious of themselves.' "

Along these same lines but in different terms, Herbert Wilner, colleague and friend of Clark's, has focused on what he believed to be the central theme in Clark's fiction as well as in his own life — the need to achieve "wholeness":

Humankind, in general, in its limited time and by its limited
views, puts itself in the center of all things. Nature does not.
In nature humankind simply bears the particular burden of
consciousness, and they bear it best who come to understand
it most, to understand that between humankind's desire
and nature's necessity there must be balance. . . . If human
beings, believing in their own supremacy, disturb the balance,
they only delude themselves with ideas of power and self-
fulfillment. . . . A vision of balance must be made to operate in
human relationship with other persons as well as in life with
and in nature. The one leads to justice; the other leads to order.

It should be added that one of Clark's favorite authors was
Joseph Conrad, who frequently wrote about nonintegrated per-
sonalities—in particular the actual physical split of a personality
into two people in "The Secret Sharer," as well as the split within
the entire ship's crew in *The Nigger of the Narcissus* and the split
between failure and hero within the central character of *Lord Jim.*
Clark had taught *The Heart of Darkness* so often he had it memo-
rized, and one might think at the end of *Ox-Bow* of that line from
this Conrad novel, "Oh, the horror!" In the Conrad novel, the narrator finds that his predecessor in the jungle, Kurz, has given way
to ego, and rather than his holding on to the ideals with which he
came to the Congo, his wholeness dissolves as he succumbs to the
worst, very bloody aspects of the native life around him. He loses
his balance and is adrift in the swamp of the darker side of the unconscious, the "heart of darkness"—or as Nathaniel Hawthorne
might say, the darkness in the human heart. (Critic John Milton
has noted images of light and dark in *Ox-Bow* that suggest the
conflict between good and evil, operating much like similar details
in Conrad's *Heart of Darkness.*)

Wallace Stegner, friend and admirer of Clark's work, uses the
term *reconciliation* to describe the thrust of Clark's fiction, rather

than Wilner's *balance* or my *integration*. Stegner, in writing about Clark's career, has said that he "was trying ... to marry sensitivity and philosophical ideas to the half-primitive western life he knew." He adds, "Civilization is Walter Clark's theme; the West is only his raw material. What else is the burden of *The Ox-Bow Incident?*" Rather than *civilization,* the theme is expressed by Charlton Laird in a somewhat different way. He suggests that there were three basic drafts of the novel. The first was a spoof of the stereotypical Western; the second was Clark's anti-Nazi version; and in the third Clark produced "a true novel" rather than a tract-like study of society, a "story that is first of all a work of art, delineating the problem of human morality." As the writer Stegner has said of the writer Clark, "I sense a fellow moralist in him."

Clark may have been a moralist at heart, but he was even more essentially an artist. He has said, "Fiction, all fiction, I think we can say, has one basic purpose, no matter what kind it is or what particular realm or subject it is dealing with: to create the illusion of experience." In light of the frequent misinterpretation of *Ox-Bow* as simply another, albeit different, Western, it may come as a surprise that Clark thought its greatest weakness was that its themes were stated too overtly — that is, not hidden, not converted fully enough into the reader's sense of experience.

With the publication of *Ox-Bow* in 1940, Clark became famous and suddenly his short stories were in demand. Most of his published stories came out during the next five years, appearing in major magazines and journals such as *The Atlantic, The Saturday Evening Post, The New Yorker,* and *The Yale Review.* Many of the stories had been written earlier and filed away.

One of these was "Hook," which has probably become the best known of his stories, having been included in a number of anthologies (it was also made into an animated film version for TV). The story is something of a tour de force. It follows the life of a hawk from birth to death and does so from the hawk's point of view, although it is told in the third person. Although Clark may be accused of personification, he walks a tightrope, making the hawk's thoughts and emotions understandable while at the same time carefully converting them into a hawk's perspective. What is striking about "Hook," however, is that it is the story of the life of an animal without the slightest hint of sentimentality. We might think back on Jack London's animal stories, such as *The Call of the Wild*, which are very realistic in detail yet touched with pathos.

Clark's telling is very matter-of-fact — as if to say, this is just the way it is. Hook is tough, a survivor who leads a tough life, but the bird's life is not tragic — his life is simply what he has to go through in order to survive. By telling such a realistic story, Clark reverses popular expectations, as he had reversed them in *Ox-Bow* — there is nothing cute or even noble about the nature or behavior of this animal. The emphasis is on the wild and the hawk's representation of the wildness in nature. But still there is something grand about the endurance of the hawk and the feeling, as the hawk is used in Jeffers's poetry, that it is somehow connected to the primordial and enduring. The hawk as symbol is so common in Jeffers's poetry that it would seem his use of it must have influenced Clark in writing his story. In an essay on "Hook," Ann Ronald points to a specific poem from the first Jeffers book that Clark purchased (*Cawdor*, 1929) as containing the germ of the story. She quotes from "Hurt Hawks":

> The broken pillar of the wing jags from the clotted shoulder,
> The wing trails like a banner in defeat,
> No more to use the sky forever but live with famine
> And pain a few days . . .

This picture matches well the picture of Hook as his life runs out. He is wounded by pellets from a shotgun and only barely manages to scrabble for food, and his life ends as the result of a dog that is sent out by a farmer to kill him. As is often the case in Clark's fiction, reflecting his Jeffers-like philosophy, it is the human who is the intruder and despoiler. It isn't sad—it is just what happens, and regardless of human interference, the natural processes will go on.

But in the presence of "civilizing" humans, they will not go on in the same way. Ann Ronald sees the hawk as a symbol of the "wilderness spirit of the West," a spirit that the story suggests is being extinguished. In representing this spirit, Hook

> has nowhere to go. So Clark faces the problem of the closing of the frontier somewhat more abstractly than most writers, crippling it first with a shotgun, letting it spend a year "without flame, a snappish, dust-covered creature," and then eliminating it. A domestic pet strikes the last blow.
>
> Many analogies come to mind—strip-mining, clear-cutting, Lake Powell, the entire Colorado River. Each seems tragic in a sense unimagined [by an eastern critic of "Hook"], tragic, finally, in an inarticulate way. I would argue that Walter Clark understood this finality well, and the "Hook" represents his own rethinking of what extinguishing the spirit of the West really means.

I can only add—how about Pyramid Lake, Lake Tahoe, and Reno itself, all beloved by Clark. In this regard, the condition and fate of Clark's old prospectors, in stories such as "The Indian Well" and "The Wind and the Snow of Winter," seem to suggest the futility of greed, although his prospectors seem to be more habituated to the search itself than dreaming of wealth. And Clark's old mining towns, gradually fading into dust, would likewise seem to testify to the futility, in the long run, of man's digging, cutting, and building.

This message of man the intruder and destroyer is brought home in an even more powerful way in the story "The Buck in the Hills." However, in this story we see a comparison of a man who is at one with nature and a man who represents humanity at its worst—destructive and blindly filled with his own ego. The unnamed narrator, after an absence of several years, is hiking once more in the backcountry, the Sierra Nevada above Tahoe. His hike is an effort to refresh his spirit and reestablish his connection with the primordial. Looking up at the mountain above him, the man declares, "The peak was sacred to me, the climb was pilgrimage, and five years is a long time." The solidity and eternalness of his environment, as well as the cycle of death and rebirth, are established here, as they are so often in Clark's fiction, when the narrator tells us

> I climbed over the big rock barrier, which a million winters had cracked into terraces, saw the dry, shriveled clumps of leaves and single dead stems in the cracks, and remembered times I had come up there in the summer [it is now fall], which is spring at that height, and seen it pouring with green, like cascades, and lighted by flowers.

The man is dwarfed by his surroundings as he looks out from his mountain over the valleys to the right and left, out toward Pyramid Lake and Lake Tahoe in the distance.

The sacred nature of his pilgrimage is reinforced by his bursting into wordless song and a "baptism" in a cold mountain lake—activities that critic Max Westbrook calls "pure Clark." Westbrook compares the narrator's journey to what Jake Barnes is doing on his fishing trip in Hemingway's *The Sun Also Rises*—trying to "replenish his soul." But a closer comparison might be made with Barnes's journey to San Sabastian. After the nightmare of Pamplona, where he has betrayed himself and his friends, he dives into the cold ocean and feels cleansed and renewed. The comparison to Hemingway is appropriate in that the prose of Clark's story is continually reminiscent of Hemingway's style. At one point the narrator of "The Buck in the Hills" says, for example, "God, I was happy. This was the way I liked it, alone, and clean cold, and a lot of time ahead." Clark taught Hemingway's stories and *The Sun Also Rises* enough to know them well.

The narrator's immersion in the primordial and his ritual of renewal is aborted, however, when he learns that one of the men he meets for a camping and hunting trip, Chet, has deliberately crippled a deer rather than shooting for the kill. He has done so in order to avoid having to carry the deer and instead has herded the wounded deer the eight miles back to camp. The narrator's other companion, Tom, recalls what Chet told him about his actions, that "he thought he was real clever. He bragged about it." Even worse, as Tom tells the narrator angrily, "He told me all about how he drove it, too ... How it kept trying to run at first, and falling over so he had to laugh."

The horror of this conclusion and the total reversal of atmosphere in the story are cinched by Clark's final lines, as the narrator hikes down the mountain with Tom:

> There was something listening behind each tree and rock we
> passed, and something waiting among the taller trees down
> slope, blue through the falling snow. They wouldn't stop us,
> but they didn't like us, either. The snow was their ally.

One might call Clark a master of reversals, for not only he reverses the plot and atmosphere, but he rather subtly provides a reversal through style.

Clark imitates Hemingway's style to a certain extent, but it is not an imitation based in admiration. On the various lists of those writers whom Clark admired or thought might have influenced him, Hemingway was conspicuously absent; instead, he names writers who are quite different from Hemingway—Joseph Conrad, Henry James, and William Faulkner. However, there is in Hemingway a sense of the smallness of man and the sacredness of nature that Clark can admire and which he uses to build the early atmosphere in "The Buck in the Hills." One need only think of "Big Two-Hearted River" to see a parallel, a story in which an emotionally troubled veteran of World War I goes on a fishing trip in the wilds of upper Michigan in order to regain his balance. In the story the protagonist, Nick, after getting off the train at Seney, discovers "there was no town, nothing but the rails and the burned-over country. . . . Even the surface had been burned off the ground." Even the grasshoppers were blackened. The parallel with the war that Nick has recently witnessed seems clear. As he heads toward the backcountry, Nick finds in this environment the only constant that brings some encouragement to him are the fish in the river under the bridge that "hold steady" in the current. The contrast between the refreshment offered by immersion in nature and the destructiveness of man is one that Clark could endorse.

However, the man, Hemingway, at the end of the 1930s, was known to the public primarily as a big-game hunter and aficionado of the bullfight. This knowledge came not only through *Death in the Afternoon* and *The Green Hills of Africa* but from photos of Hemingway with gun in hand and dressed in hunting clothes or posing with bullfighters, photos which appeared frequently in newspapers and *Life* magazine. When we realize that Clark gave up both hunting and fishing before he was twenty and recall how in fiction after fiction he deplores man the killer, we can see how he has used Hemingway to structure the "The Buck in the Hills." He leads us into a world of Hemingway's nature as sacred and renewing, but as we follow the trail, it leads to the world of Hemingway the profaner. As we read about Chet, who purposely wounds without killing the deer, we may be reminded of all the times in Hemingway's work, in "The Short Happy Life of Francis McComber," for example, where an animal is cruelly wounded (although not on purpose) and the hunter must follow the bloody trail to finish it off.

In "The Buck in the Hills," Clark's emotions are closer to the surface than they are in most of his stories. Robert Clark has said about his father's writing that "Dad needed to find material that sustained some original feeling that compelled him to write, the feeling generated by the particular image that was so often the source for his fiction." Robert has noted that his father's story "The Indian Well" is "dominated by a kind of restrained scorn for humankind and its works." Restrained scorn gives way in "The Buck in the Hills" to a more overt anger. Again, as Robert has said, there was in his father "an anger a good deal deeper than the flash-point temper. He was angry at the general course of human activity."

CHAPTER FIVE

WRITER OF STORIES, POEMS, AND LETTERS

In the story "the indian well," an old prospector, in revenge, sets out to kill a mountain lion for doing what mountain lions do. Another old prospector appears in one of Clark's best stories, "The Wind and the Snow of Winter," which won the O. Henry short story award for 1945. Once again the man is set against an environment which is large and indifferent to his wishes and within a time frame that emphasizes human temporariness. And once again the prospector is presented objectively enough that he is at once an individual we can sympathize with—but not too much—and at the same time something more. On one level he represents the end of a breed, the walking prospector with his burro, a type that Clark was very fond of; on another level he represents all humans who recollect their lives as they face the end.

At the onset of winter, the prospector, Mike Braneen, with his burro, Annie, are coming in from the desert mountains of Nevada to the mining town of Gold Rock. Gold Rock is the site of the other half of his life—time spent every winter in town until spring comes once again. The motif of the story is the journey, an ancient and durable story form, and this is a journey into memory, into the past, and, it would seem, toward death. It contrasts the lonely individual of the present with the community that in the past nourished him but in the present no longer exists. Snow flurries urge Braneen onward on his journey, and as he trudges up a mountain road toward town, his head is continuously replaying memories or inventing stories. In that regard he is something like his creator.

The old prospector's memories are jumbled and confused, underlining his age and conveying to the reader a feeling of sadness and loss. Present reality is conflicted with the past, as can be seen when he calls his burro by three different names (the story is filled with such small touches as this) and when he finally gets to town, he expects to find a town that is no longer there. As he approaches Gold Rock in darkness (just as fall is turning to winter, so day has turned to night), he expects to see a lot of orange windows close together across the canyon but instead sees a few scattered white lights. Braneen has forgotten that this is the Gold Rock of the present, and the sight of the new is not a pleasant image. The white lights "made no communal glow upon the steep slope, but gave out only single, white needles of light, which pierced the darkness secretly and lonesomely, as if nothing could ever pass from one house to another over there."

The emotion that arises from this passage is not scorn or anger, but melancholy. In the images of orange contrasted with white and the flames of lamps with electric lights there is deep sense of loss, as community turns to modern society's separateness and aloneness. The town that the prospector looks for, the greetings from old friends, the comfort of familiar surroundings, and the eating and drinking with companions are the very things that Clark himself most valued. And the town, Gold Rock, is patterned after a town, Austin, that Clark knew well and loved. The prospector has deliberately chosen the dirt road up the mountain to town rather than the paved road on the other side of the pass. He knows he is absentminded and is fearful that he and his burro would be in some danger from the cars that come up the paved road from behind. But as Braneen enters town, he and his burro are almost run down by a highway maintenance truck — another complex series of contrasts. And as he approaches the saloon where he expects it to be "the same as ever," where he will be greeted boisterously by Tom the owner and welcomed by friends, he finds the Lucky Boy "dark, and there were boards nailed across the big window that had shown the sign." Instead of warmth and companionship, he finds darkness, emptiness, and decay.

Another small touch is connected to his memory of a prostitute he had been with many years earlier. He recalls that she wore a locket on a gold chain, and inside the locket was a cameo of a man holding a woman's hand very gently, with their fingers "laid out long together, and just the thumbs holding, the way they were sometimes on tombstones." This tender joining together, the warm and reassuring relationship suggested, survives only as memory (like the community Braneen remembers and values), and the tombstone becomes a prediction for the prospector as well as a preface to his gradual recognition that all the people he expects to find in Gold Rock are now dead.

He remembers too a time long ago in his youth when he stayed out all winter:

> He could remember how it felt to be out in the clear winter
> weather on the mountains, the piñon trees and the junipers
> weighted down with feathery snow, and making sharp, blue
> shadows on the white slopes.

The scene had inspired joy and a lust for life in him, and he had trooped over the snow-covered mountains, pretending with hammer and drill to be prospecting but actually celebrating being alive, "galavanting, playing colt." It is an activity in his memory that contrasts sharply with his present circumstances: "The snowy cold had searched out the regions of his body where old injuries had healed.... Sometimes he even thought, with a moment of fear, that he was getting tired."

According to Clark, in an introduction he gave as a preface to a reading of "The Wind and the Snows of Winter," the above passage about the "clear winter weather" contains the germ of the story. And from this revelation, we can learn a good deal about how he wrote stories in general. He proposes three different ways in which a story is generated in the mind of the writer. The first approach, which he calls the "foreseen," begins with "an idea, a moral, a purpose, a statement you wish to make, though you cannot make it directly or you destroy the illusion of experience." In the second approach, which he calls the "exploratory," the writer is "suddenly moved by a memory, a personal experience, an intense feeling about something." And third, there is what Clark calls the "known story," in which the writer, to begin with, is aware of the idea, the moral, or the theory—"whatever it is he or she wishes the story to shadow forth without direct statement or preachment—and the world which will give body to that idea and shadow forth the idea." He gives as an example historical fiction, wherein the writer takes some actual scene and interprets it.

The happiest experience for the writer, according to Clark, involves the second of these approaches, "the exploratory story that really works out for itself.... You touch upon a memory that moves you." You start by presenting the little scene that has mattered to you emotionally and, if you are lucky, you discover a whole story that lies behind it. "The Wind and the Snow of Winter" was that kind of story for Clark. He came across the scene that affected him after a blizzard, while he was living in Cazenovia. It was a clearing day that caught up his spirit, with a brilliant sun, two or three feet of snow on the ground, and behind his house, a little grove of spruce trees heavily burdened with snow. He recalled,

In the bright sunlight they were casting very clear, blue shadows on the ground snow, distinct almost to the needle. The whole image was one that really did not belong to upper New York State; it belonged to Nevada. It was that kind of winter, that kind of sunlight.

For some reason, he had become restless, and he was drawn to write something, possibly a poem, to relieve his restlessness. But his vision of trees and shadows in the snow led him to a series of associations. The scene brought to mind the juniper and piñon trees of White Pine County, Nevada, and that, in turn, led him to think of an incident involving him and his wife when they visited Hamilton and Treasure Hill in Nevada in an early spring with snow still on the ground. They ran across a tall, thin white-haired man, the last permanent resident, who, although carrying a three-foot drill in one hand and a heavy hammer in the other, admitted that he was not really looking for anything, "it was just the spring that got him." Clark asked him some questions about the road and the town, and it turned out that the man had made a survey of things twenty-one years before but, strangely enough, had not bothered to look at them since. In his introduction to the story, Clark goes on to say,

> This man came back to my mind after I had had the first
> glimpse of blue shadow, the sense of cold, of clarity in the air,
> of the purity of sound that would come with that. I knew I had
> to have a prospector in the piece somehow. At that point it
> began to be a story rather than just a vignette of place, a scene
> that I was to remember.

The prospector from Hamilton, with his memories of a town twenty-one years earlier and his wandering around in the joy of spring, becomes the basis for Clark's central character in "The Wind and Snow of Winter," but with some alteration. The author wanted to make him more generic, so he combined him, in appearance, with a portrait that Robert Caples had done of an old prospector, gray bearded and stocky rather than tall and thin.

As the story began to evolve, Clark realized that he would have to make the time when the story takes place the beginning of winter rather than spring, and a name came to him—Mike Braneen. Clark continues his recounting of his progress:

> The moment I was on the road with Mike, almost everything was settled; Mike took over. It was his story. I followed. I had really only one problem: to be able to write fast enough to keep up with Mike. . . . I wrote busily, happily, and furiously for something less than three hours and the story was complete.

Not all of Clark's stories were written in quite this way, but his account of the composition of this story is, apparently, in many respects typical for him. He said many times that he was inspired to write out of emotion, emotion that came from a circumstance or a scene, and that writing quickly produced the best results for him. "The Wind and the Snow of Winter" and "Hook" are among the great short stories of the twentieth century. After earlier journal publication, they were published in 1950 along with seven other stories and the short novel "The Watchful Gods" in *The Watchful Gods and Other Stories.*

———

Walter Clark was no Emily Dickinson either in having her kind of talent or in the circumstances of his life, yet he did share with Dickinson that intimate and private relationship one can have with one's own writing. In surveying Clark's life one gets the feeling that although he was proud of what publications he did have, he was not particularly anxious to publish. This is especially true of his poetry. With his poetry he seemed to lead another life apart from his writing of fiction, a life free, private, and secure—secure from judgment and secure from misinterpretation. He wrote poetry almost constantly from his late teens to very late in his life, and after some initial publication of his poems in his youth, he stopped even attempting to get them published (although he did occasionally have vague plans of doing so).

In writing poetry he would seem to have been prompted mainly by two motives. The first was the attempt to do in poetry the sort of things he did so well in prose—primarily, to describe scenes and characters and to narrate. A number of his poems are similar to such stories as "The Indian Well" and "The Wind and Snow of Winter" in that they deal with loners who are often somewhat eccentric and are trying to make sense of their lives. The second motive was to respond quickly and in brief form to a feeling that arose from a scene or experience. The narrative poems, in particular, would seem to have been heavily influenced by Edwin Arlington Robinson ("Richard Cory," "Miniver Cheevy") and Robinson Jeffers. One can see the E. A. Robinson influence as well as the influence of Robert Browning's dramatic monologues in poems such as "Mark Agnew's Cat":

> Mad, so you'd call Mark Agnew mad
> Because he had a house all to himself,
> And a black cat, and his own way of talking
> When there was no one to hear?
> Mark Agnew might as well have talked alone
> For all that you, or such as you'd have heard him say.

Tone, rhythm, diction, and manner of address are all reminiscent of Robinson here. On the other hand, in "Benedict Morales' Wife" we see Jeffers's influence as Morales describes Helga, the woman he had loved:

> the white one
> Whose voice is low and cool as the tide in the narrows
> When it is full and going under Raven's Head.

She was a daughter of the sun and sea,
A marble cup hissing with hot, white wine
As sweet as burning in the throat,
A strange white blossom from a mystery
Awash in the green surge across the channel.

Such imagery as burning, heat, the surging sea, and the mystical personae "daughter of the sun and sea," intimately connected to nature, as well as the manner of description and the tone, are reminiscent of Jeffers. A number of poems seem to combine the two influences—the dramatic monologues of Robinson, and sometimes his rhythms, with Jeffers's tone and imagery. As is the case in many of Clark's stories, the narrator or main protagonist in his narrative poems is often a loner struggling to bring into reality his dreams or desires, often involving some kind of community, a joining with another, or a striving for a deep participation in the sacred natural world around him. But for one reason or another, he has only partial success or fails.

As the critic Susan Baker has put it in an essay on Clark's poetry:

Crucial to both the poetry and the fiction is the conflict between a solitary quest for wisdom and the need for engagement in a human world.... It is possible to trace through these poems [his extended narratives] a group of related themes that invariably attend Clark's loners: sanity and fear, beauty and pain, codified knowledge and intuitive apprehension, a deadening religion and life-giving celebration.... Clark repeatedly insists on the life-enhancing necessity of participation in a human community. So these poetic studies of loners, of what they gain and what they lose by their isolation, with all the themes that accompany their essentially one-dimensional portrayals, can best be appreciated as stages toward the creation of the multidimensional, "primary realist" protagonists of Clark's major fiction.

Clark apparently felt that his poetry was often too direct, in itself too "one-dimensional," and that it was too difficult in poetry for him to bring the reader into an experience far enough that the implicit idea or message could be felt.

Clark's second motive for writing poetry was to use it as a kind of shorthand response to something, usually an emotion, so that his short poems are often almost a kind of note taking but also a relief valve for someone driven to write. (A character in one of Clark's short stories is described as "the man who needed to write.") This motive would seem to be somewhat similar to Emily Dickinson's, but the problem for the fast-writing Clark was that he didn't usually take the time to refine and polish his poems into the little gems that Dickinson produced. Furthermore, Clark did not have Dickinson's talent for truncated metaphor. Most of his best metaphors tend to depend on extended description within a narrative context.

In his introduction to "The Wind and the Snow of Winter," he says that his first response to the scene at Cazenovia when "in the bright sunlight [the trees] were casting very clear, bright shadows on the ground snow" was to write "a little bastard poem that would serve as a note or relief." There is no sense here that he was going to write something to communicate his emotion to an audience by refining it until he felt that communication would be indirect but successful. Again, the key to Clark's uses of poetry, as well as his turning away from it as his primary writing strategy, would seem to be his deep concern for writing things that an audience could experience.

Walter Clark was a severe critic of his own work; some would say too severe. Wallace Stegner has speculated that Clark's lapse into publication silence during the last twenty years of his life may have come from a "perfectionism" — Clark himself thought that he was too much a perfectionist. Certainly, it would seem that he did not feel his poetry met the standards of what he thought literature should do. Maybe he came to feel eventually that his fiction was not accomplishing what he wanted it to accomplish either—that is, stimulating the reader response he hoped for. The "standard" by which he judged his own work, both fiction and, implicitly, narrative poetry (although he speaks only of fiction here) is stated in his introduction to "The Wind and Snow of Winter." The most literature can accomplish is an illusion of reality, he says, and continues,

> When I say "the illusion of reality," I mean essentially this: that the effort of the fiction writer, always, is to create the experience, to seek, in the first place, to put himself in the position of a major character or characters in a story and, by way of that, to coerce his reader into the same position—not to preach any sermon, not to state or expound any idea or theory—but whatever idea he may wish to present, to make it inherent in that experience. Implicit but not stated.

To put it briefly, Clark apparently tended to keep his poetry to himself because it was difficult for him in poetry to lead his reader into experience—to avoid bald statement and "make whatever idea [the writer] may wish to present" inherent. And it may be that since most poets constantly refine and revise their work, Clark realized that his preferred method of composition—to sit down and write quickly—was not really suitable to that form.

———

Walter Clark during these years would seem to have been writing almost constantly, and since in his letters or notes he seldom identifies a work by its title, it is difficult to know when the final version of any particular work was written. However, his letters, speaking in vague terms, often mention work completed, in progress, or planned. For example, during a vacation to the West in 1937, he wrote to his wife, who was at the Morse summer home in Essex:

At Virginia [City] we took separate rooms in a box-like structure of B street (one up the mountain from the main drag) and
during the whole time we were there Robert [Caples] drew
(he's using colored chalks for these sketches) sometimes from
his window or mine, but more often from various points of
vantage around the town. While he was drawing I was writing;
finished two more short stories, one of them rather long, on the
... theme we talked about, the other somewhat humorous,
unpublishable, and for my own amusement. I hate to confess
that I haven't touched the novel yet [probably *Ox-Bow*], or
even thought seriously about it; doubt if I will. Have two or
three more short stories I can get off in the next week, I guess,
and then I want to take a fling at a play in verse; it would be
good for my morale, if not for anything else. (7/26/37)

When Clark says that "while he was drawing I was writing," he
was speaking literally—he might stay in his room and work,
but he also might take his yellow pad and pencil, find somewhere
to sit near where Caples was drawing, and simply scribble away
happily.

Clark never really felt at home in the East, and he had traveled
back to the West during this summer of 1937 in order to refresh his
spirit. Stopping off to camp in the desert near Albuquerque, he
wrote to his wife:

This is home country—the air is dry and thin, and quick to
change from hot to cool at sundown. Tonight, outside our
camp, the wind is wuthering in a fashion I haven't heard—in
I didn't realize how long—and it smells of stony passes and
piñon trees. And all day, over the upland mesas, the clouds
tumbled in bulky and sunlit shapes, making the familiar black
shadows, like racing burnt patches, over buttes and valleys.
(7/7/37)

Clark had made at least one previous extended visit to Virginia City with his wife during the early thirties, but it was during a weeklong stay with Caples on this trip that he would seem to have fallen in love with the town, and that, in turn, would lead him eventually to make it his home. At the same time he was attracted to Virginia City, he was becoming disenchanted with Reno. Again, writing to his wife, Clark says that

> Virginia City is waking up again, somewhat, though it's no roaring metropolis yet, thank God. The tourists only find it in harmless trickles, most of them being too broke after one night in Reno to go anywhere but home if they can do that. There are over ninety clubs in Reno now. But you remember how Virginia looked when we last went up together, about four hundred people, and every other house vacant. Now a lot of the houses have been torn down, or have finally blown down the canyons, and there isn't a place to be had, population fifteen hundred, Comstock mine and a couple of others operating to some extent. No real changes in the appearance of the place, though, except the gaps.
>
> We took in several houses while Robert was looking for likely sets, old places with high stone foundations, solid iron shutters, a couple of miles of corkscrewed, elaborately railed stairs, and tall, tin chimneys with little caps. We poked around in the "millionaire's club," the big, as yet unchanged room over the Crystal Bar, where Mackay, Sutro, and all the other gold watch chain boys used to play Faro and Poker at a thousand bucks a throw. (7/26/37)

After Virginia City, Clark and Caples went on to a week at Tahoe, and then Clark went to Reno to visit his family. Taking up residence in his old room in the president's house, he told his wife that he was writing to her "under the most decadent of circumstances, with a phonograph right beside me, upon which I'm play-ing one of my favorite things, the Grieg Sonata in C Minor." The day before, he had spent the afternoon and evening with old friends, and he confessed that for the first time since he had been in Reno, "I've pulled my once in so often spell of talking altogether too much, and about everything, whether I knew anything about it nor not." But his best time while in Reno was a day he spent alone in the mountains, "Wearing moccasins, a sleeveless shirt, and swimming trunks. Had a small lunch along in a paper sack" (8/1/7).

Just as Clark sometimes talked a blue streak in conversation, he would sometimes write letters that were much like long monologues. During his lifetime he would write a great many let-ters — sometimes newsy, sometimes businesslike, but more often reflective or descriptive — to friends, colleagues, editors, and par-ticularly to his wife. As we shall see, part of his pattern of living after leaving Cazenovia in 1945 was to spend a semester here at one university or a year there at another as a visiting professor teach-ing creative writing, a pattern followed by many writers and poets in recent decades in order to support their writing habits. It did not seem wise for Clark to bring his wife and children with him on all these temporary teaching stints, to uproot the family for only a few months. Thus, he wrote often to a wife whom he adored and missed, while at the same time writing to relieve his loneliness and homesickness. Sometimes, it seems clear, he wrote his letters just to exercise his writing muscles.

However, in the summer of 1937 Clark was not yet famous and a visiting professor but simply worn out by his long hours of work for Cazenovia Central. He and Barbara agreed to take separate va-cations — he to visit his family and friends in Reno and renew his spirits in the western landscape, she to visit her family in Essex. Among the letters he wrote, both on the road and at his destina-tion (including the excerpts above), is one that is ten typewritten pages long. Most of it recounts a day of hiking to one of his favorite locations, Mount Rose, which overlooks Tahoe on one side and the Washoe Valley, Reno, and, in the distance, Pyramid Lake on the other.

This long monologue shows a man "who needed to write," but more importantly, displays a man who could have been an outstanding nature writer. The descriptions, both of what was seen and of what was experienced and felt, are detailed and vivid. He begins with a panoramic view from a ridge that runs from Mount McAllis to Mount Rose:

> This ridge being the back-bone of that range of the Sierra, I could see during my whole tramp, innumerable small valleys below me on both sides, six or eight burning, timberless ranges to the east, and a dozen ranges, all more or less timbered and dotted with small lakes, to the west.

And then he turns to a close-up of the environment:

> The main body of the ridge was covered with pure white, large-grained sand, which caught the light on innumerable facets, and the rocks themselves, large boulders set at wide intervals through the sand, and at the end of the stretch piled up into a small individual mountain, were also white, flecked with a pepper of black particles, but more noticeably with a bitter shining salt of mica and white crystal. The dazzle was all-encompassing.

He was pleased that during the whole eight hours of his hike, he saw only one other person — a sheepherder, with two dogs and a small flock, in a meadow a thousand feet below him. But all along his route he observed much animal and plant life. He describes the butterflies, quite a variety. The largest among them was "a bright yellow one trimmed with velvety black, being about two-thirds the width of my palm. The smallest and in second place as to number, was a uniform electric blue-green in color, more blue above, more green below, and no bigger than my thumbnail." He goes on to describe other butterflies and then several flies, one of which looked like a small bee. He focuses for several paragraphs on the birds—blue jays and Clark Crows; large, slaty mountain grouse which exploded out of the brush; and a hawk:

> In the dip directly west of me, through which a strong steady wind came up from the lake, a small hawk with russet and white underpinnings hung suspended to watch the slope. I'd never seen a hawk do just that before; he wasn't circling or coasting, but hanging fixed at one point, about fifty feet above the saddle-back, tilting a little to make use of the air currents, but never moving his wings or turning. He must have been there nearly half an hour.

There are several paragraphs of descriptions of the flowers, some of which he knew the names of and some not. High in the mountains, they are all close to the ground; lower, they are taller. It is a colorful catalog—no, a series of descriptions, a series of experiences. Then he also takes a long paragraph to describe the doings of two ants that come to carry off a crumb from his sandwich while he is eating his bag lunch. I quote it in full, because it displays his sharp vision, his interest in nature, and, above all, his sense of humor:

> I poked my bare feet out in the draught, and watched some fiercely active ants make away with the crumbs from my bread. Two of them got hold of one crumb about half an inch long, but one of them was much larger than the other, so that finally he lost his temper, put forth all his power, and upended the huge crumb, with the smaller ant balancing on the top of it, and departed belligerently up the face of the boulder. The little fellow was smart, however, and had the best of the contest. After

resting during the first part of the ride, he suddenly braced down where the ascent became steepest, and with the aid of the incline forced the big boy to stumble and lose his grip. By the time the latter had recovered himself the little fellow was well off on the down grade, and maneuvering so outrageously that by the time he reached the ground his opponent, casting wildly all over the face of the rock, had lost track of him entirely. It made a fine tussle to watch, but I couldn't make out why there had been so much earnest debate. There didn't seem to be any individual profit in the matter, for all the crumbs eventually, and rapidly, seemed to follow on trail up over a little, needle covered rise and beyond to the ant holes under a second boulder. It was obviously a community endeavor. Maybe there's some system of awards and demerits. Or perhaps it was purely personal pride, and the little fellow couldn't bear the thought of being carried into camp ingloriously on top of the crumb. (8/1/37)

All in all, this long letter is obviously the report of a person who not only looks around him, but *sees*—notes the colors of the various butterflies, the activity of birds, the shapes and colors of the mountains, ridges, and valleys, and the colors and shapes of the sand and rocks, even focusing for an extended period on the activities of two ants. Here is someone who is living in the now, experiencing everything possible around him. And what shouts out to the reader—he does so with such a spirit of joy. He was in his West.

CHAPTER SIX

THE *OX-BOW* MOVIE
AND *THE CITY OF*
TREMBLING LEAVES

THE IMMEDIATE SUCCESS OF *The Ox-Bow Incident* brought a demand for stories that Clark had already written. Right after the novel's publication in October of 1940, he sold "The Pretender" to the *Atlantic Monthly* and "Trial at Arms" to the *Saturday Evening Post*. The $450 he received from the *Post* equaled the advance he had received for the novel from Random House. Six additional stories were sold and published before the fall of 1941. He had one story included in each volume of the O. Henry prize stories from 1941 through 1945.

Clark took the money he received from *Ox-Bow* royalties and invested it in a year off from teaching at Cazenovia. At the invitation of Robert Caples, Clark spent his year near Indian Springs, Nevada, in the desert north of Las Vegas. Caples's second wife, Shirley, had purchased a ranch and converted it to an art colony. According to Clark's son, the colony provided

> housing, evening dinners at a main house, and even living
> expenses in exchange for a percentage of the profit that would

Indian Springs, Nevada. Barbara (his daughter) and Robert Clark
on Hannah, their burro. Courtesy of Robert M. Clark

theoretically ensue from the labors of the assortment of resident artists, mainly painters and sculptors, though WVTC insists on paying his own expenses.

In addition to several short stories and poems, while he was in Indian Springs Clark worked on a satirical novel based on Little America, a motel-resort on U.S. 40 in Wyoming that had gained some notoriety in the 1940s. And for a second time he started on a draft of *The City of Trembling Leaves,* completing the first half—the remainder was finished later in Cazenovia.

In March of 1942, during the second semester of his school year off, Clark's agent sold the movie rights to *Ox-Bow* to Twentieth Century Fox for $5,265. After leaving Indian Springs, Clark visited his family in Reno in the late summer of 1942 and then went back to Cazenovia, this time to a house on Fenner Street. The movie version of his novel came out in 1943, and it was given a special showing at the Town Hall Theater in Cazenovia. Clark invited all his friends, colleagues, and neighbors to the showing, which

Indian Springs, Nevada. Clark with burro he brought back from a ranch in the back seat of his car, 1941. Courtesy of Barbara Clark Salmon

Barbara Clark (Walter's daughter) on horseback, Indian Springs, Nevada. Courtesy of Barbara Clark Salmon

came late at night after the regular movie program was over. Barclay Webber remembers that his father, also an English teacher at the school, and his mother were invited and that "it was a big event for them." At the end of the showing, the audience applauded and Clark stood up and was given an ovation.

Clark was very pleased with the movie and said later that he could remember "only two changes [that] had occurred in the mutation from book to film: Gil's reading of the letter in the last sequence, and Sparks' singing of the spiritual following the hanging." The director, William Wellman, and writer and producer Lamar Trotti had created one of the most faithful renderings of a novel that Hollywood had ever produced. This, of course, was in large part a tribute to the dramatic and graphic potential of the novel. It was, despite the ambiguities surrounding most of the characters, a very coherent work of fiction, classical in its form, with a tension that built from a beginning, through a middle of complications, to a dramatic ending. Although he did not write the screenplay, Clark's long experience in directing plays likely influenced him in the creation of his novel's dramatic force and structure.

In his book *Novels into Film,* George Bluestone chose the film *The Ox-Bow Incident* as one of only six such transformations to examine in some detail. The film became a classic, although it did not originally make a lot of money. Ironically, it gained its very large audience not through theater play but through repeated showings on late-night television. Not only did it have skillful direction and production by Wellman and Trotti, but its stars and supporting cast were outstanding in their roles. The film starred Henry Fonda as Gil Carter, Dana Andrews as Martin, Mary Beth Hughes as Rose Mapen, Anthony Quinn as the Mexican, William Eythe as Gerald, Henry Morgan as Art Croft, and Jane Darwell as Ma Greer.

George Bluestone has called the movie "a critical coup in the American cinema," going on to say,

Where films are taken seriously, *The Ox-Bow Incident* consistently appears as one of the industry's significant events. Except for a few precursors like John Ford's *Stagecoach* and James Cruze's *Covered Wagon*, *The Ox-Bow Incident* became the first western to treat a moral theme with the high seriousness of tragedy. It is entirely possible that without the bold innovations of Wellman's film, later productions which carried on the tradition of the serious western (*Red River, Yellow Sky, The Gunfighter, High Noon, Shane*) would not have been possible.... Wellman's unit, going outside the pale of convention, achieved a cinematic equivalent of Clark's literary model.

Despite the critical adulation for the film, Clark's son wonders about his father's praise for it, since it obfuscates one of his father's principal themes in the book, namely,

the schizophrenia of modern man.... [This] manifests itself with those sensitive enough to recognize and feel the moral problems [but who] lack the physical courage to uphold them or have too marginal a social role/authority to affect things (the black man, Sparks), while those with physical courage lack insights and are easily prompted into destructive action in the name of manliness/courage (Farnley, Gil).

If his main theme was voided in the movie, why did Clark praise it? Possibly because he didn't pay much attention to the movie or because he thought it was well done but had to be different from the book. The latter would seem to be closer to the case, since Clark insisted that the director, Wellman, also do his other novel which was adapted for the screen, *The Track of the Cat* (ironically, a movie which turned out to depart so far from his novel's themes that he hated it).

After coming back to Cazenovia from Indian Springs, Clark resumed his heavy schedule of teaching, coaching, and directing, made even heavier by a shortage of faculty due to the war. (He had tried to activate his ROTC commission in the army but was rejected again because of his bad knees.) After long days, he continued to push himself to late-night writing sessions, "writing," as he recalled in words he used on several occasions, "into the small hours of the morning, with too much coffee and too many cigarettes to keep me going." He managed to finish *The City of Trembling Leaves*, which was published in 1945.

Soon after the publication, Clark moved to Rye, New York, following his brother-in-law, who had moved from Cazenovia to become the school superintendent in Rye. Clark was appointed head of the English Department and tennis coach. However, he was forced to resign at midyear by complete physical exhaustion, an exhaustion amplified, as he discovered later, by a touch of TB. His weight had fallen from its normal 180–190 pounds to 140 pounds, and he was a mere shell of his former self. His daughter recalls that he fell asleep at the dinner table on several occasions and that one day when he started up the stairs, he couldn't make it all the way to the top. Nor could he go back down. He sat down and could not move. The doctor's advice was to quit all of his jobs and take a year off. The strain was not just physical but mental and emotional as well. For there is no doubt that the success of *Ox-Bow* had put a pressure on him to follow up with another success. It was a pressure he was not used to, no doubt making his composition of *The City*, his most personal and perhaps most deeply felt book, even more filled with anxiety.

The City of Trembling Leaves had been in progress for many years, and it is hard to say when Clark started on the first version of the novel. There is evidence for two autobiographical works, written and destroyed, in the mid-1930s, and a draft of *The City* still exists that was probably started when Clark was in Indian Springs in 1941 and continued on his return to Cazenovia. This draft might have become the basis for Book I and part of Book II of the novel, although Clark has insisted that all previous attempts were discarded and the final novel was a fresh start.

Considering Clark's work habits, it is quite possible that rather than working from the draft, he had the material so firmly in mind that he didn't need to consult it. He often thought about a project for months, and on a few occasions even for years, not only coming up with ideas about theme and content but composing in his head the imagery and much of the language as well. When his mind was full, there was a kind of a compelling impulse, a triggering mechanism, which pushed him to sit down and write furiously. Robert Clark has described what I would call "a triggering mechanism" as his father's mounting emotion in response to an image:

> To be at his best, Dad needed to find material that sustained some original feeling that compelled him to write, the feeling generated by the particular image that was so often the source for his fiction.

He would know after the first page or so whether his ideas had jelled or not, or to put it another way whether he felt that what he had written was able to "work on our [the reader's] feelings." As noted above, sometimes after completing a draft if the resulting story or chapter didn't come out satisfactorily, it was then only a "pass" which was thrown away. He might try again, or he might abandon the project. This was a very dangerous method of writing, since quite often, month after month, the triggering mechanism didn't go off, and he found it impossible to work his way into a story or novel. Although he did revise on paper, he always felt that his best writing came in that sudden, inspired emotional rush that produced his first draft. It was something he looked for, waited for, and hoped for — sometimes desperately.

In any event, *The City of Trembling Leaves* was not a first novel that was set aside until after *Ox-Bow* was published, a misconception put forward by several reviewers. It was Clark's favorite novel because, more than any other published work, it said the things about which he felt most deeply, and because he had taken chances with it, trying out many new techniques, many so new that he really had no models for them. Yet he was always conscious of the work of other writers and felt deeply that good reading contributed to good writing. If one can pick out any one work that influenced him, it may be Henry Fielding's *Joseph Andrews*.

Both Clark's and Fielding's protagonists are bumbling innocents—Tim Hazard has been called a "sacred fool"—and both protagonists move through a series of amorous adventures. Like *Joseph Andrews, The City of Trembling Leaves* employs a variety of tones and styles, a variety that adds to its complexity and may put off the reader, who likely expects a consistent and recognizable voice.

As critic Max Westbrook has pointed out, in his novel Clark "employs at least five distinct styles: lyric, dramatic, ironic, satiric, and farcical." But the dominant tone, as in *Joseph Andrews,* is that of irony. Joseph Andrews is constantly aware of his own feelings (often bewilderment) but seldom aware of the real feelings of others—just like Tim Hazard. The similarity to the tone of Fielding's novel is most apparent in Clark's lengthy chapter titles, such as that for chapter five: "About the Small Things Which Can Create and Maintain a Major Alliance, and About the Virgin Mary of Pyramid Lake and Willis the Worldly."

As much as Clark was pleased with his book, for reviewers and critics conditioned by the tight form of *Ox-Bow* it was a disappointment. One reviewer called it "formless and sprawling," and another, "uneven and generally too long"—not uncommon sentiments. However, several did like it despite its episodic, sprawling form. One of those was Edward A. Laycock, who wrote in *The Boston Daily Globe*:

"The Ox-Bow Incident" established Walter Clark as a first-
rate writer. "The City of Trembling Leaves" should add to his
readers who shy away from "Westerns." It is an imperfect but
vital piece of work, tremendously moving; long-winded but
never dull. It is not tight and compact, but formless and sprawling, as is America.

But perhaps more important than the mixed critical reaction was
that the novel, although gaining many devoted admirers, never
achieved popularity with readers at large. It does not do what most
readers would expect a novel to do — it does not march in a coherent way from a beginning, through difficulties, to a resolution and
satisfying conclusion.

The circular, apparently fragmented structure of the novel can
be baffling. The prose is not hard to read (indeed, it is often a joy
to read), but since so much is implied or only partially revealed,
it is difficult on a first reading to fathom the book's ideas and
themes. And Clark was primarily concerned with ideas. As Charlton Laird, colleague of Clark and critic, has put it:

> Idea permeates Clark's work, all of it. Some kind of moral, or
> principle, or admonition, or something thematic and symbolic
> can be found in all his writings, even the briefest. . . . He wrote
> with people and place, with talk and action, but he wrote for
> theme.

While readers may have been disappointed in *The City* after
Clark's tightly plotted first novel, Clark himself was disappointed
in their response. Although he felt that he wrote to satisfy himself
and not to gain popularity or approval, the apparent rejection was
bound to hurt, and it became clear to him that what he wanted
to write was probably not what the public wanted to read. This
feeling of rejection was reinforced by his submission of a number

of manuscripts over the postwar years that his publisher felt were not suitable for publication (that is, as books they likely would not sell). And the realization that what he wanted to write was not what the public wanted to read seems to have put even more pressure on what he called "the critic at my elbow" that inhibited his writing.

The City has been compared to such artist-as-a-young-man novels as Thomas Wolfe's *Look Homeward Angel,* and critic Ray West in reviewing the novel called it "Portrait of the Artist as Westerner." But readers will find themselves in unfamiliar territory if they tend to relate the book to other books rather than to their own experience. Accessing *The City of Trembling Leaves* may depend on our attempting to rejoin our own childhood and growth toward maturity — recalling our emotional connections to our environments, our naïve reactions, reactions leading to wonderment and disappointment, joy and embarrassment. And what embarrassments. These were reactions that were often so strong that they overwhelmed us with their power. The novel is one of recovery — recovering the memories and feelings that most of us have repressed, forgotten, or outgrown. To experience the novel, then, one must cast aside the cynicism, the logic, and the emotional defenses that gradually insulate us from the "real" or what Clark in the novel calls the "nuclear." In this book we should be exploring, rather than traveling.

Thus, one way of looking at the novel is as a memoir of the growth of consciousness, an inner life reconstructed artistically. The essence of the book is the way Clark felt while growing up and what he discovered — and only in that sense can it, as a whole, be considered autobiographical. In this regard it might be thought of as a dramatized memoir. That is, it is figuratively autobiographical rather than literally so — Clark's life provided much of the material for his imagination. Nevertheless, the material he recalled (and he had an exceptional memory for detail) was extensive. Several of Clark's close friends have been able to point out many counterparts in Clark's life to characters and events in the novel.

Still, Clark himself, in a preface to the early draft of the novel (a draft significantly titled, "Autobiography: Or the Biography of Flesh Become One With the Intellect with the World"), wrote

> I am not Tim Hazard, nor did I ever behold, nor did ever exist, the people and deeds which will probably encumber and shine upon his slow circular progress. And what's more, I shall even do my best to make the love and life of Tim Hazard himself a befogging vision of absolute unreality, not a voice to be heard, not a place in it, in spite of their names, to be actually found. I shall even do my best to mix up time, to so indissolubly entangle past, present, and future, and never was, that finally even the most ancient and alert citizen of Reno will give up, and understand the eternal nature of his city.

Clark was sensitive to the possibility that something he might write would hurt those he had known.

Robert Clark has said that his father tended to romanticize all people and places that he came to love, and that the novel may be "anti-autobiographical," with Tim and other characters acting as Clark and his friends had not, but as the author wished they had. Clark obviously had, despite his disclaimer, ambivalent feelings about the relationship of his novel to life. On the one hand, it was not really autobiographical, and yet on the other, he became upset in a dispute with a friend over an episode in the book that his friend claimed did not happen quite that way. According to Clark's son, his father declared, "That's exactly the way it was!" And his son adds,

> He thought he was rendering it the way it was. He didn't intend it to be idealized in any way. Yet, a very common feature of his

stories or his talk about other people was to turn people he liked into the paragon of whatever it is that they did.... He always elevated—and he does that in his writing.... They turn into emblems.

Robert Clark, commenting further on the connection between the novel and his father's life, has pointed out that one of the main differences is that in life Clark came from an aristocratic family, whereas Tim Hazard comes from a working-class family. This change, he suggests, was one of his father's main strategies for hiding the autobiographical basis for the book. Robert Clark adds that in Tim's family,

the mother is a little strange; cultured as she is, she doesn't fit too well. A little bit more of his [Clark's] own real mother got in there, I think. But Tim's family was not Dad's at all. They [Clark's family] had their mother encouraging every kind of artistic effort and everything else, yet he disavows all that in the book. I think he disavows it for a thesis.... What bothered me in trying to deal with that book is that it seemed to me that he was allowing himself to bypass some personal difficulties, emotional things. I mean Tim Hazard has a lot of trouble loving anybody. He doesn't do it—he doesn't have to do it, thanks to the thesis for the book. He doesn't have to give much of himself to anybody else....

The City, it seems to me, is the critical book. It's the one that is autobiographical, and yet it's not. It does seem to me revealing. I don't know how self-conscious Dad might have been about it. To me, there's a couple of pretty sinister things in that book ... It's always seemed to me, for instance ... that he has to kill a mother in that book. It strikes me as important.... Talking about [Clark's] relationship with his father— in that book, the father kind of dismisses Tim Hazard as well. The father goes off to San Francisco, you know, and Tim Hazard doesn't worry about him, and he doesn't worry that much about Tim, and they don't have much to say. But he's got to kill the mother. He's got to get rid of her. I always thought there was something about the relationship between Dad and his mother in that happenstance fact. In the book, he also, to be practical, he gets rid of her because she's a complexity that's going to screw up this theme of the search for artistic wholeness. She's the one character that Tim Hazard has to deal with as a person; he can't use her as a symbol. Everybody else [in the novel] is kind of used as a symbol.

Robert Clark, after majoring in English as an undergraduate, continued with it as a graduate student and tried to write his doctoral dissertation on his father's work, but found himself stuck:

The City of Trembling Leaves was kind of a rock upon which my dissertation crashed and drowned, because I didn't know what to make of that book. But it does seem to be pretty revealing to me about the kind of lack of interest in other people that that character [Tim Hazard] had. And I think that Dad saw it in himself.

Again, commenting on the relationship of the novel to life, the son has observed that

one of the obvious points of conflict with reality in The City of Trembling Leaves [is] ... the emphasis that Dad puts in that book for Tim Hazard on naturalness. On being just naturally whatever the hell it is. Naturally the musician. Naturally the composer. Naturally the runner. He doesn't get trained by a coach; he just does it.

The emphasis on naturalness has implications for Walter Clark's own life, particularly in regard to his philosophy of composition. His later difficulties with writing may well have had their roots in his belief that his fiction should evolve naturally, in a rush, rather than by steady application.

As a form, the novel might be said to be an attempt, through artistic composition, to organize life and thereby make sense of it. But although *The City of Trembling Leaves* follows the life of Tim Hazard and things do happen, one thing does not necessarily lead to or cause another. What the novel would seem to explore is the question, What is the experience of life? — not as it may be rendered by the typical novelist with order and clear consequences, but as it is actually lived, haphazard, fragmented, ordinary, and disconnected. There is a rough chronology throughout, but the structure is cyclical rather than linear, which fits the novel's philosophical implications and its meditative tenor. The cyclical structure also ties together with the extended musical metaphor that Clark employs. As he reaches adulthood, Tim Hazard strives to write a symphony, "The City of Trembling Leaves," which is of course the title of the novel but also provides the structure of the novel as a "symphony." At the beginning of the book, we are told that

> the trees of Reno have regional meanings, like the themes and transitions of a one-movement symphony. It would be impossible to understand Tim Hazard without hearing these motifs played separately before you hear them in the whole.

As a memoir of the growth of consciousness, the novel presents a series of experience snapshots to which Tim Hazard reacts or fails to react (in fact, Laird points out that "superficially, the tale suggests home movies more than a powerful epic of the West). What ties this series of snapshots together is, in the first place, art — art as a means to get behind facts to the nuclear and art as a medium by which both Tim and the reader experientially develop and grow. We may, through art, be enlarged, be made more sensitive, or gain understanding. If the art is true, it can lead us behind appearances. It is not an easy or a clear path, but one of frustration and occasional confusion. Clark thought of himself as an artist, not a psychologist or philosopher, and writing for him was an art form. In *The City* art is the method by which Clark develops his ideas, and art is given to the reader as music (Tim's symphony), graphic art (Lawrence Black's drawings and paintings), and of course writing (the novel is narrated by a fictional "Walt Clark"). The novel might be said to be Clark's attempt to present a broadly artistic view or interpretation of life rather than a novelistic or journalistic view. It is important to note that art in the novel, particularly as demonstrated in the efforts of Tim and Lawrence, always attempts the impossible and more often than not fails. The nuclear is hard to reach, but, as Clark would insist, worth the effort — indeed, it is the only thing worth such constant effort. As several of Clark's critics have pointed out, the author felt deeply that humanity was on the wrong track, both ecologically and socially.

The snapshots are also tied together by the theme of trembling leaves, which, as Laird points out, is associated with "expectancy and creativity." Again, according to Laird,

> Clark explains that it is identical with the Mary Turner plus the Rachel plus the Margorie [*sic*] Hale plus the Eileen Connor plus the Mary theme. It is various enough to encompass the book, from the first two sentences to the last two, and in various circles between.

The novel moves through a series of Tim's love affairs, each with a different quality. The affairs provide romance in a specific sense, but more generally, considered together, they generate a romantic attitude or view of life throughout the novel. They provide the mystery, magic, and hope to Tim's life. He is constantly reaching out for something intangible and indefinable that he feels the girls and women he is attracted to may provide. Mary Turner is the subject of Tim's first love, a childhood crush on a girl he idealizes when the opposite sex is a tantalizing mystery. Rachel is the subject of a totally spiritual adoration, an object of courtly love. Marjory and Eileen provide a more down-to-earth love involving the flesh. Then at the end of the novel, in a chapter called "In Which the Circle Closes," Tim and Mary Turner are married and the spirit and flesh are brought together. On the one hand, in a joining of their flesh they have two children, and on the other, Mary is compared to Saint Francis and Tim's spirit is lifted so high that he is finally able to write his symphony. One of Clark's basic ideas, which he expressed both in life and in his writing, was that the flesh is just as important as the spirit and should not be ignored. It is this principle that has led some readers to compare him to D. H. Lawrence.

The connection of Mary, Rachel, Marjory, and Eileen with the trembling leaves would seem to represent the duality of spirit and flesh. The physical, the leaves, moves mysteriously in response to the unseen, in a sense expressing the spirit. To a child, the leaves may seem to be alive in an animated, expressive way. And with this theme, as with Mary, we go from the end back to the beginning. The novel begins by describing the various sections of Reno as characterized by their trees. Tim Hazard lives in a house with three big poplars in front of it, and daytime or night, winter or summer, "he heard the poplars … and saw them." At the very end of the book, we see Tim's daughter: "Little Mary reached up and stopped a leaf from trembling, letting it lie flat against her small palm. … Mary withdrew her hand slowly from under the leaf, and it began to dance again, by itself." Once again the circle is closed, and it would seem that in that trembling leaf we can find what Clark called the "nuclear" — that is, an apprehension, largely unconscious, of the essential spirit at the heart of life.

Max Westbrook, who has written a book about Clark and his work, would seem to have a deeper understanding of *The City* than most other critics. He sees the pervasive irony of the novel coming out of a conflict in Tim Hazard's experience between the profane and the sacred: "*The City of Trembling Leaves* is a study of a sacred youth who lives in a profane age.... a story primarily of spiritual growth in a moribund city." Although there is obviously a conflict as Westbrook describes it, there is also, as he points out, another, complementary movement in the novel toward unity as Tim Hazard strives throughout to bring the sacred and profane together.

Bringing the two together, Tim is able to reach the "nuclear," but that goal is only reached occasionally and momentarily and not by conscious application of will. The best example of this, cited by both Laird and Westbrook, takes place when Tim, in high school, goes out for the track team to run the mile and half-mile. He has often, on his own, run long distances and has learned that occasionally he finds a natural, unlabored pace that seems to transport him beyond himself. It is something like, but beyond, that "second wind" many of us may have felt when running distances. Our pace seems effortless; our wind seems inexhaustible. Tim calls this "running with the wild stallion," a state which Westbrook finds to be "symbolic of that balance which is so essential to a realization within one's self of an alignment with the eternal." But in telling contrast to the metaphor of Tim's imagining of the stallion, an image beautifully physical, there is the intangible, essentially spiritual metaphor of music which Clark also uses to indicate Tim's achieving of that balance which leads to the nuclear.

One night, after finishing his gig of playing in a dance band, Tim watches Rachel, the girl he has longed for, go off in a car with Red, a high-school classmate — and not toward the middle of town. His upset (exasperated by the fact that he, himself, doesn't have a car, only a bicycle) leads him to go to the university stadium, where he begins running on the track. As he runs, he has a desire for roaring sound that gradually becomes "a blaring and martial quickstep inside him." He runs lap after lap,

Then, during one lap, the music in him began to be sadder
and slower, and became a big music, like an orchestra, not a
band. . . . He felt a deep content in this music, as if his body
slowly turned and plunged in it as in dark, cool and heavy
water; it was a turning like the motion of the full boughs of the
cottonwoods in the spring night, moving separately, one after
another, as the wind slowly played over them. The size of
spring surrounded him, so that he was suddenly as nothing in
the night.

Here, not only are the physical and spiritual brought together, but
the metaphors of music and the trembling leaves are once again
joined as they are throughout the novel.

On the sidelines of the track, two unnamed observers of his
running have timed four of his laps, a mile, with a stopwatch at an
amazing 4:39. After inquiring and learning that he is still only in
high school, they are disappointed he is not at the university but
advise him that he should go out for track at school — "You can
run, boy."

On the track team, Tim becomes the rival of Red, who is the
school's best runner and something of a school icon, a tough-look-
ing kid with an inscrutable stare. He also just happens to be going
steady with Rachel. In the big race, the competition between the
schools or even between Tim and Red for Rachel's favor becomes
less important than the contest of Tim within himself. As Westbrook puts it, "the real contest is the alignment of self with primordial reality."

In the first race, the half-mile, the competition between the two
boys is fierce. But Tim does not find that natural stride that comes
to him without conscious effort, instead trying to will himself to
run with rhythm and then to push himself harder. He barely loses
to Red, and he has pushed himself so hard that after the race, he
collapses and almost loses consciousness. Recovering for the sec-

ond race, the mile, Tim "felt a steady determination to outrun Red. That was practically all he was thinking about."

But this time, rather than forcing himself he hangs back, letting several runners go ahead of him. He knows that in order to "roll" and "go faster each lap, the way he had that night," it must be done "only by working up smoothly, until the joy of flight came." That joy does not come quickly or automatically. On the third lap, "He could feel that he was running stiffly, that his spikes were jarring him when they hit" and he despairs "of ever getting it right."

However, at the end of the third lap he feels the tension passing from him:

> A kind of golden anger of triumph poured into him. Second
> wind it is generally called, and it is made up as much of
> smoothness, of getting the inner and outer runner together,
> as it is of attaining an oxygen balance.

"Now I've got you," he thinks, as he pulls abreast of Red at the start of the final lap.

As when Clark connects music with spring and the trembling leaves in describing Tim's nighttime run, here again he connects Tim's joyful release with the same elements:

> The spring sunlight was wonderful.... He rode before the
> wind.... Now he could imagine his stallion, now he could
> imagine a pale antelope skimming level backed through the
> gray brush.... Tim drew into the pole.... The poplars in a
> clump beyond the north-east turn bowed and rushed under
> the wind.... Tim exulted about the blowing in the poplars.
> He loved the poplars. They were a shout of triumph whiten-
> ing against the deep blue sky.

But his sense of triumph is short lived. Red, after being passed by Tim, fades and fails even to win third in the race. Something has gone out of him, permanently, and he never performs again as he had before. When Tim passes Rachel and Marjory waiting for Red in the car, they look worried and neither of them will speak to him. Suddenly, Tim "felt as if he had cheated Red. He felt as if he had cheated Rachel."

If this long account of the races were just about how one boy loses the first race and wins the second and another boy loses both a race and girlfriend, then it would be an example of poor plotting on Clark's part. This is especially so, as Charlton Laird points out, if the account only tells "how Tim grew a little closer to a girl whom he was eventually going to forget about anyhow." As Laird comments,

> But the scene is not about winning or losing high school track meets; it is about the nuclear, human nature, the futility of triumph, and probably some other things. It has its place in the "slow circular progress" of the novel.

Therefore this account, like so many others in the novel, does not forward plot but forwards theme. The race is a parable of self-discovery, and since that is a process that continues and does not end, the account can be said to be a paradigm of the entire novel. Tim must evolve naturally, not through will but by relaxing into the natural and letting the unconscious take over. It is his spirit that must evolve, and when he reaches a certain point where he is able (as in the race) to bring spirit and flesh together on a more long-term basis and trust his unconscious, he will be ready to create his symphony. That symphony, "The City of Trembling Leaves," will give expression in tangible form to the trembling leaves as a symbol of the powerful unseen that influences all life — that is, what Clark calls the "nuclear."

Laird talks of the circular progress of the novel, but another way of looking at the novel's structure is to see it as a system of intersecting, overlapping, and repeated figures, figures that include metaphor, allusion to myth, paradigm, parable, and ritual. (Several of these are demonstrated in the turtle episode in *The City*, discussed in chapter 1.) As we have just seen in the accounts of Tim's running, Clark seems to particularly favor animal metaphors and those that employ music, trees, and the seasons as well as images of light and dark. He can use metaphor to convey Tim's feelings, reactions, and state of mind effectively, as in his response to the living room in Marjory's house: "Tim had felt, during his few visits, that some very old person, almost too frail to speak, was sitting unnoticed in one of the shadows, and querulously resenting his intrusion upon remembered dignity."

The ultimate effect of Clark's dependence on figures, particularly metaphor, in his novel is to impose upon the reader a sense of timelessness — discrete yet interconnected moments that come together in a unity of theme. Tim lives his life in art and through art. And the novel (one almost hesitates to call it that) is an attempt to communicate through art (as both medium and content) a sense of life beyond words as a unified whole. Experience is not words, and while the latter can be used to describe the former, it is only art that can reproduce the experience.

As we have seen, unity was an important concept to Clark. In this regard it should be noted that Eastern religions had a strong influence on him, and a good part of his attraction to them was his sense that they were unifying. In answer to a question sent to Clark by Max Westbrook about Clark's religious beliefs, he

> declared his preference for "oriental faiths and philosophies,"
> which he preferred generally to European thinkers whom he
> considered "divisive," and added to the list of his favorite read-
> ing "all primitive faiths, philosophies, folklores, especially
> those of the American Indians," which he characterized as
> "unifying and inclusive."

Westbrook feels that Clark's book is a "sacred vision" which calls for a style like that of the Japanese Haikai, one that "uses the sense to evoke a meaning which is profound and ... not subject to conscious analysis ... some image beyond words, a sense of unity which is nonverbal."

The City of Trembling Leaves is then a book about many things, but particularly about unity—unifying body and spirit, the conscious with unconscious, the human with the natural, and the sacred with the profane. This emphasis on unity had deep philosophical roots in Clark—he thought it so basic to our lives that it meant the difference between disaster and survival. In regard to our place in the natural scheme of things, he wrote in his autobiographical statement:

> I believe ... that the two most important concerns of the
> human race, all of it everywhere, must be birth control and
> natural conservation, the preservation and even, where possi-
> ble, the restoration, of other forms of life and of all natural
> resources. Unless we make big gains in these realms, and make
> them promptly, too, we won't last long enough to let our con-
> cern about anything else matter much.

Of course, the opposite of unity is division, and about that he wrote in equally apocalyptic terms:

> There are a great many kinds of division, and all sides of all
> of them seem to me bad when they get hostile, greedy or so
> concerned with their own interests that they can't even recog-
> nize anybody's else's rights or problems. ... I have no more use
> for the haters among minority groups than for the haters in any
> larger group. Hate means division, and all division, from that
> between people that can't get along to that between nations, is
> evil. In an atomic age it is also the seed-bed of doom.

CHAPTER SEVEN

BACK TO NEVADA AND
THE TRACK OF THE CAT

*T*HE CITY OF TREMBLING LEAVES may have been Walter Clark's sentimental favorite, but it was little appreciated by either the general reading public or the critics. The sales were so poor that even though he had one story included in each volume of the O. Henry prize stories from 1941 to 1945, Random House declined to publish a collection of his short stories. Following publication of his novel in 1945 and his one-semester stay in Rye, New York, Clark moved with his family to Taos, New Mexico, in February of the following year. The Clarks had saved some money, and he and Barbara decided that he should take a year to recover his health, while at the same time he hoped to get back to his writing.

He had been invited by Mable Dodge Luhan to stay, rent free, in an adobe house on her ranch, but although he accepted the invitation, Clark insisted on paying rent. There was a pattern during Clark's life of insisting on his independence and freedom from obligation to others. Perhaps it had something to do with a Western sense of honor. A remarkable fact about him was that throughout his life, he never applied for a teaching job — he waited until he was asked — nor would he apply for a fellowship. He refused to do these things even though, after he left Cazenovia, the Clark's finances were often shaky, sometimes very shaky, causing them some worry. In the decade of the 1950s, Clark was frequently away from home, having accepted several temporary teaching positions, and in his letters he frequently reported to his wife, who took care of the family's finances, how much he had spent. He usually stayed in inexpensive rooming houses or even in student dormitories and treated himself only sparingly now and then to a steak dinner and a movie.

In Taos, Mable Luhan had set up a colony where she housed or periodically entertained a number of artists — writers, painters, and photographers. She apparently became interested in Clark because she had seen a connection between his writing in *The City of Trembling Leaves* and the work of D. H. Lawrence. At Mable Luhan's, Clark made the acquaintance of a large number of local artists, including Frank Waters, and he had fun getting back on the stage, playing the ghost of Kit Carson for a local little-theater production. He also met Frieda Lawrence at the Luhans', and along the lines of ghostly activities, he was invited by Mable Luhan to observe seancelike ceremonies for Frieda's deceased husband, D. H. Lawrence, which Clark attended only reluctantly.

But he was happy and relieved to be back in the West and enjoyed his surroundings. He remembered,

> [I was] in Taos ... for a year exploring that magnificent valley, the Sangre de Christo (Blood of Christ) mountains east of it, the San Juan forest and mountains west of it, the long, deep gorge of the Rio Grande, and the little Spanish villages and Indian Pueblos along it, while I recovered some energy and interest in life.

As he recovered his health, Clark was able to help fight a local flood and a more distant forest fire.

Walter, Barbara, Robert, and Barbara (their daughter) in front of rented house in Taos, New Mexico, spring 1946. Courtesy of Robert M. Clark

Attracted, as we have seen, to the cultures of Native Americans, Clark made friends among the Taos Pueblo Indians and developed a close friendship with one Indian (significantly, an artist) who was a silversmith. Mable's husband, Tony, who was chief of Taos Pueblo, invited Clark to observe some Pueblo ceremonial dances which were usually closed to whites, and Clark attended these with great interest and a feeling of being privileged.

But as happy as he was with his natural surroundings and pleased by his contacts with Indian culture, Clark and his family encountered a good deal of conflict in Taos. Clark's daughter Barbara was in the second half of the third grade and her brother in the second half of the first grade. Barbara remembers that

they had a private [Presbyterian] school there, but it was full.
And, of course, the public school was about ninety-five percent
Hispanics who didn't care for Gringos. And the Indians and
the Mexicans hated each other. We had all of that going on
with [us] who were being raised in this "don't base people on
their color" kind of thing. My brother and I would stand back
to back and fight it out.... For raising children, it wasn't the
most ideal situation.... On Friday nights, if my folks were
entertaining—we had a two story adobe house and ... [we
would] get up on the big screened-in porch in the back and
watch the night fights between the Indians and the Mexicans.
Things were a little tense.

For someone like Clark, who believed that all divisions between
people were evil, the atmosphere in Taos must have seemed at
times painful.

The children also had a problem with their father's writing
situation while they were in Taos: "When people looked at my
father as an accomplished writer," Barbara recalled, "my brother
and I used to hate it, because he would write at the kitchen table,
right in the middle of everything. Everything had to be real quiet."
In fact, Clark was able to get very little writing done. After several
months the situation for Clark himself became nearly untenable
when Mable Luhan seemed determined to run his life by putting
notes of instruction under his door in the early morning hours.
The Clarks decided it was time to leave, and in the late summer of
1946, they went to Nevada and rented a house on a ranch in the
Sierra Nevada foothills. It was the old pioneer Lewers ranch in the
Washoe Valley, a place which, as Clark has taken pains to point
out, was "named after the Indian tribe, particularly fine basket-
makers, who were living there when the white man came." "We
were," he adds, "back in the country where I'd grown up, and
which I loved most." The Washoe Valley runs along the east side

of the Sierra Nevada between Reno and Carson City, and the Lewers ranch sits against a partly forested mountain. It was a location that roughly matched the setting for his next novel, *The Track of the Cat*.

It was a joyful return home. He resumed his two favorite activities by becoming active in the Reno Tennis Club and the Carson City Chess Club. On the ranch there was a separate building, a barn called the "apple house" (because the ranch had had an apple orchard in the Comstock days) in which he was able to make a study. At last he could get some writing done, and his daughter rejoiced that she could invite friends over and make noise. Nevertheless, Clark did continue to use the kitchen table on occasion for his writing. Seldom did the studies he worked out for his writing in any of his residences really take entirely.

Clark's nephew David Chism recalls his family during this period visiting the Clarks by taking the narrow-gauge train from Reno down to Carson City, getting off, and then walking a long distance across grassy fields to the ranch house. In the last months of 1946, while at the Lewers ranch, Clark wrote the first version of his novelette, "The Watchful Gods." And during the first half of 1947, he finished two novellas involving chess, "The Queen Is a Powerful Piece" and the satirical "Ambrose, the Chess Playing Poodle." This latter work he polished and sent to Random House, but his editor, Saxe Commins, advised against publication and Clark abandoned it.

He started on *The Track of the Cat* at the end of 1947 and finished the typescript revisions for it in December of 1948. In the meantime, during the summer of 1948, he taught at his first writing conferences at the University of Kansas and then at Stanford (where he renewed acquaintance with Wallace Stegner, who in 1954 would invite him to take his place in the graduate creative-writing program for the spring quarter while he was on leave).

In a letter to Ray B. West Jr. (editor of the *Rocky Mountain Re-*

Christmas 1946 in front of house in Washoe Valley. Back row: Jim Santini, Walter E. Clark (Clark's father), Euphemia Santini (Clark's sister), Walter V. T. Clark, Marjory Clark, Miriam Chism (Clark's sister), David (Clark's brother). In front of David, Barbara Clark holding David Chism and Euphemia Clark (Clark's mother). Row of children: Robert Clark, fourth from left; Barbara Clark, fifth from left. Courtesy of Robert M. Clark

view, which in 1943 published Clark's story "The Buck in the Hills"), Clark reviewed his teaching at Stanford in the summer of 1948 and his writing progress:

> My summer was a thoroughly chopped up one, but in retrospect it has telescoped, plus September and October so far, into one long session on the typewriter. The Stanford session turned out to be no such rough one as I'd expected on the solo basis [at Stanford he taught for a week alone]. I was busy enough not to sit around gnawing my nails or any such — with a party of some sort almost every afternoon or evening,

Lewers house, Washoe Valley. Courtesy of Barbara Clark Salmon

and something like thirty individual conferences — though I
brought more than half of those on myself — you can't help it
when you see a bunch as intimately as you do on their plan.

But there were only two talks before big groups — and I
cheated on both — used the fable [from the timing this would
seem to have been the allegory "Chuangtse and the Prince of
the Golden Age"] and the conservation theme again (I'm in
danger of getting really hyped on that — I see erosion and
beefy chicanery everywhere) for my windup — which was
public (there were more questions about where could they find
the fable, and much interest when I told them you were going
to print it) and for my conference talk read a story of my own
in an unfinished stage — just draft only partially revised — as a
point of departure for what they wanted, a craft talk on genesis,
methods of revising, etc. The story is one I like better than
anything I've done in a long time — *The Little Gods, the*

Walter and Barbara Clark with their son, Robert, at Lewers ranch,
Washoe Valley, 1947. Courtesy of Robert M. Clark

Watchful Gods—the only short piece I've done in all this time
of wrestling with the novel [*The Track of the Cat*]. It's about ten
or twelve thousand words, and I believe it worked pretty well
for the purposes desired—having come out strongly enough in
the first draft to get home pretty well as it stood, and yet with
several revisions points of a structural nature still needed, and
fairly complicated ones too. But you can see how easy I made it
for myself—for the thing was thoroughly alive for me still—
and I still knew pretty completely how it had happened. It was
interesting and useful to me too to read it in that state. The one
projection made clear to me the chief revision needed, and I've
been a bit vague about it before. So actually I milked them as
much as they milked me. . . .

Meanwhile, the book [*The Track of the Cat*] progresses
slowly. Only the last section of three chapters remains to be
re-worked—and then the final cleanup, where I hope, I vow,
I turn plain typist this time. But the MS runs around 600 typed
pgs. So that will still be a long chore. I hope to have it in to
Random House by the end of November if not sooner. They're
planning, so Saxe [Commins] writes, a June publication—
tentative—meaning, politely, they'll wait till they see the MS.
By now they're onto old four-year Clark. The title—also still
tentative—it doesn't get me, but neither does anything else
that's popped up yet—"In October Snow." I think it's a pretty
solid piece, though I'm so far under it by this time that I
wouldn't really know. I'm sure of advances over anything else
I've done in some phases of it, anyhow. As to the all-important
question of whether the spook is really there, I'll have to get a
little farther from it to be sure. (10/15/48)

Teaching at writing conferences and taking temporary profes-
sorships became an important source of income for Clark over

the next decade, especially during the last two of the three years (1946–49) that he spent on the Lewers ranch when he was without a regular paycheck. In the summer of 1949 he taught at the University of Utah and at Stanford, and for the school year 1951–52, he taught in the Writers' Workshop at the University of Iowa. Then in June of 1952 and through much of the summer, he taught in writers' conferences at universities in Nebraska, Missouri, and Arkansas. Beyond providing needed money, these teaching stints provided Clark the opportunity to meet other well-known writers, such as Allen Tate, William Carlos Williams, and Irwin Shaw; journal editors; and other creative-writing teachers. Such acquaintances led him from one job to another, as well as leading to requests for reviews and articles. He began to get manuscripts from publishers for review, mostly from Random House but from others as well, and this also contributed to his income.

In a Christmas card to his editor, Saxe Commins, at Random House sent in December of 1948, Clark wrote,

> I think—I think—I think it is coming. It is the cat story at
> last—bitter of flavor and coming fast. Begins with the coffee
> and ends when I fall over. After two weeks it is well more than
> half-done. More, we shall wait and see. It is time. I was a long
> time on the mountain, and it is beginning to show. I debate
> titles—The Cat and the Shadow, Shadow of the Cat. Trail
> of the Black Panther. Forest of the Night—well, perhaps one
> will grow on me. I don't care. Right now I'd as soon call it X^2.
> Or use a nuclear fission equation.

The Track of the Cat was published in June of 1949 to mostly favorable reviews and good sales. *Kirkus Reviews* said, in part,

> In his first novel since 1945, the author of *Oxbow Incident* [*sic*]
> again recreates a mounting drama of high tension in mental

as well as physical domains where emotional geography is carefully explored. . . . Rates "excellent" in western fiction, in the slow and steady building up of character and emotional atmosphere.

What is interesting here is that *The City of Trembling Leaves* is not mentioned in this review, only "*Ox-Bow*," and that it confirms the frequent pigeonholing of Clark as a writer of "Western fiction." It was a categorization that Clark chafed at, writing, as we have seen, other kinds of fiction, but he had to give up eventually in the face of the insistence on the category by critics and, more importantly, by his publishers. Yet he trusted his publisher and his agent completely and, in a show of loyalty, never considered changing either one during his entire career. Being branded as a Western writer was one of several factors that over time was demoralizing and made it difficult for him at a certain point to continue to write fiction. (Such pigeonholing was the main complaint that John Steinbeck had against critics — once they had put you in a certain box, they refused to accept anything you wrote that was outside that box, and, like Clark, he was frustrated because he wanted to do something different with every book.) Fiction was always a somewhat borderline activity for Clark. In his devotion to metaphor and imagery, he was, perhaps, most inclined toward poetry. His son, Robert Clark, has said that in looking back he is surprised his father turned to fiction at all, since his mind was essentially philosophical by nature and his father, unlike most novelists, had no interest at all in gossip and little interest in the inner workings of other people's lives.

Still, it is worth noting that Max Westbrook, expert on Western literature and the author of a book on Clark, has called *The Track of the Cat* "perhaps the finest Western novel written." Unlike *The City of Trembling Leaves,* this new novel was more or less traditional in form and dealt once again, as in *Ox-Bow,* with Old

West subject matter—cowboys, horses, cattle, guns, the hunt, the old ranch house, and a mystery at the heart of nature (a black mountain lion—was it real or a hallucination?). Although he went back to the traditional overall form and subject matter, the novel was still experimental in many ways. Clark seemed to find it impossible not to go beyond what was expected in manner or content (as in his chess novellas). And at the same time, he used the form and Old West material to express many of the key ideas that were dear to his heart. He took the conventional and what was expected and adapted them to his own purposes, adding layer upon layer of meaning—although by his skill with metaphor, the casual reader might not detect this. That was part of his plan—to make what he wanted to say palatable. He could be a very sly writer, a trickster, a son of the wily coyote. He seemed determined by the popular failure of *The City*—a failure that might be attributed at worst to self-indulgence or at best to an attempt to escape from his box— to say what he had to say, this time, to the widest possible audience.

The Track of the Cat is a haunted and haunting story, one that is likely to stay with any reader for a long time. It is the story of a family and the story of a hunt, and the two are woven together in a number of ways. The hunt takes up almost the entire novel, as one son after another goes out into the blinding snowstorm or deep snow and darkness to pursue a black mountain lion that has killed the family's cattle. The lion, called the "painter" by the characters in the novel, was the subject of some carping by critics. There were objections to the blackness of the "painter," but as Clark himself affirmed, mountain lions come in a variety of colors, including black, depending on the season and terrain. There were also a few complaints that mountain lions do not attack people nor are they capable of bringing down steers. Mountain lions can get up to nine feet long from nose to tail tip and weigh two hundred or more pounds, and while attacks on full-grown cattle may be rare, there have been many instances of mountain lions attacking people. But since we are talking about fiction, these matters are trivial, not to say irrelevant, especially if one looks at the book as a kind of ghost story (a way of reading the story which is supported by much of the imagery).

The cat is obviously a symbol, but the question is, of what? Several reviewers have suggested a comparison with the white whale in *Moby-Dick* (a book that Clark frequently taught, was fond of, and may well have been inspired by). One parallel with Melville's novel certainly is that Clark's hunt takes place in a setting that is also a microcosm. In the whale book the setting is a ship at sea and the sea just around it, the physical limitations of the setting intensifying the drama; in the cat book the setting is the ranch, isolated by a snowstorm, the action taking place either in the ranch house or in the mountains nearby. Another parallel is that Melville's Ahab is obsessed by the hunt and dies as a result of his obsession and Clark's character Curt, who spends the most time of the three sons hunting the cat, is similarly obsessed and also dies as a result of it.

However, to compare the cat to the whale is, according to the author of *The Track of the Cat,* a "parallel that is dangerously misleading." For one thing, the challenge for the humans in his novel is to understand, to get in touch with the "primitive," not to overcome or dominate nature. For another, as Clark explains, there are actually two cats in his novel which "are quite separate—the one—not like Moby Dick—quite real and killable—the other an invention of the primitive mind and everlasting." As in his story "The Indian Well," Clark's sympathy is with the cat, and the cat in his novel, whether in its real form or as an imagined phantom, is a test for the human characters. "The relationship," Clark adds, "between the real and legendary cat ... [is] that both are avengers against man's evil." (How clever of Clark to give us not only a ghost but also the physical reality of what that ghost represents—

that is a real switch on the ghost story.) By making the cat black, Clark leads us to think of it as evil, tricking us again, for as he has said, "the cats come near to being good, since they act against the one conscious and disproportionately destructive force in nature — man."

The ranch family — the Bridges — is, in current jargon, dysfunctional, to say the least. Most of the members of this family, particularly the three sons, are given well-rounded characterizations, but all play symbolic parts related to Clark's themes. The father spends most of his time sitting, drinking, and complaining. He looks back to a past in San Francisco when there was wealth and opportunity to gain wealth. There is no love between him and his wife, a bitter, narrowly religious shrew who disapproves of her husband's drinking and sloth and also disapproves of everyone else in and around the family and just about anything they might do. The only exception to her general disapproval is Curt, her second oldest son, who is also favored by the father. Curt has more or less taken over the lead for the family and is strong, tough, and practical, but — of particular importance to the novel — he is a materialist. He, like the father, is primarily concerned with gaining wealth and is impatient with and makes fun of his older brother, Arthur, who is gentle — a dreamer and reader. Hal, the youngest son, is to a certain extent a combination of the two other sons: he has the strength and determination of Curt, but his practicality is modified by a willingness to tune into what Clark calls here the "primitive."

An old Indian handyman on the ranch, Joe Sam, representing the primitive, is, in Clark's words, "the very central character of the action, although he is inarticulate." After Arthur, who recognizes the truth of the primitive but is according to Clark the "ineffective idealist," is killed by the lion while accompanying Curt on the first hunt, Curt goes after the cat himself. One of Clark's most remarkable narrative performances is his hundred-page description of this hunt and Curt's mental and physical journey into the black-and-white environment, the snowy darkness. Westbrook comments on this episode by saying,

> He [Curt] is, like modern man, disoriented in space and time,
> out of touch with his dark and inner self, alone in the universe
> with only his pathetically inadequate intellect to guide him
> among the ancient realities he is now about to meet. . . . This is
> the first time in his thirty seven years that he has met the cat
> that cannot be killed with bullets, the cat, that is, which makes
> him confront himself.

Clark discussed the novel in a letter to a book group that had written him to ask the novel's meaning. However, sometime later he wrote across the top of the first page, "Never sent—told too much." In the letter, quoted several times above, he discusses the two cats and describes the part played by each of the three Bridges sons:

> The idealist, the dreamer [Arthur], because he cannot act, is
> killed by reality, and the realist, the materialist, the "conqueror,"
> the man of action, is killed by the dream cat, the vision—i.e.,
> he goes mad, and acts madly, because he won't think.

As for Harold, the youngest son, he has only begun to think as Arthur does, but

> he is beginning to see, and he realizes that there is a valuable
> kind of "understanding" in the primitive Joe Sam, which he,
> like Arthur, must learn to understand, or else act as blindly,
> and finally fatally as Curt.

And with that understanding and by combining idealism with realism, Harold is able to kill the real cat while coming to terms with the phantom. In other words, he achieves a wholeness, or unity (harking back to Tim in *The City of Trembling Leaves*).

—

The Track of the Cat was published in June of 1949, and that summer the Clarks went back to Cazenovia for a visit and then on to the Essex house in upstate New York to vacation with Barbara's family. That fall, on their return, the Clarks moved to Virginia City, a place that Walter had visited often, knew well, and had wanted for years to live in. To understand Walter Clark, the path of his life and his choices, you have to know about Virginia City, about the history and romance of this old mining town that so attracted him throughout much of his life. In many ways it is the ultimate Western town, a fitting setting for what, in many ways, was the ultimate Western man. It was dear to his heart, the one place above all in which he felt comfortable. During the last years of his life, he would give lectures about some aspect of it to various groups on a number of occasions. Forget about ghost towns; this one is still alive and kicking, although it is full of ghosts.

To get there you head south from Reno on the freeway toward Carson City and then turn eastward on a two-lane road that winds up Geiger Grade into the mountains, a road that runs parallel to one that a hundred and forty years ago was a pack-animal track used for bringing supplies to the miners. The "new" Geiger Grade joins the old track at Five Mile Flat near the summit, where it then runs on into town. The surrounding mountains are roughly cone shaped and relatively low at seven thousand feet, but they are steep. They are dotted by only a few trees, piñon pines—most were cut down a century ago to make timbers and firewood for the mines. And here and there on the sides of the mountains are the remains of old mine shafts, dug out by prospectors and then long abandoned.

With many curves, the two-lane road runs up into the mountains where finally it becomes C Street, the main street of Virginia City. The town is built on the side of Sun Mountain (also called Mount Davidson), and the slope is so steep, one wonders how a town could be there at all. In fact, Virginia City on occasion has slipped downhill due to cave-ins. The town is situated on top of the Comstock Lode, the largest and most important silver deposit in North America. Under the town there were four hundred miles of tunnels, at a maximum depth of three thousand feet. (At that depth the heat for the miners was so intense that the mines had to bring down large blocks of ice, and still the men could work only fifteen minutes at a time.)

C Street has an Old West look, with board sidewalks, false fronts on the saloons, and wooden overhangs to posts at the street that could serve to tie up a horse. It is hard to tell how much of this is authentic and how much may have been rebuilt to match the sets of movie westerns in order to attract tourists. In the center of town, many of the buildings are constructed of brick or stone, but quite a few of the houses and other buildings are made out of wood, and today much of the wood is worn, cracked, and unpainted. Despite the beauty of the occasional restored Victorian house, one does not get the impression of a wealthy community. It is almost as if the town revels in showing off its age and wear. Driving down D Street below the main street, one can look up and see the backs of the buildings running down the hill, several stories, to what at one time were loading docks and storerooms. At the back of some buildings are tall wooden ladders fixed to the structures near the windows—presumably to be used as fire escapes.

Fire was the main scourge of the area, and there were disastrous fires both in the mines and in the town. The 1869 fire in the Yellowjacket mine beneath Gold Hill threatened the lives of a thousand miners, took the lives of forty-five, burned out of control for two months, and then, after the mine shafts were sealed off, smoldered for three years. The great fire in Virginia City occurred on October 26, 1875. Its origin was discovered when a column of smoke was sighted above a rickety wooden boarding house on A Street, Crazy Kate's, that barely clung to the steep slope of the mountain. (Where else but in Virginia City or some other boom-town would you have a boarding house named Crazy Kate's?) With a stiff west wind and tinder-dry wooden buildings, the fire spread more rapidly than the volunteer fire department could deal with. Several of the main structures were devoured by a wall of flame—the courthouse, Piper's Opera House, and the International Hotel. Blasting crews were called in to try to stop the fire with dynamite.

As the fire approached the newly completed Catholic church, a crowd gathered to try to prevent the dynamiting crews from getting near the brick church building. Bishop Patrick Manogue, who had labored long to get the church built, stepped forward, had an animated conversation with the mine superintendent who was in charge, and then motioned the anxious crowd away. With a deafening roar the church collapsed into rubble, and as if by a miracle the flames that had approached the church flickered and died down. The firemen were able to stop the fire's progress and save the rest of the town and all the producing mines. A new St. Mary's of the Mountains was erected in less than two years on the ruins of the old church.

The Comstock developed in the late 1850s out of several gold strikes, but as it turned out, the area was much richer in silver than in gold. There is a story that the residents of Johntown, near Virginia City, were dismayed when they learned of the discovery of silver on the Comstock. They realized they should have paid more attention to a Mexican miner who had been working in Gold Canyon in 1853. Other miners had watched him resting on his shovel while he waved toward the brown outcroppings along the mountain peaks:

"Bueno," he would say, "Mucho plata, mucho plata." They couldn't understand Mexican and the word plata meant nothing to them. The Mexican, they thought, was referring to gold buried in the mountains. As long as the weather held out, they worked the placer gravel, eking out two dollars a day, all the while damning the "blasted blue stuff" that covered up the quick in their rockers and interfered with amalgamation.

One of the main early strikes on the Comstock was the Ophir mine on Gold Hill just south of the present Virginia City, and a ragged, makeshift community grew up around the mine. This community got its name in 1859 from a veteran placer miner by the name of Old Virginny who had made the original discovery of the Gold Hill claims. A contemporary account of the town's first winter describes the situation for the early arrivals on the scene:

> Tents of dirty, ragged canvas pieced out with tattered clothes coated with grime — hovels of pine boards roughly nailed together and pierced by bent and rusty stovepipes — heaps of broken rocks with shapeless crevices into which men crawled like lizards — shallow pits partly covered over with boards and earth ... dark slimy holes into which the melting snow dripped with a monotonous plash.

In the meantime silver ingots cast from ore taken out of the Ophir had been shown around San Francisco, and thousands of men from all walks of life infected with silver fever gathered in California waiting for the Sierra Nevada passes to open. In the spring, the flood of people brought bankers who provided capital, businessmen who brought wagons and mules loaded with goods to sell, and miners and laborers who had quit their jobs elsewhere to join the stampede. "It has been estimated that 10,000 people came to the Comstock in 1860, but less than half that number stayed."

In 1860, also, a very important improvement to mine construction in the shafts and drifts began to be employed, the invention of square timbering by Philipp Deidesheimer. This was a matter of cutting lumber in a standard size, generally a foot or more square, with a large square peg at the ends and then placing the timbers so that four of them met from each direction at the top of an upright. No nails, bolts, or cables were needed. The horizontal beams at the top were covered with sturdy planks. This practice allowed the mines to go very deep and extend their drifts for great distances in following the veins. At the top of the mine shafts with their cages were shaft houses with adjoining "works," machinery for bringing up the ore, huge fans for ventilation, and pumps. Eventually the greatest danger became not cave-ins or even fires, but the flooding of the mines with water, which could get as hot as 170 degrees. The mines, as they were dug ever deeper, encountered more and more water, and they began to use the largest pumps then in existence. But these were not enough, so the men from Cornwall, England, who were experienced in deep mining and had used large pumps in their deep copper mines, brought that technology to the Comstock. The Cornish pumps were widely put into use by the early 1870s:

> An example of a typical pump is one used in the Yellow Jacket mine, which had a vertical shaft more than 3,000 feet deep. The pump had two fly wheels weighing 125 tons, a pine pump rod 16 by 16 inches and 3,055 feet long, and when in operation raised more than a million gallons of water daily.

In addition to all of this machinery, there were huge sheds with stamp mills that crushed the ore prior to the extraction of gold or silver. Then in 1869 the Virginia & Truckee, a narrow-gauge railroad, was built from Virginia City to the reduction mills on the Carson River (water on the surface had been in short supply and needed for the reduction). Thereafter, the line was extended to Carson City and finally to Reno to connect with the Central Pacific Railroad. At the height of its activity, the V & T ran thirty trains a day over the twenty-one-mile route between Virginia City and Carson City. At this point in Virginia City there were also railroad yards, maintenance sheds, and ore chutes which adjoined the tracks for loading the ore. Today, all of the huge sheds with their giant machinery, as well as the railroad (except for restored pieces of it kept as a tourist attraction), are gone. There are a few large piles of mine tailings, but of the machinery itself the only remnant is part of a stamping mill, which can be seen in front of the museum on C Street.

The history of the Comstock has been characterized by a repeated cycle of booms and busts, as people rushed in and then left as the prices of mine stock soared to inflated heights and then plunged to the depths. In 1860 the San Francisco Stock and Exchange Board, which was the first exchange in the country devoted to mining stocks, was organized to take care of the demand. Investors began pouring money into silver stocks. There was a downturn in stock prices and demand early in 1860 because of reports that the mines were not producing as well as expected. But then in 1861, the prices soared once again. This up-and-down cycle continued through the next decade and beyond as the mines seemed disappointing and then promising and financiers manipulated the price of stocks and battled each other for control.

The worst downturn occurred in 1865 with the great Comstock panic of that year. All the major mines had played out at depths of five hundred feet or less, and fifty working mines, which had levied millions of dollars of assessments on their stock, had to close or severely cut back their activity. Recovery came in the next year when a number of mines hit new deposits of good ore, but the economy of the region bottomed again in 1870 when production dropped off steeply as one mine after another encountered water-flooding problems. Investment in the mines was a great gamble, since most of them did not usually pay any dividends but instead often assessed the stock in order to finance further exploration.

Then on March 1, 1873, the local newspaper, *The Gold Hill News*, announced a major strike in the Consolidated Virginia mine. As one historian has put it,

> This was no small pocket of high-grade, as had been found in other Comstock mines, but it was the granddaddy of all Nevada orebodies. Located 1,200 feet directly below the streets of Virginia City, the discovery soon came to be called the "Big Bonanza" and its discovery sent shockwaves through mining and financial circles.

Among those who rushed to Virginia City in the spring of 1860 were those who came to make money not directly from mining but from the miners. The first saloon of many was set up in March by John L. Moore, who had secured a pack train to carry 2,100 pounds across the Sierra Nevadas, including blankets, tin plates, brandy, gin, whiskey, rum, and wine. When he got through the remaining snow to Virginia City, he was cheered by miners lined up along the streets. He set up a fifteen by fifty-two foot tent, put up an American flag at the top of the ridge pole, and divided the tent into two rooms. One was a "hotel," and one was a saloon. In the hotel, Moore put his guests, up to thirty-six of them, on top of the first carpet in the town, providing two blankets and charging them one dollar. In the saloon, the old sideboard of an emigrant wagon was set up on stakes driven into the ground to serve as the bar. Liquor was the most popular cargo among the early settlers. Once when Carson City was near starvation for lack of supplies in the winter, a pack train came in with liquor and flour. The population was angry, expressing indignation that space on the pack train had been wasted on food instead of all being used for whiskey. The number of saloons in Virginia City grew to more than one hundred during the town's heyday.

Virginia City became a booming, boisterous, twenty-four hour a day town. Because of the constant stream of men entering and leaving the mines, many businesses, and certainly the saloons and bawdy houses, never closed. Prostitution was a big business, not legal but tolerated. Almost all the men in town were single and a long way from what they considered home, and the ratio of men to women was about twenty to one. Prostitution was permitted in three areas of town—the main red-light district on North D Street, the Barbary Coast of South C Street, and Chinatown. There was a class system among the women. At the top were those who lived in fancy brothels, establishments that had a parlor and a musician who played the piano. These "parlor houses" were used as much for their social amenities as for the opportunity to have sex. Next down the line were the single prostitutes who lived alone in rented cabins. "These women were usually quiet, discreet, of 'good' character, allowing one customer a night." Near the bottom of the ladder were the women who worked in the disreputable brothels in the backrooms of the saloons and dance halls of the Barbary Coast. At the very bottom were the Asian women who had been sold into slavery and put into the Chinatown brothels and who had to turn over all their earnings to their masters.

The most famous of the Virginia City prostitutes was Julia Bulette, who, over time after her death, became a legend. She was a middle-class prostitute who lived alone in a rented cabin. Good looking and buxom, she built a reputation as a kind, considerate, and generous person who became known for her acts of charity. She was made an honorary member of a volunteer fire company, Virginia Engine Company, No. 1. Such engine companies were a social and political force in town, and they showed their clout, for example, in vociferously supporting the Union during the Civil War.

On the morning of January 20, 1867, Bulette was found murdered in her small frame house on D Street. A week later a Frenchman by the name of John Millian was charged with crime, tried, and hanged in front of a crowd of three thousand people. The Storey County district attorney summarized the feelings of the town:

Although this community has, in times past, seen blood run like water, yet in most cases there was some cause brought forward in justification of the deed, some pretext. But on the morning of the 20th of January last, this community, so hardened by previous deeds of blood, was struck dumb with horror by a deed which carried dread to the heart of every one — a deed more fiendish, more horrible than ever before perpetrated on this side of the Sierra.

Because of her good looks, her kindnesses that seemed to contradict her profession, and the sensational nature of her death, Bulette seemed destined to become a legend in a place that loved legends. It was said that she owned a fancy bordello or gambling house, that she was always attended by servants and always rode through town in a coach and four, but these and other such glorifications of her were false. Many stories about her were invented, leading to totally erroneous books that purported to tell her life story and even a fictionalized episode about her that was televised on *Bonanza*.

Over the years as the mines closed down and the population of the town dwindled, the prostitutes moved on to more lively locations, and by the 1940s there were only a few left. In 1947 prostitution was outlawed in Virginia City, but two decades later, as part of the effort to attract tourists, the Storey County Commission voted to legalize it — the only county in the country at that time to do so. (Earlier, the state legislature had voted to make legalization of prostitution a county option.) It confined the business to the extreme northern part of the county, miles away from Virginia City. There, the infamous Mustang Ranch flourished for several decades until it ran into problems with the IRS.

CHAPTER EIGHT

VIRGINIA CITY AND
THE WATCHFUL GODS
AND OTHER STORIES

BUT VIRGINIA CITY DURING THE boom years was not just a city of bars, bordellos, fights, murders, and public hangings. While it may have been a wild place, even at times and in certain places dangerous, it was also, strangely enough, a city that developed quite a social and cultural life. It had live theatre productions; many newspapers, including two dailies; a number of fraternal and social organizations; and the card and billiard rooms of the dignified Washoe Club.

Hardly had the rush to the Comstock begun before a theatre was built in the raw town, and within three years five different companies were playing every night to packed houses, while at the same time six additional song-and-dance variety shows were packing overflow audiences into large tents. Piper's Opera House, the premiere theatre venue, attracted almost all the well-known performers of the time, including General Tom Thumb, Edwin Booth, Clara Morris, James O'Neill, Frank Mayo, and Madame Modjeska. Piper's presented a number of contemporary plays, such as "East Lynne," "Davy Crockett," and "Under the Gaslight," as well as the frequent staging of Shakespeare (usually a single scene rather than an entire play).

For two decades during the boom years, Virginia City became the cultural capital of the West. Even San Francisco could not dispute that claim. The Comstock was where the money was. Virginia City and latter-day historians have made much of the Comstock's cultural life, but the truth was that "the intense young people on Sun Mountain were impatient for quick fortunes, and... [what] they [really] loved [was] the colorful and the sensational." It was common for enthusiastic audiences to toss coins up on the stage following a performance of which they approved. Piper's, rebuilt after the great fire, still operates in Virginia City today, and other theatres around town regularly present western melodramas during the summer season for the entertainment of tourists.

Altogether the Comstock mines produced about $320 million in the twenty-one years between 1859 and 1880. A number of financiers, brokers, and mine superintendents were made wealthy; some like John Mackay, who headed up a partnership in the Big Bonanza mine, the Consolidated Virginia, became very wealthy indeed. The incredible wealth made Virginia City a place of extremes:

> Some of the very wealthy were not content with building mansions and ornate mine offices, but were known to order silver and gold trimmings for their carriages, put silver shoes on favorite horses, and give away small silver ingots as gifts.

The last mine to stop pumping water was the Combination in 1886, and immediately its lower levels were flooded, as were adjoining mines. From then on, through the nineteenth and into the twentieth century, efforts to revive mining in the area, one way or another, continued off and on, and sometimes with success. One strategy that worked was to refine with cyanide in mills the low-grade ore that had been ignored, discarded or used to backfill. These efforts continued for several decades. There was even an effort to pump out some of the mines again, but milling costs for refining the low-grade ore and pumping costs to revive deep mining were so high in both cases that the profits were relatively low. In the middle of the depression, the U.S. government raised the value of gold to thirty-five dollars an ounce and silver to sixty-four cents. In response several companies began a new technique for the Comstock — open-pit mining. These operations were profitable and continued until World War II broke out and a government order severely curtailed the mining of gold and silver. By 1950 all mining had stopped, and the population of Virginia City went down to an all-time low, declining from a peak in the late 1870s of twenty thousand to the present level of about seven hundred.

Today Virginia City is supported primarily by tourism, although it is also the seat of Storey County. The early promotion of tourism is credited in part to two high-living writers from the East who wanted to revive the excitement and romance of the old West, Lucius Beebe and Charles Clegg. They dressed extravagantly, like tinhorn gamblers out of a Technicolor western; acted like impresarios (many of the locals thought they acted like idiots); and stirred up publicity for themselves and for the town through reactivating the defunct *Territorial Enterprise*. The articles in the newspaper were funny and irreverent, often running to spoofs and Western tall tales. The paper was very entertaining and managed to circulate widely, spreading the fame of the town as a real relict out of the western past. The town responded by opening new museums and a good many new saloons with waitresses dressed like dance-hall girls and, of course, slot machines. The town also got in the spirit of the revival by staging quick-draw contests, camel races, and endurance rides.

For Walter Clark, Virginia City provided a way of life that

At the Silver Dollar Saloon, Virginia City. Left to right, back row standing: Walter Clark, Duncan Emrich, Roger Butterfield, Len Haffey, Charles Clegg, Lucius Beebe. Front: Irene Bruce and Marian Emrich. Courtesy of Hugh Gallagher

matched the way he wanted to live. As we have already seen, he loved the old mining towns and knew many of them well but loved Virginia City most of all. While he resented the kind of phony westernness that tourism had brought (the retiring writer Clark did not like the show-off writer Beebe, whom he did not consider a writer at all), the town was still very much alive, and there was a genuine western spirit at bottom that he responded to and a neighborliness that he could relax within. No one thought he was special; he was just another guy that you would see around town.

The Clarks lived first in Virginia City in a rented house, the Chollar Mansion, now a historic site, on D Street in 1949. It was not really a mansion, but a relatively small house by today's standards that had been used as the Chollar Mine office. The Clarks spent some time fixing it up to make it livable. Walter could walk two blocks north and then one block east up to C Street, where there were saloons that he would go to in the late afternoon and evening. Every day his trip up to C Street became a break from the lonely business of writing. Saloons had always been the social clubs of the town, and Clark was a very social man. He liked to drink, liked to talk, and liked to get to know people. Two of the places to which he went most often were the Sazerac (now called the Ponderosa to cash in on the fame of the TV program *Bonanza*) and the Union Brewery. Gordon Lane, who owned the Union Brewery and ran it for thirty-one years, met Clark for the first time in 1937 when Clark was in town visiting Bob Caples. According to Lane, one of the things that Clark and Caples had in common was that neither one cared about money. It just wasn't important to them. Another was that both loved the desert. Lane remembers Caples as quiet but very funny and Clark as talkative, someone who could get along with just about anybody.

Once Clark had moved to Virginia City, he frequented "Gordy Lane's place" and became a good friend of the owner. His saloon, Lane recalls, "was kind of a meeting place, mostly locals, no tourists at all. And other than Saturday nights when a piano player would happen to drop in or something, relatively quiet. It was a good saloon. It really was. We had some good conversations." Although they talked about many things, Lane remembers Clark talking to him and others about sports, any sport, it didn't seem to matter. When arguing about some particular sports point, Clark could get very adamant, although never hostile or nasty. In fact, if he could dispute sports trivia or strategy, it would make his evening. Lane remembers Clark leaning against the bar and drinking his boilermakers throughout the evening, but they never seemed to have any effect. He would be as steady leaving as when he arrived.

Up above the Sazerac Saloon (a name that came from a New Orleans drink), the Sharon House Restaurant opened up in the early 1950s. Named after William Sharon, it was a restaurant that served Chinese food and became Clark's favorite eating place (by contrast with the number of saloons, there were only a couple of dinner places in town). Both the bar and restaurant were in the old California Bank Building, the bank having been started by Sharon and used in his efforts to monopolize as much of the mining activity as possible. Sharon, with his bank, also built the Virginia & Truckee Railroad in 1869, doing so in order to increase his mining profits. He wouldn't have to pay to haul the ore down to the mills or the wood back up for the mine boilers.

Among those who were Clark's good friends were Clint Salmon, who was the local grocer, and Clint Andreasen and Ole Hart. (Clint Andreasen and Ole were the owners of the Sazerac. Clint was a good-sized man whom Clark liked and admired. In pioneer days earlier in the century, he had been in drilling and mucking contests and had done a lot of mining.) Clint Salmon's son Ross eventually married Clark's daughter, Barbara. A number of writers and artists moved to Virginia City after World War II—among them Katie Best and Katie Hilliard, who wrote for women's magazines—and they often attended the Clarks' parties. After a couple of hours at a party at someone's home, it was almost automatic that everyone would go downtown and finish up the evening at the Union Brewery. Clark would sometimes invite friends up from Reno to a party, either at his home or to meet them at Gordy's.

The Nevada novelist Robert Laxalt, who became a close friend of Clark's, recalled their first meeting. At the time, Laxalt was a journalist and aspiring creative writer, and he had read a feature story in the *Nevada State Journal* entitled "Walter Clark Does It

The Sazarac, Walter's favorite bar, Virginia City, 1951 or 1952.
Robert Laxalt, in the back, center; Walter, at the bar, center, with glasses;
Robert Caples, in the back, second from the right; Clint Salmon, in front
of Caples, leaning on the bar. Courtesy of Barbara Clark Salmon.
Photo by Kelly Lyon, Virginia City

Again" about the publication of *The Track of the Cat*. He thought,
"There's the man I need to talk to," and a few months later, in the
winter of 1950, got up the courage to call Clark on the phone. He
told Clark that he had written a short story and asked him if he
would look at it, evaluate it, and give him suggestions. Clark was
somewhat hesitant but ended up inviting Laxalt and his wife up
from Carson City to meet him in his new home in Virginia City.

Laxalt, in his preface to the paperback edition of *The City of
Trembling Leaves,* describes the occasion and his impressions of
the writer:

> Virginia City and the Chollar House, really the old Chol-
> lar Mansion of the town's mining-boom days in the 1800s,
> were both worn and frayed around the edges. Despite its size,

I believe the house had limited space in which to live—a warm kitchen that was the living core of the house, bedrooms for Walter and Barbara and for their children, Babs and Bobby, and an upstairs room where Walter wrote.

There was a knocker on the door. It made a resounding noise that echoed through all the chambers. The tall door opened and an unmistakable Walter Clark stood there framed against the dark hallway. He was taller than I had expected, with athletic shoulders and arms. His face, tapering down from black, curling hair tipped with gray and a wide brow, could be called almost skeletal in a strong-boned way. But when I remember Walter now, I see first those startling blue eyes boring into me like a drill. The navy blue woolen turtle-neck set them off even more brilliantly. There was a magnetism about the man that flowed like a physical force.

If not effusive in his greeting, he was at least courteous. We learned that insincerity was no part of his makeup. In the kitchen, we met his wife, Barbara. She was an opposite of Wal-ter, small boned but wiry, with a bird-like face framed by gray-ing hair. She talked about horses and her New England rearing and one did not need to look far to know she was putting us at our ease. She had a New England face for sure, but there was warmth and compassion in those eyes.

We had a drink and then Walter led me up a creaking stair-way to the room in which he wrote. Lost Generation writers in Paris could not have asked for a better setting. There was no furniture except for Walter's worn desk and two old chairs of uncertain stability, but there were plenty of cobwebs.

Clark sat down at his desk, while Laxalt sat in one of the rick-ety chairs. Clark held out his hand and took the manila envelope with Laxalt's story in it, opened it, looked it over and then said that they could talk about it later when he had had a chance to read it.

*Walter Clark on the steps of Chollar House in
Virginia City. Courtesy of Hugh Gallagher*

Then Clark asked his visitor how much writing he had done, what
kind he wanted to do, and finally what he had read. After talking
for awhile, they went downstairs, and the two couples walked together through the light snow to the Sazerac on C Street.

They sat and drank and talked for a time, Clark now and then
jotting down notes a slip of paper. As they were leaving, Clark
handed the paper to his guest, suggesting that the list of books he
had written down might help him with his writing. "Walter Clark,"
in Laxalt's words, "believed that serious reading was the foun-
tainhead for serious writing." The list contained the following:

Joseph Conrad, *Heart of Darkness* and *The Nigger of the Narcissus*

D. H. Lawrence, *Sons and Lovers* and the first *Lady Chatterley*

Stephen Crane, *The Red Badge of Courage*

W. H. Hudson, *The Purple Land* and *Green Mansions*

Knut Hamsun, *Hunger* and *Growth of the Soul*

Turgenev, *Fathers and Sons*

Dostoevsky, *Crime and Punishment*

Faulkner, *The Sound and the Fury* and *As I Lay Dying*

Rolvaag, *Giants in the Earth*

Graham Greene, *The Heart of the Matter*

Richard Hughes, *High Wind in Jamaica*

Willa Cather, *Death Comes for the Archbishop*

During the summer of 1950, the Clarks moved from the Chollar Mine office into a house they purchased at the top of Virginia City on Stewart Street, the first home of their own. And during that same summer Walter got an unexpected offer. Among Clark's many friends in town was Hugh Gallagher, who was the principal of the elementary and high schools. One afternoon Gallagher ran into Clark downtown and asked him if he would be willing to teach in the high school. Gallagher told him that they hadn't had an English teacher for several years. The Clarks could use the money, although it was only two hundred dollars a month for teaching half-time, but it was the school's need that convinced him. That and the fact that he was asked—which was always important to him. Why would a famous writer (and at this point, after the publication of *Track of the Cat*, he *was* famous) take on a two-hundred-dollar-a-month job teaching in a small-town high school? Some clue to the answer to this comes in a statement he made in his short autobiographical summary:

I also believe that education, both formal and informal, is the only thing which can really lead to a large enough recognition and practice in all three of these huge, basic all inclusive neces-

Walter Clark with Duncan Emrich (left) on the occasion
of the donation of the manuscripts of The Track of the Cat *and*
The City of Trembling Leaves *to the Library of Congress, ca. 1950.*
Courtesy of Robert M. Clark. Photo by Jack McCann

sities of survival, voluntary birth control, natural conservation, and the reduction of divisions, to matter, so I also believe
that equal opportunity in education is the most important of
equalities.

As was his habit, he turned a half-time job into a full-time
effort. The grade school and high school were located within
walking distance of his house. They were in attractive, low brick
buildings that had been constructed in 1936 by the WPA. He would
teach two English classes, an hour and a half each. When he started
teaching, Clark encountered a number of students who could
hardly read and hated English. He began by bringing in comic

books, piles of them, to get the kids interested in reading. As time went by, he gave them more advanced comics that had more reading than cartoons. And he told them stories — stories he had heard about pioneer people in the area — as well as stories out of the literature he had taught. Then he had them write.

The other thing that Clark introduced, as one might expect, was chess. As we have seen, he and his wife were both great fans of chess and played frequently. Clark owned a number of chess sets, large and small, and he brought them all to class with him. He got his students involved in playing, with the idea that it taught them concentration and thinking ahead. Then there was the other typical component of Clark's teaching character — sports, the mind joined to the body.

Principal Gallagher recalls,

We didn't have enough boys in high school for a basketball team. . . . So we went to a community, Dayton, down in the desert, which is eleven miles from here, and they didn't have enough either. So, I remember Walter and I going around to various schools to see if they would permit us to have one team, a Dayton-Virginia City combined, and we went to Coalville and Smith Valley and all of them. Had a great day, and talked to all the principals. They said, "Sure, go ahead." This gave us the opportunity to go to the Nevada Interscholastic League, and they permitted us to do this. Walt coached that team. We had an old army surplus van, a Chevy van that we got from the Marine Corps for nothing, and that's what he traveled in. He only had six kids. He would go down to Dayton and pick [the Dayton kids] up in the early afternoon and bring them up to practice in our gym. When they were through practicing, he would drive them down — most of them were ranch kids — drive them right down along the river to their homes and then pick them up for games.

Clark's other sport, of course, was tennis. His was a tennis family. Not only was he a good player, but his sister, Miriam Chism, was a top player in Reno. His father had taught him tennis, and now he was teaching his son, Bobby, how to play, having started in Carson City when the family was living in the Washoe Valley. In Virginia City, however, there was a problem. They had a tennis court that was put in by the Lions Club in 1942, but they let it go to waste and ruin. Right after construction it had been a beautifully laid-out court and even had lights, but now no one played on it. One day, as Gallagher recalls, Walter said to him, "We ought to do something about that tennis court. But we don't have any money. I went through this one time before in Reno and helped them with the tennis courts and so I know what to do. Somehow we can raise a little money. Let's try it."

Gallagher recalls further, "So we went around to some business places up here and raised some money for supplies, got the supplies, and he and I did the work. Tough work too. But we did the work, and we made that tennis court first class." What the work amounted to was digging out weeds, filling potholes, and laying down a new surface with their own hand-mixed asphalt, painting lines, putting up a new net, and replacing the old bulbs in the light standards. Just the two of them—no greater love of tennis could have been demonstrated. Clark did it for the town and for the schoolchildren, but also for himself and in order to use the court to teach his son.

Because of the success of *The Track of the Cat,* Random House finally agreed to publish a collection of his short stories, *The Watchful Gods and Other Stories,* which came out in September of 1950. It would be his last major publication, and sadly it got little attention and had small sales. Typical of the response to the book was this summation in a review in the *Chicago Sunday Tribune*:

The final judgment on this collection, so far as I am called to give it, is that here are some good, sincere, appealing stories mixed up with some that display an over-reaching for emotional content, and some so nebulous they just don't jell. You'll find some good reading in it, but don't be surprised if you find yourself wondering, at times, just what the author is trying to say.

In the *Bulletin of Bibliography,* however, Robie Macauley compares story collections by Irwin Shaw and Mary McCarthy with the Clark collection. Early in the review he states,

> In a sense, every story of Shaw's is a sure thing and everyone of Clark's is a gamble. Clark usually takes on a subject that is dangerous and likely to go wrong at any moment.

And then he concludes,

> Any critical judgment about Clark's writing would have to be tentative and conditional. Irwin Shaw and Mary McCarthy are unlikely to become a great deal better or a great deal different in the future. Clark has a chance to be both.

There is of course great irony in that "chance," as following this publication, Clark tried but could not take up the challenge. No one knows quite why. He wrote nearly constantly for years—there are many hundreds of pages of unfinished drafts that remain, and how many pages burned or thrown away, we don't know. But none of this material was ever put into publishable form. He just wrote.

The Watchful Gods and Other Stories was a mixed bag of unrelated stories. In addition to the western stories that we have already looked at—"The Wind and the Snow of Winter," "The Buck in the Hills," and "The Indian Well"—the collection included "Hook," the story of the birth, life, and death of a hawk, perhaps the best story Clark ever wrote. Also included are five stories, most of which tend toward humor or satire and which are clearly not as successful as the others. Clark was attracted, more than he should have been, to satire—a form that usually led him into a mode of writing that was too symbolic and abstract when his forte was descriptive detail. Characters became types rather than individuals, and their humanity was abbreviated or lost.

This problem with characterization is apparent in the first of these nonwestern stories, "The Rapids." Here the central character is a "man of the City," as Galsworthy or Dickens would say of a character from London's Wall Street. The man, named John, is described as an extreme type:

> A man appeared, walking by himself. He was thin, and wore spectacles, and his legs, when they showed through the flapping wings of his red and blue dressing gown, were very white. He carried a towel in one hand. Walking carefully, for his slippers were thin, he came down between the fir trees, then between the alders and the willows, and stood at the edge of the river.

He has apparently come out from a country house down to the river to bathe, and there is hardly a touch that Clark could add to this description that would have made him any more out of place. The natural surroundings that he is immersed in, however, are described in convincingly realistic detail, and the contrast between the man and his surroundings—he simply does not fit—couldn't be more obvious. Once again Clark is saying something about man as being part of or separated from nature. The man's alienation is emphasized even further by his attempt to join his surroundings by rescuing an old, half-sunken boat and his comic attempt to ride it down a rapids. Then it is underlined again by the appearance of his wife, who wants to know what in heaven's name he is doing and thinks him crazy. It is impossible for him to be in or a part of nature; the city calls him back to his normal role. His wife cries out to him as he splashes around in the boat, "D.L. called you ... He wants you back in town." And adds later, with some irony for the reader, "D.L. will be wild." It is to some extent a story like one that might have been written by John Cheever, "The Common Day," for example, except that Cheever gives his attention to the internal life and injured humanity of his central character. That character in the Cheever story, Jim, is certainly a type, but he is also an individual. We can empathize with his feelings.

Other stories in Clark's collection include "The Anonymous," about an Indian boy who has his identity stolen from him by a wealthy Anglo woman. Written in 1941, the story has its setting at the Stewart Indian School just south of Carson City. Here, once again, Clark is more interested in the situation and the theme that is illustrated by that situation than in the human dimensions of the small tragedy described. The central character is an Anglo teacher, a Mr. Gates, at the Indian school, who is the observer of the boy. At the denouement of the story, Gates, who has been puzzled by the boy — his Boston accent, and the fancy dress, the elaborate furniture, and separate residence that have been provided for him — finds out that he has been "captured" by the rich woman, who met the boy on a dude ranch. Another character explains to Gates that "he don't even know he's nothing but a toy." To end the story, the teacher's response to this revelation is simply to go back to correcting his papers. We don't know how the boy feels, nor do we know what emotional reaction Gates may have had — we can only suppose that the teacher's response, like ours, may be sorrow or depression. In its own way the story is effective (as is "The Rapids"), but the reader may well mourn the missed opportunities to make the story richer and even more powerful.

Then there is "Why Don't You Look Where You're Going?" This is a humorous story that is more like a cartoon than a short story — although, once again, it does illustrate a theme. A big liner almost runs down a small sailboat out in the ocean, and one of the points of the story is presumably that the large mechanical monster separates its passengers from nature and is careless about the fate of the "little man" (a phrase often used by Clark) in the sailboat, who is in nature. Civilization, particularly its technology in the form here, "White as a sainted leviathan, but too huge for even God to have imagined it," can separate us from our surroundings and destroy our sensitivity to our place in nature.

Another story which is also comical and satiric is "The Fish Who Could Close His Eyes," about a boy, Tad, working at an aquarium who becomes entranced by a particular fish, romanticizes it, and begins to think of it in human terms. A remark by his boss, "What are you fussing about that damned fish for?" turns the boy's sympathy for the fish, which he has named Hamlet, "into violent partisanship." The boy's romantic notions about the fish are deflated when his boss, Dr. Litter, tells him that the fish's strange behaviors—his closed eyes and his failure to eat—are due to a fungus. They are not demonstrations of loneliness or any other human emotion. At the end, nature becomes nature, and there is an almost Jeffers-like recognition: "Tad stood there for a long time, staring out at the bland, happy, heartless sea in the morning freshness." It is a story that may well have come out of Clark's work at the Scripps Institute of Oceanography years before.

And finally, there is the story "The Portable Phonograph," which for many years was one of Clark's most popular. It rather graphically illustrates the author's devotion to theme over any other story element except physical description. Written at the beginning of World War II in 1941, years before the atom bombs were dropped on Japan, Clark's story takes place on the prairie somewhere in this country in the aftermath of a catastrophe, perhaps a devastating war. The situation is reminiscent of a number of after-the-bomb stories and novels written in the period after the war ended (George Stewart's *The Earth Abides* and Eugene Burdick's *The Ninth Wave* among them).

In Clark's story four men gather in a cave in a desolate and ravaged landscape at the outset of winter. Ragged, dirty, and bearded, they have gathered at their host's invitation in a ritual of remembrance and a struggle to carry on something of civilization. Since they talk of those "who will come after," their continuation is understood to be only temporary. The host, a Professor Jenkins, had just read from Shakespeare's *The Tempest*—Shakespeare's works, along with the Bible, *Moby-Dick,* and *The Divine Comedy,* were salvaged by the professor as he fled the disaster.

After the reading, the guests—including a musician and a writer—all hope that the host will play a record on his portable phonograph. He has also salvaged several classical records. The host is reluctant to use the phonograph, since he is running out of needles and the records are becoming worn, but he does so, and the listeners are deeply moved. The guests leave, but Jenkins thinks that one of them is lurking outside in the shadows. He nervously opens a hole he has dug in the dirt wall above his earthen couch and places the phonograph, records, and books in the cavity, covering the hole over with a board and then dirt. At last he gets up on his bed and covers himself with his worn blankets. The story ends on an ominous note: "On the inside of the bed, near the wall, he could feel with his hand, the comfortable piece of lead pipe."

Even for a piece of science fantasy, if one can call it that (it is also reminiscent of several stories by Ray Bradbury), this story would seem to be all too neatly arranged, too pat in order to make its points. There are the representative characters—professor, musician, and writer—and the representative selection of great books and great music. Nearly everything in the story would seem to be symbolic, and for some readers the tale is barren and artificial. One of those is critic Vernon Young, who thinks that the basic problem goes back to the way Clark composed his story. Young refers to an article by Clark, "The Ghost of an Apprehension," in which he explains how he set up his composition.

Clark states that an apprehension, indeed, was the source of the central idea and that the story took shape in his mind "somewhat as a play might, the intention producing the scene, the scene and the intention selecting the cast, and all three, ... dictating the action." After quoting this, Young comments,

> The unsatisfying totality of "The Portable Phonograph" may well derive from this same production of scene and cast by intention rather than by the opposite method. Why did not Clark's "ghost of an apprehension" suggest or recall concrete, realizable people within a scene of devastation, thereafter creating the atmosphere of devastation from the viewpoint of the people experiencing it? Instead, the apprehension created the scene and Clark then had to manufacture the *personae* for the scene. And manufactured they are.

But Clark's mind did not work the way this prescription would require.

Clark's story does not fit the pattern that Young wants, but who is to say that there are not other satisfactory patterns—a story, for instance, that is thoroughly symbolic? Clark was obviously almost obsessed with the use and power of symbol. Robert Gorrell, who was chair of the Department of English while Clark was teaching at the University of Nevada, recalls taking over an American novel class for his colleague, who had to leave town for a conference. Gorrell was not in the classroom more than a couple of minutes before a young man in the back raised his hand and asked, "Can you explain to us what symbol is?"

Nevertheless, as attached as Clark was to symbolism as a way of communicating theme, his attachment was something that worried him. According to Robert Clark and Charlton Laird, Clark's lapse into publication silence at the end of his career may have been in part due to his worry during composition that "his concern for the allegory behind the story should derange the fiction." As we noted earlier, his son, Robert, has commented that in looking back at his father's career, he is surprised that he turned to fiction at all, since his mind was essentially philosophical.

According to Robert Clark and Laird, "He [Clark] conducted dialogues with himself on the subject [of allegory], and even left little notes about symbolism and how to control it, admonishing himself." On unpublished manuscripts written during these later years, he jotted down such notes as "Learn to incorporate an organized (allegorical) symbolism within a natural context," and "You know that symbolized meanings must be inherent in the real meanings — enlarging them, not saying something else."

This conflict was uppermost in Clark's mind during his composition of the novella that gives its name to the collection, *The Watchful Gods and Other Stories*. The story is about a day in the life of a twelve-year-old boy, Buck, and a journey he takes that is combined, as we have seen in other Clark stories, with a hunt — and as before, the human is the predator. The themes once again are the discovery of the nature of nature, man's place in nature, and the desirable unity of body and spirit. And in connection with all of these, as we shall see, is the primary theme of the evolution of religious consciousness, both in the individual and by extension in humankind.

The day of the story is the boy's birthday, and in this family birthdays are celebrated at breakfast. With great anticipation, Buck is looking forward to receiving one present above all, a .22 rifle. The receipt of such a gun has been a traditional rite of passage in this country, particularly, of course, in rural areas. A boy, in receiving such a weapon and learning to use it wisely, is on the road to manhood. Clark uses this tradition ironically, since for him there is no such thing as a wise killing of animals except in the dire need for food. If we know Clark's work at all, we have a sense of foreboding as the boy takes his present out into the countryside to try it out.

The story in many ways is similar to other initiation stories —

Steinbeck's "The Red Pony" and Faulkner's "The Bear"—as in all of the stories the boy learns he must go beyond his romantic view of life, his daydreams, in order to find his real place in the scheme of things. All the boys in these stories learn about responsibility and the reality and finality of death. Like Tim Hazard, who dreams of Rachael in terms of Tristram and Isolde, Buck dreams of Janet Haley. And just as Tim lives in a world inhabited by gods and spirits, so Buck has conflicts in his mind, internal arguments, which are developed in dialogues between him and the watchful gods, the fog god, and the sprites who are the little "gods of life."

These spirits, which colleague Robert Gorrell has said that Clark "almost really believed in," come to represent the various aspects of nature—the fog god, for example, representing nature's opposition to human will as well as the sinister, threatening aspects of nature. The story is set on the coast near the ocean (the setting is the Morse summer cottage at Essex, New York), a foggy location, and the fog god obscures that which the human tries to understand and attempts to block that which the human tries to achieve. Critic Vernon Young has commented in response to this kind of material,

> Tentatively, [Clark] is essaying an American myth but up to now it is a myth in which the gods are more clearly construed than the heroes.... The hallucinations in *The Track of the Cat* and in *The Watchful Gods* have more substance than the victims who suffer them.

He clearly exaggerates, but it is true that aside from the boy's internal voices and his visions of the watchful gods around him, Buck remains outwardly a rather ordinary boy, almost stereotypical—very little individualizing substance is given to him. On the other hand, outward individualizing is not to Clark's point. Robert Gorrell has written that the novella "is more than a story of a boy's dreams and problems; the dreams and problems are pressed toward universality by the machinery of the story: the gods and the mythmaking." The question is whether Buck is individualized enough for Clark's purpose—and what is that purpose? To even write about the boy as a boy seems to Vernon Young a mistake: "I have no final conviction that Clark is denatured more by his mind than by his discouragingly juvenile emotions."

Buck's journey is from his home after the birthday breakfast, through the coastal canyons, to his "secret beach" (which because of its isolation and riptides he has been forbidden by his parents to visit). The journey through the canyons is rendered with the kind of naturalistic detail that Clark excels at—we feel or see every rock, pebble, bush, animal, and turn of the path. The two crucial incidents of that journey are Buck's shooting of a rabbit and his encounter with a rattlesnake. A rabbit may be a convenient, even typical target for a young boy with a rifle, but it is a convincing symbol here for the helpless innocence that is victimized by a boy's pride and mistaken notion of manhood. He wants to prove himself to his father, who has given him the gun, and also show evidence of his skill to his sister, who mocks and doubts him. (Tim in *The City* is often motivated to action, as in his race against Red, by what he believes are women's opinions of him.) He can't return without a trophy, Buck thinks at first; but after the kill he is so ashamed that he plans a ritual burial for the rabbit out in the wilderness. The rattlesnake, which Buck thinks of as a servant of the fog god, almost bites him, an action that he believes comes as punishment for his "crime."

"The Watchful Gods" went through two revisions and three versions. In an article, "Problems in 'The Watchful Gods,'" Robert Gorrell compares the three versions and concludes,

Comparison of the versions reinforces my feeling that Clark approached "The Watchful Gods" strongly preoccupied with his desire to make a significant statement about the world....

The revision reveals Clark's awareness of the dangers of giving the story too many of the characteristics of a philosophical
treatise, and he reworked the manuscript with the skills that
had made the shorter stories successful—rendering experience
with accurate detail, selecting and ordering events so that they
made the abstract statements for him.

"The Watchful Gods" was not the kind of material that Random House hoped for from Clark, and Clark was aware of this resistance. In sending the manuscript of the collection to his publisher in 1950, Clark included a covering letter to his editor, Saxe
Commins, explaining what he was trying to do in the novella. He
begins by noting that the first version was written in 1948 but was
little more than an outline for what he wanted to say. The enclosed
revised manuscript, he says, comes very close to what he had in
mind for the story (the phrase "very close" suggests once again
Clark's perfectionism). He mentions that the central incidents of
the killing of the rabbit and the rattlesnake came out of his own
childhood, although they were not so closely related, and for some
reason "they have always haunted me as something I had to use
someday."

He goes on to explain the philosophical basis for his novella:

> The theme I finally used has also interested me for a long
> time—made me watchful of many pertinent manifestations in
> youngsters while I was teaching, and since, and as an explorer,
> insofar as memory can be trusted—and mine is pretty good—
> of the same things in my own childhood and adolescence. You
> will recollect hints of it—the running and the kind of prayer
> Tim Hazard used, for instance, in *The City*. Very roughly
> speaking, the idea is that religious development is a continu-
> ously repeated experience of the race—each individual in his
> childhood and early adolescence ... recapitulates in capsule

form, as it were, the religious history of the race, from primitive anthropomorphism, through the more regular and limited classical pantheon ... into the simple two-force (good and evil) conception basic to Christianity, and finally, given a sufficiently strong urge to unity and honesty in appraising the events of life, into the complete unity of mysticism—a spiritual evolution comparable, that is, to the recapitulation by the fetus and infant in the womb of the biological history.

For many readers, particularly those who have not read Clark extensively, "The Watchful Gods," would appear to be a very strange document. What to make of the gods and sprites that Clark "almost really believed in"? And that Buck is obsessed by? Of his dreams of Janet, of mythic heroes, and of running like a football hero—what do these daydreams lead to and what is the point? What can one make of his ritualized burial of the rabbit? Or of the strange, ambiguous conclusion?

At the end of the story, when Buck finally reaches his "secret beach" after burying and praying over the rabbit, he sees that the sun has broken through the fog and has reached the sea in "a long, slanting column of white light." He is nearly overcome by a sight that makes him at the same time want to weep and to burst out in "triumphant song." With steely determination, assuming the "expressionless countenance of the fighter advancing from his corner," he begins to wade out into the dark water. As he presses forward, "The betraying voice spoke again in his mind. 'You aren't going home ...' it began, but he cut it off there." Is he simply going into the water, previously labeled as dangerous, to perform a ceremony of cleansing himself? Or is he so overcome by his "crime" that he is determined to tempt death or even die?

Certainly this is a boy with a very rich inner life, and that is Clark's main concern—one that with naturalistic detail he must try to make believable. Here is the split in Clark between the writer and the philosopher. It was a split that he recognized and one that he even expressed in a dialogue, in an essay that he wrote called "The Writer and the Professor, Where is the Little Man Inside?" The professor (the philosopher side of Clark) discusses art as communication by saying,

> Certainly all primitive art was essentially religious in source and intention, suggesting in turn that even now the primary impulse of the arts was religious, ritualistic — their central hope, however much diluted by time and civilized detachment and irrelevant rationalization, the same old one of propitiating or enlisting Nature, the Gods, or God, or whatever name one wishes to give to the encompassing and still mysterious whole, and of acting, as it were, as the shaman, the witch doctor, the intermediary, between poor suffering man and the occult powers which control him.

The writer part of Clark in response points out that he, himself, wrote all of this long ago: "[The] story of a twelve year old kid shoots his first rabbit without proper respect and fellow-feeling, and loses touch with nature. Stuck all by himself then, like idiot modern man."

This is a rather blunt summary of a story that Clark had labored over, revising it with an intense motivation to get it right, to communicate the present condition of mankind in respect to the whole. Max Westbrook has commented that "the first solo hunting trip of a twelve-year-old boy has turned into a religious experience so powerful it melts the only ceremony he knows to offer." As a whole, the stories and novels, Westbrook adds, are in his view "centrally concerned with the incapacity of words to capture the primal and religious immensities assigned to them." Why did Clark turn to fiction? Probably because in fiction he could say things, through symbol and allegory within a created experience, that one could not say as effectively in words of the philosopher. Finally, it must be said that Clark believed in art and the power of art to enlarge our minds and extend our sympathies in an intimate and organic way. As a teacher he used art to teach; as a writer he used art to educate.

❰❰ CHAPTER NINE ❱❱

AWAY FROM HOME—
FRUSTRATION AND LONGING

CLARK'S TEACHING AT THE HIGH SCHOOL in Virginia City lasted only a year, 1950–51. He got an offer to teach the following year at the renowned Writers' Workshop at the University of Iowa. Reluctant to move from Virginia City or take the children out of school for a year, he and Barbara decided that he would go on by himself.

In many ways it was a very difficult year for him, but there is no doubt that at this point he needed the money. He wrote to his wife frequently, sometimes every day, and expressed in every letter how much he loved and missed her and how unhappy he was about not being home with her and the children. He also describes repeatedly his difficulty in getting any writing done, although he tries over and over again. The letters altogether tell the sad story of the onset of a writer's block that would not go away for the rest of his life. He refused to think of himself as through, as a teacher of writing who could not write, and he fought to find a way of breaking through the barriers that he had largely set up against himself.

After arriving in Iowa City in mid-September, Clark complained of not feeling well, with a variety of ailments, and throughout his stay he tended to blame the high humidity in his new low-altitude, nondesert environment. He wrote to his wife on September 15, 1951, that "probably it's all—ankle, fever, head—just psychosomatic. Down psyche." He goes on to describe settling in, including locating the English Department buildings and, of course, the tennis courts. He got all his paperwork done and wrote that all of these arrangements had

> just about [fixed me] up on all I wanted to be fixed up on—
> except getting going on the book. I have made four tries at that
> [he had been in Iowa City only a few days]—one still hanging
> around, ten pages long. No better than an effort of will, yet—
> but it may get me into it. Then I can throw away the surplus.
> If only I could get the book going, then I could really feel that
> I am here for a purpose, which, I admit, I don't so far. It still
> seems like a strange interlude—a pointless passage in another
> and not altogether real world. The will is not enough—
> definitely not enough—or it is a strange but sure thing that I
> have worn mine down to where the gears slip getting started.

Two days later he wrote from 120 East Market Street, Iowa City, to tell his wife that he had looked in the papers for a place to rent and made a foot tour of the downtown. He couldn't find anything at all suitable, and, discouraged and disgusted, he almost wrote Hugh Gallagher to rearrange the schedule at the Virginia City high school. Finally, he settled for a small room in a men's rooming house among sixteen other residents, all students. It was relatively inexpensive, an important consideration at this time, and had the advantage, from his point of view, of being in walking distance of the tennis courts, the stadium, and the basketball pavilion. He concluded, "I'm all settled in now—a good reading chair, a good work table, another table for the typewriter and I have a notion that between the town, which offers no temptations, and my schedule, I should get a lot of work done."

A day later, he wrote another long letter. It would appear that he was spending more time on letters than writing anything else. Perhaps it was loneliness; perhaps it was procrastination. He reported that he had been tramping around the campus all afternoon and found "the buildings are gray stone reminders of the Metropolitan Museum—just about as inspiring as that oversized tomb would be, empty." He found the English Department, housed in army temporaries on the lower campus, and was "glad to find the department there in the outside shanties. Much more human."

On the 23rd of September he wrote again to "Bub Dear,"

> I've met the other regulars of the workshop group now too— Martin and Cassill, both about thirty—but seem to me much younger—that sign of time grows in me—most of the undergrads here look to me like school kids. I met my first section— the normal class, twenty-five of them, all but one graduate students, most of them ex-G.I.'s—no kids—a promising looking gang. I can only hope I can give them something. It troubles me that there still seems to be no juice in my battery. I've made two or three abortive attempts at starting the novel— but still no go. And I don't seem to care whether school keeps or not. No ideas, no interest, no sparks. A little homesick, very aimless, and profoundly disgusted with myself. I keep coming to and discovering that I have been sitting for half an hour or more doing nothing, not ever really thinking anything. I don't know how it feels to be dead, but I don't think it could be very different....
>
> This is a rotten letter. I'm sorry. Anyway, I am gradually finding my way into things. Given a little time, I'll get moving where it counts, too. I'd probably do it faster if I'd quit kicking myself—but that I can't seem to do, so I must kick a little

harder. God help the tale that is written by will alone—but if nothing else is working, I guess it has to be that. I have the soul of a frozen turnip—my apologies to the turnip.

His worry about a lack of writing progress was almost constant. On September 28, he wrote,

So far I am still distinctly on the surface, and feeble and vague in my thinking. My mind plays little tricks . . . even with what is visible before it—I cannot write a sentence that seems to have the true light or color—I even forget the names of characters and the shape of scenes I have made copious notes on and pondered, on and off, for months and even years.

On October 2, he wrote that he'd got his first paycheck, and it was not as much as he'd thought it would be. With withholding and social security it was only $434, so he promised his wife he would be more careful in his spending this month and try next month to send more money home. The weather, he reported, was oppressive: "Always it is damp—the kind of constant, heavy damp that grows a fungus on the soul as well as the flesh." And then once again, he turned to his condition in regard to his writing:

Now that I have let the writing strictly alone for three or four days, and the Iowa numbness is beginning to wear off (I still say this must have been wonderful buffalo country) I feel an occasional nudge from the personal friend—a sentence or two shapes up now and then and seems to have found better words, a character makes a small move in the back of my mind—starts to lift a drink, maybe, but doesn't taste it yet. And I begin to feel something a little besides the constant yearn for you and mountains and thin air—at least a little pity for the character who can't get his drink up. Also I begin to look at things a little bit that way—to see people and hear what they say and guess at what goes on inside them. So I get a little—secretly—hopeful.

In the meantime, he had received his first workshop manuscripts, and he reported that perhaps reading them would "assist in the necessary reincarnation of my spook." He had a conference that afternoon with the student author of a novel manuscript. Although the writing was mostly good, the structure was impossibly involved. Such conferences, he wrote, were "always tough, and no real way to plan beforehand, how to give encouragement, and still tell the truth." Three days later, he wrote, "I might well let you know now, though, that I don't intend to be away again—at least not this long—if I can help it. I will learn to tend bar first."

By October 10, he was beginning to try to figure out how he could leave Iowa in midyear. Some small amount of money was due to him from a return of his retirement contributions at Virginia City, and his wife had some inheritance money due to her from her parents' estate. He wrote, "Right now I regret I didn't take the last offer from the U. of N. We'd have made almost as much money out of it, I'd been there instead of here, and if I hadn't quite as much time, it would have been more use to me." The situation at Iowa was getting worse:

> The dominant attitude of the Iowa workshop toward literature, and that of one W. Clark are highly incompatible, so that I walk like a spy in an enemy camp, ever watchful and cautious. The differences became evident very quickly, but I thought for awhile that, as in most cases, if I just mildly maintained my own views and emphasized what I thought should come first in writing, we would find gradually, that we weren't so far apart. But it hasn't worked that way. I have been subjected to a number of malicious, secretive personal attacks, and feel the antago-

nism always heavy in the air. . . . I have not yet managed to
cut myself free from the brooding depression, even when I
am away from the workshop, and it makes writing very hard.

Paranoia was not typical of him, so there must have been a combination of his loneliness, depression, an unpleasant physical environment, and some basic disagreements about how to approach literature. He couldn't figure out, if the faculty at the workshop had
known anything about his work, why they had asked him to come
to teach at all. Apparently, the dominant approach to teaching literature and writing at Iowa at the time was a Freudian one, and Clark,
as well as most recent major western writers, was not inclined to
use Freudian concepts as a basis for his thinking or writing.

The approach of writers like Walter Clark, John Steinbeck,
A. B. Guthrie Jr., Frederick Manfred, Mari Sandoz, and Frank
Waters, if psychological at all, was more likely Jungian. Their
close identification with nature and the land, their sense of the sacred unity of life which they inherited from the Indians—and in
some cases, from Eastern religions—and their sense of the importance of the unconscious all led these western writers toward a
Jungian interpretation of the human place in this world. But this
label describes a way of thinking, and in Clark's case and that
of many of the others, it did not involve a deliberate embracing
of Jungian philosophy (Clark never used Jungian terminology
as such). Nonetheless, Clark's commitment to myth, archetypal
symbol, and allegory obviously set him apart from the Iowa main-
stream. How much the hostility toward him that this apartness
generated was real and how much was an impression that was generated out of his depression is impossible to know. However, the
hostility could not have run very deep, since Iowa, at the end of his
year, asked him to stay on a permanent basis. Regardless of his approach, they must have recognized that he was a hell of teacher.

Toward the end of October, however, he was beginning to weaken in his determination to return home, somehow, in mid-year. There were some signs, he wrote his wife, that there was "some thawing of the ice—a suggestion that we may reach at least a workable compromise," and he thought he should wait to inform Paul Engle, the chair of the department, that he wanted to leave. This change may have come from an alteration in circumstances but more likely was caused by a shift in his own attitude, since, for the time being at least, he was optimistic about his writing:

> Also—there are signs—I dare not speak more confidently yet—that the writing may be beginning to move—which by now is the only really important thing to me, except being home with you.... Over the weekend I made a five or six page new start on the novel, and yesterday I wrote ten hours and wound up with better than twenty double pages in the note-book—not just what I would wish but still, something from which I can go on, and which may be mended in revision well enough to hold, I think. Anyway, the difficult and intricate expository and allegorical problems are straightened out in this final chapter [his most recent attempt]—and I have past reasons to hope that the rest may move more easily and truly ... I am setting myself, though not yet too confidently, the improbable goal of a completed first draft by Christmas.

He had really decided to stay on—they needed the money—and he noted that "I can take anything for a year, or let's be specific, eight months—that's a big difference. I cannot remember having counted off days on the calendar like this since I worked in the Imperial Valley at the ripe old age of seventeen." In the meantime, he reported, he was finding company in books, especially those he was very fond of, *Wuthering Heights, Green Mansions, Moby-Dick,* and *The Heart of Darkness.*

But a week later his optimism about his writing evaporated, as it would over and over again:

> I have been a bit depressed all day, because it became evident
> that the new start on the novel—into the fifth chapter—would
> not do either. So I have been brooding about it all day, lying on
> the bed, getting up and making notes, arguing with myself and
> refiguring that, until finally I could make the new outline—
> which I have just finished. Now I feel more hopeful again.
> (10/30/51)

Clark's social activities during this period were limited—as one might suspect knowing his strained relations with some of the other faculty—to going out occasionally with his students. One evening, after a long talk with a graduate student about his writing, the two of them went to dinner at the Ox-Yoke Tavern, twenty miles north of town. It had a big dining room with a fireplace, old lamps suspended from the rafters, and two old Germans, watching each other and smiling, strumming zithers. Clark dutifully reported to his wife that he had splurged and ordered a steak (11/3/51).

A week later, November 9, his spirits had plummeted again. He continued to search for some formula, some beginning to his manuscript that would catch fire and move him onward, but he found himself going around and around in the mechanics of the first chapter. "I am numb," he told his wife. "I am in a secondary stage. I have hung up my feelings, apparently, for the duration. I am a thing of words and theories, a sock with no foot in it."

His struggle within himself and with his projected novel continued, and on November 18, he wrote to "Bub Dearest":

> I feel more cheerful all around tonight. To begin with, I have
> spent the weekend wrestling with the book—and thrown away

nearly two chapters of beginning again, but because I believe
I have at last seen the light. I know I've thought that a good
many times before but this seems like it—not only feels like
it, but looks like it. I haven't a word written on this book, as
a result, but I'm sure of my starting place, of the manner that
belongs, and of my overall pattern. I have it all in rough outline
already—new ideas, new glimpses of scenes have been spring-
ing into the notes and working in my head all afternoon.

In the same letter he reported that "young Richardson, my
chess vis-a-vis here at the house," had taken him out to a little steak
house near the airport and then drove him around while he
checked on the prices of bus, plane, and train tickets back to Reno.
Having given up the idea of quitting at midyear, he now hoped to
go home for a couple of weeks at Christmastime. From his research
he found that he could afford to go if he went by train, and the
prospect lifted his spirits: "I already have enough in the local sock
to get my ticket. You have no idea how much that certainty bol-
sters my internals—practically a tie with new hope of the book."

But eleven days later, on November 29, he was down in the
dumps again, telling his wife,

> Probably I shouldn't be writing you. After all my fine rush of
> enthusiasm, here I am back at the beginning again, not a line of
> writing to show for nearly three months of working any time I
> was free. Not even in the dismal struggle to get the *Cat* going
> did I ever feel as terribly encumbered, the life so gone from
> even particular words.... But as it is, I am even now confident,
> if somewhat determinedly so, that tomorrow I will go back and
> try a different starting point, and really get it under way.

In his letters, Clark often made reference to his sports activities. Physical activity was important to him, but as November
went by with little progress on his writing, he found himself pre-

occupied and having just about given up on tennis and pickup basketball. He worried that he would be "a pretty flabby job by spring" (11/9/51). Desperate during one of his down periods, he asked his wife (daughter of a preacher) to pray for his getting through the first three chapters—since her prayers would be much more effective than his.

Then, having tried prayer, he later turned to "magic":

> I wish I had some kind of talisman of you, a ring, or pin, any kind of gadget that definitely means you. I have wanted one frequently. It is not by any means the only reason, but the only reasonable reason I can give is that I want to hold it in my right hand while I try to write.

Although he was counting his "supper pennies as usual," he would, he told his wife, treat himself to supper that night and go to a movie, *Tales of Hoffman,* and "then I shall come home and see if I can make another stab on the *Man in the Hole* [the novel he was trying to write]. (I've got a sneaking suspicion who the real man in the hole is.)

Lonely and depressed, he found a friend. In a hole in a tree just outside his window, he discovered a big gray squirrel. As Clark sat by the window, trying to write, he would see the squirrel sitting on a limb or just poking his head out of his hole, looking around at the world in general or staring at him through the window. He was pleased that the squirrel did not care to talk about writing, nor did it even read. Yet one day he was surprised to see the animal tearing up a big piece of newspaper and carrying it column by column up the tree and into his hole. He was relieved to see that it wasn't concerned with the contents, but stuffed the paper in the hole and jumped up and down on it, not in rage or desperation but just to make it fit. "Neither," he reported, "have I ever seen him smoking a cigarette, drinking a cup of coffee, or sitting with his head in his hand. I believe that, without ever getting into burdensome intimacy, without ever relating each other's private souls, we shall be very well acquainted by spring" (12/5/51).

He had his train ticket all paid for, and with great anticipation he was beginning to count the days until he would be going home during the Christmas break:

> Two weeks from today — that's what I keep thinking about — two weeks from today. And I'd love to go to the movies with you, any movie, or no movie, or anywhere. Just with you, that's all. I love you very much. I am getting so restless I can hardly sit still or keep my mind on what I'm doing. (12/7/51)

Then in his last letter before going home, on "December 13 (8 days to go)," he wrote,

> I am cleaning up to come home now — finished the Christmas cards ... today, and winding up *Moby Dick* — somewhat arbitrarily, tomorrow, and next Monday and Wednesday am doing a quickie discussion — by request — of *The Cat* — deliberately put it there because it can be a quickie, and I will have Christmas vacation to get over the lack of reaction. ...
>
> I have not had time to write on the book for a week and feel very guilty — which only goes to show how ridiculous a conscience can be — since I have done quite a lot of various sorts — and all the previous writing has only been thrown away. I began to suspect, however, that the black first chapter is coming home with me — and I had sworn at least to have that done. Well — maybe you and house and hills and C Street now will untie me and get me over the hump. ...
>
> Well, nothing really matters to me now except to get these odds and ends cleaned up, and get onto that train next Wed. at 5:50.

After not quite two weeks in Virginia City, Clark returned to Iowa City, refreshed and once again optimistic. He had returned with Christmas presents — a Navajo rug, a Mexican blanket, and a framed photo of his wife and children. There was "a new and hopeful start on the book," but of course it was "not ready to use as it is, but something near what I have wanted." He couldn't go on with it, however, because it was near the end of the semester and he was inundated with last-minute term papers and manuscripts from the writing students.

On January 11, he wrote,

> No notes and no Christmas cards from anybody at Random
> House. One is alive or otherwise according to his production,
> I guess, and there's something in that, all right. But from MCA
> (his agents) ... an encouraging note to prove the *Watchful
> Gods* not quite stillborn — a French outfit has taken it for trans-
> lation (though cutting it for length by dropping "The Anony-
> mous," "The Rapids," and "Why Don't You Look Where
> You're Going?" I seem to be the only person on earth who
> likes those last two little stories).

He mentions, in the same letter, that he had heard from Bob Gor-rell, department chair at Nevada, that he couldn't offer him a sum-mer-session job but that there was a good chance of a job for Clark in the fall. He also got offers for teaching at conferences during the summer at the University of Omaha and the University of Mis-souri. By taking these up he would not be home until the first of July, something he regretted, but they needed the money: "Until I really begin to produce again, I guess I'd better teach and see the world."

By the end of January, hearing that the snow had gotten very deep at home, he worried about how his wife was coping, and he wrote to her, "Records are fine things, but if v.c. is going to break any all time ones — I'd rather be around." It was indeed a record year — drifts and piles of snow from shoveling grew higher than the people. Snow in the Sierra Nevada broke the flume that brought water to the town, so that Virginia City was without running water for six weeks. Tankers brought in water, and townspeople melted snow to get more. Hay was airlifted and dropped to cattle in the eastern part of the state. "It was," according to Robert Clark, "a winter that quickly became legend to the residents of the Comstock," and Walter Clark, while worried about his family at the time, was later sorry he had not been there to experience it.

Out of a need for money and possibly out of frustration with his novel, Clark, in Iowa, had signed up with Random House to do a history of the Comstock for a series of histories on various topics designed for teenagers. He wrote his wife that he would have a week between semesters, and if he couldn't get the novel moving, he would go over to the Comstock book right away. Since it was nonfiction and the material was familiar to him, he thought that writing it would be a straightforward job and that the exercise of writing might even help him to break out of his creative dry spell. "I really don't know—what keeps me sterile so long" (1/25/52).

On the first of February, he wrote to Bub,

> I've had no classes this week—between semesters—but for all the free time I don't seem to have got much done. New, still futile, tries at the book—papers, reading ahead, and considerable being dined and wined—the meals being all very good and substantial and the whiskey a relief, but the talk, invariably, about the workshop. Can't seem to escape that little inferno anywhere. It is obsessive with everyone involved. . . . Besides being wined and dined, I've seen a number of movies lately—too many—but that's an Iowa habit.

The next day, he wrote that he had made a new start on the novel and was hopeful once again, but he didn't want to talk about it yet. Then a week later he told his wife that he wasn't totally cut off, that he still touched the world here and there. He had been at

Robert Clark shoveling out a path to the Stewart Street house in Virginia City during a blizzard. Courtesy of Barbara Clark Salmon

a party with four fellows in the basement apartment—two novelists from his workshop group and two painters from the artists' workshop. One of his students, an Italian from Massachusetts, made spaghetti with a special three-hour wine sauce and spiced meatballs. "We had wine, and chewed the fat—less artily than otherwise, thank God, until one a.m. or thereabouts" (2/6/52).

Over the semester break, his rooming house had changed its residents from mostly graduate students to undergraduates, "way under," he commented and added, "my tolerance is wearing thin." On February 19, he moved to a new address, 222 East Market Street:

> As the above address signifies, I finally, just today, got desperate and moved. It's going to cost me a little more, but if I can get the writing going—which I have not and have not and have not at 120 [Market Street] (and the mid-year personnel changes were all for the worse—the intrusive kind, that just walk into your room and start blabbering, without even both-

ering to knock, and no matter what you're doing). It will be worth it several times over. I should have moved sooner, if anything.

Now, he told his wife, he could at least lock the door and had "a bed with a Simmons mattress, not a broken-backed army cot."

He had begun the school year of 1951 in September with a plan to finish a first draft of his novel, "Man in the Hole," by Christmas; then he planned to get a good start, a chapter or two, by Christmas; at Christmas, he began to look toward a start of some kind before the end of the school year in June. But by the end of February 1952, he was so discouraged that when he wrote his wife, it was a cry of despair out of complete frustration—a painful letter to read. If there is a special hell for writers, Clark was in it:

> The new room is much pleasanter—but unfortunately that does not seem to be all that is wrong with the writing. I have made several days more of persistent, fierce, savage, grim, desperate and forlorn efforts at starting the novel—often with new and hopeful notions as a take-off—and still nothing happens but a terrible waste of paper, ink, pencil and self for a new paragraph of prose which does not either look or sound at all as I want it to. And I go to bed late and exhausted (I have written this year first chapters and pieces of first chapters enough to make five books in mere dead word count) and all tied up, and lie there sweating, and cursing myself and the Iowa workshop (which interferes all right—much too much talk and theory— but it is not the real trouble—for barring the *Watchful Gods*— on which I already had a sufficient start—I have been this way for nearly three years now) and wishing except for you and the kids, that I was dead, and wondering, all the time desperately trying to figure out just what in hell is the matter with me. But I don't know.

He decided just to give up—the hell with it. The struggle wasn't worth it. He would devote his time and energy to his teaching and student manuscripts. The theme of "The Man in the Hole" had begun to seem too personal, as if getting his character out of the hole was the only way to get himself out. He was tempted to go to the library and take out Fitzgerald's *The Crack Up*, which he had never read, to see if he could discover anything about his own bog-down from what happened to Fitzgerald. He had decided to give up, at least for the time being, but still worried:

> All the time I keep thinking, I am forty-two, going on forty-three. I should be at my best, my freshest, my most productive now.... I feel the winds of time whistling just past my ears and all the little financial figures of our needs hurrying through me.

His other common theme in these letters was, of course, his love for his wife, and he concludes this letter to her by saying, "I am going to think about you instead, every time the book starts trying to talk again. That is much pleasanter thinking—my favorite kind ... It is also the only subject I now possess which can now eliminate the book."

One of the ways he tried to appease his frustration besides making love to his wife by mail was to go back to physical activity. On March 1, he wrote,

> Dearest—
> I ventured up to the field house last night ... as planned, and engaged in a little one-handed, free-for-all basketball with a pick-up gang. There were a few minutes when I didn't think even Iowa, counting all the soot and fog, had enough air to keep me going—and I shamefacedly took a time-out, all for me....
> We finished up Dostoevsky's magnificent *Crime and Pun-*

ishment yesterday — the last king-sized struggle of the year, and there are left just Virginia Woolf's *To the Lighthouse* and Henry James' *Turn of the Screw,* of the novels — both intricate jobs that take a lot of looking into, but both favorites of mine, and short enough so we can do a fairly thorough examination of them without going on too long about it. . . . I keep listening for some stir of the spook within me — especially a short story idea, something clear apart from the novel . . . but so far not a trustworthy whisper, so I leave him squat in his darkness, which reduces my active vices to four, reading too much, smoking too much, drinking too much coffee, and thinking too much and too closely about my wife, whom I love very much and miss very much and want almost constantly.

The next day, he wrote,

Sometimes I get like Mr. Ramsey [from Virginia Woolf's *To the Lighthouse*] and his foolish recitations — all wound up in the frustrations of my writing. Then I think much of it goes into these frantic gestures. I must seem to you often like a bully of the worst sort. I have seriously thought — often — that I should just quit writing entirely — or trying to. It does not matter, any of it, dearest — this writing, nearly as much as you and your love do. It is not even real compared to that; and I know it. . . . I have felt guilty concerning you . . . because I often think you got cheated on the whole deal — just didn't get the kind of a man you really wanted — a rancher, an engineer, a more objective and active kind of a guy. Or even that may be once, way back, you had him, and I just haven't worked as a replacement.

CHAPTER TEN

FROM IOWA CITY, TO OMAHA, AND TO COLUMBIA, MISSOURI

IN THE MEANTIME, THOUGH CLARK continued to be blocked in his writing, he found some solace in his teaching, his situation having evolved into a much better one this second semester. His improved relations with his colleagues were important, not only for his peace of mind but for some sense of accomplishment during a difficult time. Satisfaction in teaching and his love for his wife were the two things he could hold on to. He reported to Barbara,

> My relations with the workshop group seem to have become,
> rather suddenly, much easier this half. Perhaps it is just because
> I stayed, I don't know. . . . One improvement I notice—we
> have entered into far more general discussion in the weekly
> meeting of the whole group, and, I feel much less like a vaude-
> ville end man. I think everyone is easier. The whole trouble,
> perhaps, wasn't just me, as a presence—one alien drop in the
> mixture and now it is wiped—we understand each other better,
> and tolerate the differences better. (3/7/52)

As preoccupied by his writing as he may have been, he still worked hard at his teaching and made a sterling impression on many of his students. One of these was George Bluestone, who became the author of several books, a film producer, and a professor at Boston University. He remembers Clark as "an exemplary man":

> In the year I studied with him in the Iowa Writers Workshop, I never heard him speak harshly to a student. He seemed endlessly available for conferences and reading. Tall, handsome and athletic, he was easy in his skin, could arouse erotic feelings in his students. Staying in shape was as natural as breathing. He was up at 5:30 every morning to run his four miles. He was an avid tennis player and swimmer. In his shell rimmed glasses he could look like Clark Kent. His idea of high style was putting on a mauve or peach t-shirt. He would meet with students at watering holes like Kenney's. He seemed more comfortable there than in the plain quarters he was renting that year. What did we talk about? Although Clark could be a penetrating philosopher . . . his natural style went toward the anecdotal. He was a natural-born story-teller.
>
> The one time I saw him in a rage was at Kenney's. Seems a hunter had gone after a cougar, and had successfully brought it down. For reasons no one could understand, the hunter had returned [with] the big cat on his back. Holding the cougar by his hind legs, the hunter had displayed him ostentationally [sic] for all the world to see. [Clark said something like] "they ought to ban this kind of killing. Not only does he kill for nothing, he has to brag about it. I'd like to see how *he* likes being trussed up." The beauty of the cat's tawny pelt made its destruction insufferable. It was clear to all of us that there was much more at stake than a single caught cougar. The killing had violated some fundamental tenet of Walter's cosmos.

How to characterize Walter's worldview? ... To me he has always seemed a pagan moralist who defies any system. In this he reminds me most of Henry David Thoreau.

Another student, Ruth Prigozy, who audited Clark's creative-writing seminar because of his reputation (and because she was going out with a man who was in the Writers' Workshop), remembers that

he was tall and rangy and held people spellbound — indeed, he would talk to groups of students all night long — into the morning. That was one of the things people admired about him — he was a natural storyteller. He told a story about [a] venture into New York City — saw the tall buildings, the crowds and the subways, and headed promptly back west and vowed never to come east again. [A story that stuck in Prigozy's mind because she *was* a New Yorker.] ... To me — and I was very young — he was a mythic figure, but what was interesting was that he seemed that way to those who knew him well.

———

As the spring semester at Iowa ran down, Clark's letters became more and more love letters to his wife, suggesting continuing dismay and depression despite his better adjustment to the school and his colleagues and a sense that he was accomplishing something with his students:

Almost continuously is a total-you deprivation, empty arms and empty rooms ... many voices in echoing corridors and through the walls, but never the voice that inside of me I'm listening for ... never you to just sit with and touch, and know that so much more is said. Which is why I keep writing too much to you, I suppose. Still trying to make words do what they can't. (3/12/52)

Some of his letters were quite passionate, and Barbara apparently felt that they sometimes went too far and that he was coming close to an unhealthy obsession, for he replied to her, "For awhile, at least—I will try, as you suggest to write quite objective, informational letters" (3/12/52).

His next letter, March 21, was objective and informational:

> Yesterday I finally got the desk cleared down to the point where I began outlining and organizing my material for the Virginia City book [the Comstock history]—and as I suspected, it's proving a bit baffling—and a little tough because I can't really get up much interest in it in this form—not after having, on and off for so many years, accumulated information and shaping ideas—which still work in me every now then— for almost a dozen novels, and of the same stuff. [The material for the history was basically the same material he had been gathering for at least two novels that he had in mind, including the one he had been working on during this year, 1951–52.]

In his next letter, March 24, he could no longer stand being objective, and thinking back over his life with Barbara, he wrote,

> All these associations keep leaping around in me, and spearing me in the middle with a great loneliness like the end of the world—first meeting you (hitting you, in fact, at the tennis courts), so many things about your apartment, our summering place on the Pyramid [Lake] around where the sheep ran over us, the night among the pines in Montana, the times at Essex, the honeymoon [at a borrowed cabin in the Adirondack mountains]—oh, so many—there's no listing them—and other things, all the way along—our worry when Babs [daughter Barbara] was in the hospital with pneumonia, first seeing you, so white and tired and hurt, but all you, and still there, after

Bobby was born, summer nights in the pool room at Essex, sitting with you in the infernal Gold Plate Limited coming out to Reno from New York, late at night on the upper porch in the spring at Taos, beside the duck pool at the ranch, and at American Flat poking around together—anywhere and everywhere, by ourselves and with others. And each time I see you in any of these times and places, I love you so much.

He followed this up on April 4 by returning once again to wondering what was wrong with him:

[I] am doing so badly at the writing this year that I'm really getting scared something has happened to me that I don't understand. I've never been blocked up like this before. At least I've written whole books before I threw them away. And it's three years now with nothing but the rewrite on *The Watchful Gods* to show for it. That's the longest I've ever gone. As if I had fallen into something like that paralysis Robert [Caples] had about painting when he came out of the Navy....

I suddenly feel time whizzing by—the way I do when I think of all this time without you too. Well—never mind—I'll write something this summer, no matter how bad—and I'll get this little Virginia City monstrosity [the Comstock history] out as a bad ace in the hole, even if I can never shave with a mirror again.

He was signed up to do a writers' conference in Columbus, Ohio, during spring break in April, and just before leaving, he reported to his wife that he had packed his suitcase and had given his room a thorough cleaning. He went on to say,

[I] cleaned up all my necessary MS [manuscript] conferences also—and saw the lady from Iowa State—the visit turned out no particular trouble save that some of her curiosities about

The Cat were a bit on the far-fetched side. I don't like to talk
about my stuff anyway—and unless people begin to see Yin
and Yang forces and geometric symbolism in it, I have to work
a little not to be impatient [he is not serious about the Yin and
Yang and geometric symbolism, which may be echoing the
lady from Iowa State].

As the end of the second semester approached, Barbara told
him that if he were offered a regular job at Iowa, possibly taking
over as the head of the workshop for the following year and then
staying on as professor, she thought he ought to consider it and the
family could relocate to Iowa City. It was not something that ap-
pealed to him:

> I don't want to stay at Iowa, if the offer comes, or anywhere in
> the Middle West. It would be much better with you and the
> kids—but not for you—and it isn't to be thought of as com-
> pared to the mountains—and Virginia City, and our own
> house. Besides which it would entail all sorts of executive and
> social nonsense of the kind I particularly abominate. Little as
> what I produce would show it, I really do think writing all the
> time. As far as occupation is concerned that is all that matters
> to me—and after it, teaching—but not, God knows, manag-
> ing. (4/14/19)

He added that he had received a letter from Bob Gorrell, chair of
the English Department at Nevada, who was still working to get
him hired.

A few days later he told his wife that he was again "morbid." It
was "due to the fact that the first page of this damn Comstock book
is trying to be as stubborn as the first page of the novel" (4/19/52).
It was depressing. He had been working day and night on what he
expected would be a simple project, one that he thought might help

him break through his block, but try as he might, he could make no progress. Then, in a super act of will, he reported,

> I went back and cracked that infernal first page that afternoon, and today I wrote steadily surrounded by geology books and the history of the Comstock Lode, from eight until five, and finished the first chapter, which is to say I got the Comstock Lode born and brought it up to the first mines. . . . It's the first chapter of anything, hack work though it is, that I've been able to finish all year. I keep the fingers crossed, but I hope the block is at least cracked.

He hoped against hope that he could talk his wife into joining him for his conference stint at the University of Missouri. He wrote on April 25, trying to talk her into the trip even though he knew she didn't like to travel. Then again on May 1 he told her that she shouldn't worry about the expense, since he figured that the check from Omaha should take care of the two of them just as well as him alone — it would cost no more to run the car with two in it, and the difference between a single room and double would be negligible. "My meals will come way down, because with my love in bed with me, I will never get up in time for breakfast and during the other two meals I will eat much less because I will be holding her hand under the table most of the time." And, after all, he had taken on these conferences precisely so that he could get the money for her to join him. He reached out for her like a man reaching for a lifesaver in rough seas.

The end of the semester was approaching, and he wrote his wife,

> I'm gradually making at least sufficient gestures towards clearing up my social debts here. Two dinner parties in the last week. It is not properly grateful of me, I'm afraid — but

I feel almost obsessively bound not to leave a single uncanceled obligation behind me here. Or to incur a new one from here out.

On the same day in another letter, he reported,

I received our official confirmation from Bob Gorrell today — teach first semester at Nevada for $2200 — which is really almost what they're paying me here, and will actually amount to more for us when the old man is home and spending only his legitimate share. That may work into a permanent proposition too — alternating semesters with Larry Laird, and once I get just one book ahead, and we don't spend it all, either moving or buying a place — it should be all we'll need to keep things evener. . . .

Maybe I can work something out with Hughey [at the Virginia City high school] for the second semester if we need it. I'm even contemplating going spendthrift myself to the extent of a new pair of shoes and a light weight suit or slack outfit for these conferences anyway. (Though I really believe I'm thinking more about being dressed up to meet my girlfriend.)

He followed this up on May 8 with,

I really begin to believe I am going to see you. It's still six weeks off, but it makes my hands want to start reaching out right now. You will have to look very severe and restrained, or hold a suitcase up in front of you, or I am likely to crush you entirely on sight.

Then, at two weeks before the end of the semester, he wrote,

Dearest —

I'm in among last doings — only one more story to prepare for class — and one more for the general session — next week is the last full week. Finished reading twenty-one stories in the

annual undergrad contest—to a happy and easy conclusion—
most agreement with the other judges. Last week MS piling in,
and the long term papers also—but here and there daylight,
green fields, a less moody future to be glimpsed beyond them.
And I seem, with the aid of a little early morning tennis (which
I have resumed, with no more than natural creakings) to be
holding up fine, still able to read and make sense....

Let me know what time your train comes into Fayette-
ville—if one can—or wherever I should meet you, so I'll be
sure not to have any conferences or teas or any kind of insignificant goings on then. I would bust with chagrin to think I had
wasted even five minutes of seeing you.

With the close of the semester, there were many social events
for the faculty to mark the occasion, receptions and dinner parties.
Clark reported on one such dinner to his wife, telling her that he
feels ungrateful when he goes and eats and drinks somebody's
extra-special goodies and remains bored. "But what else is one
to be with academic gossip, which what most of it was—like pick-
ing on your neighbors in their absence, only I didn't even know any
of the neighbors." He declared, "I get tired of talking"—a different stance for someone who loved to talk and loved companionship.
Perhaps no one at the dinner wanted to talk about sports (5/22/52).

As the meeting with his wife at the University of Missouri approached, after the conference at the University of Omaha,
Clark's anticipation became more and more intense. His longing
for her led him to reflect on their relationship and on the times
when he had not behaved very well toward her:

I ... know that although you don't love me any more than I
love you, because I don't think that's possible, you have, oh so
many times, loved me better, more steadily, more wisely than I
have loved you. I have a rather terrible list of times I have been
unkind to you—that all seems to focus, in a way, on two times,

the one when I came back from Reno so late, and you were cry-
ing, and the other time (it shocked me almost as deeply and
gave me the same kind of not very enjoyable glimpse of myself)
when, after I can't remember what cruel, distracted thing I had
been saying in front of the kids—probably something ridiculous and atrocious about getting out of there—you said, very
quietly, but with an insight of only too well merited bitter-
ness—that they needn't worry, because I wouldn't really go to
all the trouble it would take to leave—as if that were the only
reason I didn't leave. So I do know—darling—that you have
loved me better than I have loved you. Time and again, I know,
I have been mastered by the furies of frustration and discouragement about the writing (that is what it is—always that and
only that) I've done, and said things so appallingly heedless
that I can hardly believe them when I remember them. But the
reason I can hardly believe them is not because I have any false
vision of myself as a paragon of husbands, lovers, fathers, but
because really, even when I acted like that—I kept on feeling
inside that nothing had changed because I still always loved
you and the kids as the most important things in my life. That
doesn't excuse the things I did or said—only you and the kids
have done that—and I do, at least, know how wonderfully
and how often—but it does explain what I mean when I say
you have loved me better than I have loved you—but not
more. But perhaps my year of solitary confinement will have
improved me. I want very much, anyhow, to make up to you
for all the bad times I've given you—and to learn, as the chief
purpose of my life, before I'm done, to love you also as well,
or almost as you have loved me. . . . But there I go—probably
embarrassing you again (but still, I have owed you such a con-
fession for a long, long time, and I never seem to be able to say
it to you face to face, as I should, so I write it). (5/22/52)

Still at Iowa on May 27, he announced that he had signed the contracts for going back to teach at the University of Nevada. The schedule came with them, and he saw that he would have a lot of reading to do with a class of creative writing and two of freshman composition. These, plus two literature classes, made up a twelve-hour load, a heavy one considering his stature as a writer. It was about the same load a just-hired young professor might have, except that he or she would probably get three sections of beginning composition. And yet he was happy to be back at Nevada. The situation would

> beat Iowa all hollow ... if only because I can go home every
> afternoon and put my feet up, and have a cocktail with my
> wife, whom I love very much.... [And besides] we should be
> able to get faculty season tickets to all the football and basket-
> ball games. (5/30/52)

Missouri sent him his schedule for the conference there, and as it turned out, he was scheduled for his novel class at just the wrong time. His final session came just when he was supposed to meet his wife's train on June 21. He was understandably upset, although the people at Missouri promised him that they would send a deputy to meet his wife and take her to their hotel. Clark told his wife, "I will try to have all my MS reading out of the way, so we can idle away the rest of Saturday together. I'm almost afraid to say it, in fear you'll think I'm being foolishly romantic—but I feel as if I were waiting for a honeymoon" (5/31/52).

At the University of Omaha conference, he wrote his wife,

> To be quite frank, I do not love this kind of thing—and I had
> best make it earn the best I can. If I am going to be a pro, I had
> best be a pro. Actually I think writer's conferences have several
> times been of real use to me—for sharpening the wits, turning

up the dormant critical faculties, getting me to come alive to writing again—whether they have been of any benefit to anyone else or not.

From the Dundee Manor Hotel in Omaha on June 7, Clark reported in some detail on his conference experiences and along the way revealed some of his teaching of writing philosophy:

Bub Dearest—

So the first week at Omaha is wound up—the preliminary lectures on technique, half way on the illustrative close analysis of *Heart of Darkness,* conferences on a dozen manuscripts— nearly all into some good writing and more than glimmering of technical necessities and means—but all very young— nothing to say and a persistent tendency to go off into sentimental flights of fantasy—a good deal of roses, sunsets, dream girls and alone in the world-am-I. All very normal and healthy and more promising to my mind, than most kinds of solider work would be at this stage—but oh, how dull to read and how difficult to criticize encouragingly when they are such finalists, feeling, with all the iron might of their nineteen or twenty irrecoverable years, how time presses upon them. If they do not begin to make a living at writing in the next six months, the grave has them. Such nice kids, so earnest, so quick, so troubled, so foolish. You say, in twenty different ways, take your time, grow older, look at life, not at dreams, read, think, be patient, another ten years, art is long, life is short, but you know it doesn't take. How can anyone twenty years old conceive of working another ten toward saying anything anyone will want to hear? And at the other end there is Mrs. W.—at least in her sixties, and Mr. G.—who just two or three months ago, at the age of 72, decided to become a writer. They are in a hurry for quite other reasons—yet what they can write sounds astonishingly like what those twenty year olders are writing.

It is still roses and sunsets, and I will meet you across the border, my dear. A very different thing, "I will meet you across the border," coming from them. But unfortunately, it doesn't look much different on paper, because they don't know what they know, and haven't learned to hunt for it and set it down patiently while they write. If anything the difference is in favor of the "greensickers" [chlorosis — iron deficiency in young animals and green plants] who at least have been well taught in many respects and on the strength of that alone, do have moments. I suppose I should say, to the white-haired, "Forget it. Why torment yourself now?" and to the young, brutally, with a contemptuous mouth, and a derisive thumb on the page, "This stinks. This is pabulum. This is attar-of-roses in m'lady's cloisonne jar. You are not unintelligent. You are not certainly and utterly hopeless, but only probably so, because ninety-nine out of a hundred of you never do get work in print, outside the college quarterly. Read, read, read, look, go out and get a tough every-day job, it doesn't matter what kind. Write four hours every day and throw it away without looking at it. Keep on until you dream real, five years, ten years, fifteen years. If you really want to write well, what does it matter how long? And if you just want to write to sell, I don't give a damn what happens to you anyway." I should. But I don't. I have to go at it point by point. I have to just let it add up slowly to something like that, if they can add it. And really hoping, I think, that they can't — more than just enough to reduce their green bloat usefully. Because really, I suppose, they have to feel that rush, that almost upon it, all of those five or ten or fifteen years, in order to keep at it. It is wearing. It's like the Virginia City basketball team. You know it's foolish, but you still get involved. I'm getting older, about two for one now, I think. I'm getting much tougher and more exacting about the writing itself.

One has to believe that one result of that toughness was that as he applied it to his own writing, it became more and more inhibiting. Although he turned to teaching as a companion activity to his writing — and turned to it in some relief as something valuable he could do while blocked — it would seem to have increasingly cut away his ability to create. And he seemed only dimly aware of this internal conflict between the critical and the creative. He kept asking, over and over again, What in the world is wrong with me?

From his motel room in Omaha, Clark went on in his letter to say that writers' conferences still wore him out — it was like being in the ring every night. And he added,

> Intervals of utter boredom seem to be my only relief, and I don't like them very well. Or maybe it's just the heat. I doubt if my room has been down to eighty, even at night, all week, and the humidity fairly dripping from the sky. Or maybe it's events like yesterday's luncheon at the college with the president and his assistant, and thank God, several others. The president is a real stuffed shirt, of the pompous, this I have said variety, a former lecturer in education, whose depth and breadth of outlook is sufficiently indicated by his stated conviction that certain regular University T.V. programs were good for his faculty because they had to learn to be exact, to get it all said in thirty minutes to the second, "no more and no less." After a little of that, he said, they were always much better in the classroom, didn't waste time getting started, or let pointless student questions take up time. Yes, he did. Exactly that. . . . I sat with my hands in my pockets, and stared at my plate, watching nothing but time going by at about a tenth of its normal rate.

Although for the last year at Iowa his life had been ordinary, somewhat impoverished, and often in his frustration dismal, he was still something of a celebrity. He didn't want to be, nor did he feel like one. Yet his name still had some cachet. He told his wife of his dislike of TV interviews:

I had hardly sat down to talk to you again [to continue his letter to her]—when the phone rang—and another kind of annoyance, with a very sweet and pleasant voice, came on, asking would I do a visiting celebrity program on TV with her. I am learning. I am hardening. I would not, thank you very much just the same. But why not? Well, frankly, because I feel that the impression is always false, when I watch others, and even more when I do it myself. It is impossible to look and sound as if you meant what you're saying, even if you do. The modulated voice was hurt, because it made its living at it. I was very sorry, but it didn't get around me. I had a little reward for my negative virtue in the case of the agent.

That very day I got my first really new glimpses of problems in two of the four or five novels I have been only sluggishly brooding about, and for some four or five hours wrote notes about them. I have a small, cheerful hope traveling with me now that I have arrived at the precipitating factors of stories that have long been pretty fully foreseen, but just would not seem to fill. (6/10/52)

Having "arrived at the precipitating factors of stories" that he had been carrying around in his mind and notebook, he continued two days later in his optimism about getting back to writing:

It must be I'm getting gradually attuned to the heat, though, because I had another reasonably profitable mental morning yesterday—record weather or none—the germ of a short novel about an Indian woman, a stranger in town and a pack of wild dogs, that I've been carrying around in my note-

book for some months now—suddenly began to put out pseu-
dopodia [protrusion of a cell for gathering food] and move
queerly around in all directions by itself, devouring bits of say,
Wells, Nevada, landscape, and fragments of scenes, even to
dialogue. And last of all—it remains in a nice, suggestive mud-
dle, with just enough of a hint of where it's going to make me
really feel like exploring. Something in me is getting ready to
write. For the rest, I've been holding up against the weather
chiefly with the aid of [E. M.] Forster's tight, quiet little *Passage to India*—which one can no more read idly than he can
play chess in a daze. (6/14/52)

As the time for his wife's arrival in Columbia, Missouri, approached, he wrote to her on the day before he would leave
Omaha:

> We finished the final Omaha session last night—and
> everybody was very nice about it—in fact we ran a half hour
> overtime. . . . I have today and tomorrow [to drive to Missouri],
> and will just wander down along that way, and stop when I feel
> like it. I anticipate practicing some small medicine rites every
> morning—in hopes of propitiating the weather, now a bit
> more cooperative, toward your coming. But even if it doesn't
> listen to me (and probably my approach is all wrong for this
> again) you'll have only three or four days to wait before we
> aim for at least drier regions. You can stay at home in the
> bathtub, letting the cold water run slowly, and I can come in
> between sessions and get some nice wet kisses, and that way
> everybody will be happy. I figure it will be just one week, to
> the hour, from the time I leave Omaha, until I see you. If Mis-
> souri knew how little I am concentrating on my literary duties
> under these circumstances, they would probably send me a
> wire saying "All is over. Do not come." But once I get there,
> the prod of the presences will probably work. It had better—

or this one week, so short compared to all the time since I've seen you, is going to be the longest of my life. I aim to keep very, very busy, even if I have to invent work. The number of times I have wanted badly to see you since I first hit you in the tummy with a tennis ball at U. of N. is beyond accurate estimate even, but I am quite sure, to put it conservatively, that I never wanted you more.

Barbara hated to travel. She was subject to motion sickness on plane, train, or bus and dreaded the trip to Columbia, but she felt she had to go. Her husband's constant barrage of letters, which were largely devoted to expressions of love for her, were often, she felt, too extreme and led her to worry about his state of mind. Early on the morning of June 21, Barbara was met at the station by a member of the University of Missouri English Department, who took her to her hotel. A little more than an hour later, Walter finished his last session with his conference group and rushed to the hotel. Stopping at the front desk to find out if his wife had checked in, he ran up the stairs, strode quickly down the hall to their room, and knocked on the door. He had on his new sport coat and slacks.

CHAPTER ELEVEN

TWO RESIGNATIONS,
SON AND FATHER

By THE END OF JUNE 1952, Walter Clark was back with his wife, in Virginia City, in his beloved desert mountains. He had been offered a job at Iowa, first, as temporary head of the workshop, and then second, as a professor in the department for the following year once the permanent head returned from leave. But he had turned the offer down. Although by spring he was getting along well with his colleagues and enjoyed many of his students, he just didn't like Iowa.

He was home, but he would pay a penalty for it. The Iowa job was a good one, with a writing program that already had an excellent reputation. As head of the workshop, he would have had some administrative duties but would have taught only two classes, an upper-division class and a graduate seminar. By contrast, he would teach four classes that fall at Nevada, including two sections of freshman composition. Normally, no writer of Clark's reputation should have considered such a job.

The problem was that the University of Nevada simply wasn't

able to appreciate Clark. That resulted from the nature of the school, which at the time was a small, essentially rural state university that specialized in mining, agriculture, and engineering. The administration, primarily concerned with using its resources to develop these and other practical specialties, had tended to downplay the importance of the arts and humanities. And after all, this focus on the practical, as a land-grant university, was its mission.

Bob Gorrell, as chair of the English Department, had had an uphill battle over several years to get Clark any kind of job at all. All of the teachers in his department had four-class loads, and there were not very many advanced classes to go around. The main job of the department was not literature and certainly not creative writing, but teaching the required course of freshman composition (although some literature was offered as part of teacher education). With two advanced classes, Clark, as a new member of the department, was doing very well.

Besides the heavy teaching load, Clark had a five-day-a-week schedule, and for someone who had a tough commute the schedule was an additional burden. It was almost thirty miles from Clark's house to the university campus, all, in those days, over crowded two-lane roads. And the road up Geiger Grade from the valley into the mountains was narrow and full of curves and difficult, even dangerous, in winter snow. For much of the route, mountains climbed steeply on one side of the road and sheer slopes dropped down on the other.

As a result of his heavy teaching schedule and long commute time, Clark had difficulty getting any writing done. But he did feel that now he was on his home turf, he had a good chance of breaking through his three-year writer's block — and he was determined to try. His friend and colleague Gorrell has said that Clark often commented over the years that he couldn't really write unless he was in Nevada (the *Ox-Bow*, of course, was not written there, nor were many of the short stories). That summer, after coming back from Iowa, he started on a novella, "The Angel and the Judge," and his work on it continued, off and on, into the fall. He went back to the Comstock history several times during the year and started on an article on Nevada commissioned by the travel magazine, *Holiday*. Neither the novella nor the history was ever completed; the *Holiday* article was finished (or perhaps sent to the magazine only partially finished at its request), but it took him five years. However, during the year he did publish two book reviews, a historical sketch of Virginia City for a tourist pamphlet, and an essay defending creative writing as a valuable college course.

In the meantime, he resumed his Virginia City life, going to the Sazerac and Union Brewery those evenings he could, when he wasn't correcting papers or preparing for class or just too tired to move. Gordon Lane of the Union Brewery remembers one particular night when he and the Clarks and several other couples stayed up drinking and talking until five in the morning. They were waiting to find out if they could see the effects of the first above-ground nuclear explosion, which would be set off on the Atomic Energy Commission testing grounds about sixty miles northwest of Las Vegas. Just before dawn, the group in Virginia City could see a slight, ominous glow in the distance. The sight may have brought Clark's thoughts back to his story, "The Portable Phonograph," presciently written in 1941.

Clark had not planned to teach a full load of classes at Nevada but had hoped for a part-time job that would give him time for writing. How he would make up for the lack of income was up in the air—he hoped that he would get enough of the novel done so that he could get an advance from his publisher. Or, barring progress on the novel, he could do several writers' conferences next summer and maybe add the payment from an article or review. But Gorrell could not offer him a half-time position; it was essential that the department cover its freshman composition obligations, and by teaching two sections of composition, Clark could prove

*A Clark family Thanksgiving at the 20th Century Club in Reno
(one of Clark's mother's clubs), ca. 1952. Back row, standing, from the
left, Marge Clark, Barbara Clark, James Santini, Miriam Clark Chism,
(in front of Miriam) Euphemia Clark (Clark's mother), Euphemia Clark
Santini (Clark's sister), David G. Clark, John Chism, Walter V. T. Clark,
Vida Boyle (widow of former Nevada governor). Second row, seated, left to
right: Jim Santini (in front), Robert Clark (leaning forward, with glasses),
Betty Chism Cordes (behind Robert, to the left), Walter E. Clark, Barbara
Clark (Walter and Barbara's daughter), Gordon Chism, Clark Santini,
William Chism, David Chism. Courtesy of David Chism*

his worth to the administration in order to get a temporary appointment.

So Clark was appointed as a lecturer, a nontenured, temporary position, while at the same time he was hoping to go on the following year to a permanent professorship, with a half-time load if possible. Gorrell and others in the department seemed to agree that this kind of position might be possible in the future. But at the end of the school year in late May, the whole picture changed.

The change came as a result of the circulation by a biology professor at the university, Frank Richardson, of an article by a Professor Bester at the University of Illinois. It was an essay on entrance requirements, and in particular was critical of colleges of education. Moreover, it was critical of progressive educators who placed too much emphasis on "real life" subjects and not enough on the sciences, mathematics, and history. Richardson had circulated copies of the article in response to a call by the new president of the university, Minard W. Stout, who had asked for comments on his desire to change some of the requirements. Richardson thought he was properly responding to that request and was contributing to the discussion, but the president hit the ceiling, thinking that the circulation of the article was an attack on him. Stout called Richardson into his office and "read him a lecture on what he called sticking to your own business, various other things, and threatened to fire him" — this according to Bob Gorrell, who was chair of the faculty grievance committee.

Gorrell, along with Robert Hume and Charlton Laird from the English Department and Tom Willards from Biology, protested Richardson's treatment, and subsequently all of them received notices that they must appear before the board of regents and show cause why they should not be dismissed for insubordination. Gorrell, first on the list alphabetically, appeared at the initial regents' meeting, but at the last moment a courier from the Nevada Supreme Court arrived (not on horseback) with an injunction to stop the hearings. Subsequently, Gorrell, Hume, Laird, and Willards were called into the president's office, where Stout apologized, said the whole thing was a terrible mistake, and asked them to come back on the faculty. They agreed to do so, but at the time, since nothing had been said, they didn't realize that their salaries would be cut. However, Frank Richardson, the biology professor, was forced to face a public hearing in front of the regents and was fired. The supreme court again intervened, and he was reinstated after a year.

All of the professors involved from the English Department— Gorrell, Laird, and Hume—were Clark's friends, and he thought the whole drama was shameful. The conflict had started in early spring and then played out while Clark was absent from the campus. He had been appointed a Rockefeller Foundation Lecturer in Writing for the spring semester and went to speak at Reed College, the University of Washington, and the University of Oregon. From Eugene, Oregon, he wrote to his wife:

I remain uneasy about this sort of semi-final status of the Nevada ruckus. I am relieved, in a way, that the English dept. is out of it—yet I am not happy that they go out so easily. I don't know Richardson very well, or his associate [Willards] at all—but from all I do know of the case, they are no more guilty of anything but an expression of opinion than anyone else. Their only guilt is that they spoke sooner, and were compelled, in their capacities of Pres. and v.p. of the A.A.U.P. [American Association of University Professors] to deal with a questionnaire on administrative policy which came, unfortunately right on top of [President] Stout's ill-advised and doubtless Ross [Silas E. Ross, long-time member of the board of regents] inspired, first talk to the faculty, in which all faculty committees, even the advisory, were summarily abolished and this autocratic chain-of-command system set up, which makes it illegal for anyone but a dean to even speak to the president on any campus matter. I cannot help but feel that Ross and Stout, especially Ross, who has never yet been fully dragged into one of these messes of his own concoction, have nothing more against the remaining two [the two biology professors] than against Laird, Gorrell and Hume, [that] is nothing, but that they are hoping to save face by making their Hitler attitude stick in some quarters, so that Ross will not have to show himself, or Stout go. Their fundamental dishonesty in the whole situation seems to me still manifest in their failure, even now, to issue any particulars of their accusation.... I don't want to say or do anything that would put the English dept. on the spot again.... There's only one sure thing I promise myself—if the situation becomes one in which I feel I should talk—I'm going to make Si Ross mortally sorry he ever started throwing his corpse-fed weight around [Ross was a funeral director].

I feel also a little uneasy, however, because my position of talking back is so much better than that of regular faculty members. I don't give a damn, fundamentally, whether I stay on at Nevada or not. My chief concerns are about what such repeated maniacal stupidity ... will do—has done—to the university, and what Dad is going to feel about it. (4/21/53)

After returning to Reno and attending the regents' hearing for Richardson, Clark felt he had to take a stand publicly, and he wrote a letter of resignation to Chair Bob Gorrell:

This is to tender, through you, my resignation, as of the end of this June, from the English Department of the University of Nevada, to return, unsigned, the contract offered me for next fall, to explain to you the reasons for my delay in giving you the word, and to express my regrets to you, both for the resignation and for the inconvenience the delay must cause either you or your successor in the chairmanship in the matter of finding replacement.

The decision to resign is not one that I have arrived at either easily or happily. Both this year's teaching and past connections had led me to hope that I might find a permanent place in the department, at least on the part time basis you and I have talked about. It was a hope I could not lightly relinquish. On the other hand, the indications of an increasingly autocratic administrative attitude which I have noted throughout this year, and which are wholly opposed in spirit to all that I have long conceived to be good in the academic community, made me wonder whether, given any circumstantial freedom in the matter, I could, with good conscience, remain part of a community in which they prevailed.

In this dilemma, I decided to await the outcome of Dr. Frank Richardson's hearing. Now, having witnessed the greater part of those proceedings, and being unable to read into the regents' abrupt termination of them, or into the delay in announcing their findings until after the inauguration of the president, anything except a preconceived intention, whatever they have in store for Dr. Richardson, not only to condone, but to perpetuate and implement that autocratic administration, and thus, tacitly, also to approve the several acts which I know to have occurred under it, as well as the unwarranted and possibly damaging affronts to yourself, Dr. Richardson and three other members of the faculty which led to the hearing, I cannot but feel that the decision has practically been forced upon me.

Clark went on in a final paragraph to add,

what is obvious to both of us, that nothing whatever in my relationship with you, or with any member of the department has had anything to do with this decision. .... I feel personally indebted to you, Paul, John and Mabel for taking on the extra work which made possible my spring lecture tour on the coast. Thanks to all of you. (6/1/53)

Bob Gorrell remembers that after receiving the letter he argued at length with Clark, telling him that the thing to do was to stick it out with the rest of them and protest, to work to get things back in order. But Clark's mind was made up. Needless to say, since the job at Nevada was the one job he wanted above all others in the world (despite what he wrote to his wife about not giving a damn whether he stayed at Nevada or not), it took considerable courage for him to back up his beliefs with such draconian action.

The controversy hit the newspapers and was reviewed in some detail by the *Reno Evening Gazette,* and the essence of that article was picked up by the *New York Times.* Both of them quoted from Clark's letter. The situation at Nevada was not atypical. Most American campuses have wrestled with questions of how autocratic a college administration should be and to what extent faculty should participate in decisions regarding curriculum and personnel matters. Because it was so fundamental to higher education, the controversy found an audience beyond Nevada. The *Gazette* reported,

> The administration has been bombarded with letters, telegrams and other documents from more than 20 campuses carrying expressions ranging from indignation to dispassionate requests for more information. Many of the letters were sent in response to an account of the case mailed from here by Richardson friends, without the professor's knowledge, to campuses in other states.

The response of the president of the university to Clark's painful decision was almost predictable. When the matter came up

in a meeting of the regents, he denied that Clark had any position
from which to resign (from the minutes of that meeting):

> Regent Hardy referred to the resignation of Walter V. T. Clark
> from the Department of English, as reported in the local
> papers, and asked for information regarding the status of Mr.
> Clark. The President informed him that Mr. Clark was a Lec-
> turer, that he did not have tenure, that his previous contracts
> had been on a semestral basis, and that he had been offered a
> contract by Dean Wood for the first semester of the coming
> school year, which he turned down. Mr. Clark held no position
> at the University at the end of the school year from which to
> resign.

Walter V. T. Clark may have been something of a celebrity, at
least in literary circles, but for the regents he was most prominently
his father's son. Although his relations with his father were often
somewhat strained, he carried on many of the same values. Like
his father, Clark was a man of principle, a man whose life embod-
ied much self-discipline and a willingness to work hard as well as
a dedication to contributing to the welfare of others. Unlike President Stout, Walter E. Clark, when he was president of the university, did not think of disagreement or criticism as insubordination.
In his history of the university, James W. Hulse summarizes President Clark's contribution during his tenure:

> [He] has long been remembered with respect for his dedication
> to academic freedom. New faculty members who came during
> his tenure quickly learned that he enjoyed intellectual disputa-
> tion, and that he would defend his staff against outside hostility
> as much as possible.... Clark encountered many criticisms and
> disagreements from his faculty, but he did not resent opposition
> and he maintained the respect even of those who disagreed
> with him.

Walter E. Clark was the president of the university from 1917 to 1937 (when he went on leave, resigning in September 1938) and probably more than anyone else was responsible for taking the school from a cow college, with only two buildings, on the path toward becoming a respected modern university (under his leadership it was accredited for the first time). He did so under very difficult circumstances. He may have been brought to the university as a financier, but he never took his eye off of what the money was for. Throughout his tenure he pushed for a quality program taught by a quality faculty in quality university facilities. But his push always involved a battle. Nevada, dominated by mines and · ranches and limited financially by a small population, had never had higher education as a major priority. Support by the legislature was sometimes very meager, and there seemed always to be some members of the regents who opposed spending money on faculty and programs. Furthermore, throughout Clark's tenure as president one or two members of the board of regents were always determined to oppose him on nearly everything he proposed. On occasion they even questioned his honesty and integrity.

But there is no doubt that the hard financial times during the Great Depression not only severely limited what W. E. Clark could do for the university but adversely affected his own personal fortune as well. He had had a goal of giving each of his four children a million dollars when they reached the age of twenty-one, but the crash of 1929 and its aftermath reduced his personal fortune from eight or ten millions to little more than one hundred thousand dollars. The crash not only reduced his fortune and hopes but dealt a severe blow to his sense of accomplishment in his chosen profession as an economist.

The continuing battle waged by President Clark to improve the university, or to at least maintain the status quo during hard times, on several occasions came to a head and led to good old-fashioned Western showdowns. The most serious came in a meet-

Clark's father, Walter E. Clark, as president of the
University of Nevada, Reno. Courtesy of David Chism

ing of the board of regents on January 31, 1929, when one of the
regents introduced a very long resolution condemning Walter E.
Clark for a series of offenses against the university and demanding his dismissal. Clark was accused of having condoned drunk-
enness and poor discipline among students, of giving too little
attention to campus building programs, of misusing his entertainment fund, of forcing girls to pose in the nude for photographers,
and of other assorted improprieties.

Of these charges, the most painful and sensational was one that
described a situation that Clark had had nothing to do with — indeed, one that he may not have even been aware of until it was
blown up into a scandal by a local newspaper. As described in item
9 in the list of charges:

He has maintained a requirement that all women students, notwithstanding their objections and tears, be photographed nude, and the plates have been taken for treatment by photographers away from the University grounds. To justify this he has misrepresented to this Board, and to the public press, that this practice has long been in very general use by American colleges when in fact it has not been so in general use.

The idea of taking such photographs was apparently installed years earlier by the women's physical education department. It was a fairly common practice in colleges at the turn of the century, one designed to promote health and physical well-being among women students. The pictures would be screened by doctors who would look to see if there were any students with bad posture or spinal curvature who might need special physical education or therapy help. The procedure no doubt had been originally designed out of the best of motives but had hung on as a relic out of an earlier, more innocent time.

All the charges, including this one, were brought to the state legislature and provoked an intense investigation by a six-member joint committee of the state assembly and senate. According to Hulse's history,

> The hearings were held over a period of several days in the state supreme court chambers in Carson City, with a flood of accusations and innuendoes.... A self-appointed committee of students complicated matters by submitting their own list of grievances against Clark and [some] faculty members. Flamboyant press coverage accompanied the hearing. The committee compiled some fifteen hundred pages of testimony.

In the end the legislature found most of the charges to be "far-fetched and ridiculous," and Clark was cleared of all serious allegations. However, as affable as Clark could be in his relations with faculty and alumni, he was essentially a Victorian gentleman of the old school, upright and honest, and his integrity had been publicly challenged. The very fact that there had been a scandal on his watch was upsetting enough, but the sexual implications of the scandal were simply devastating—that he was somehow sponsoring a kind of pornography. Even though he had been cleared, the affair would haunt him throughout the rest of his tenure, almost nine years, as president of the university.

Samuel B. Doten, professor and administrator at the university for thirty-seven years, testified before the investigative committee, reminding it that this was not the first time members of the board of regents had filed bogus charges against a university president. If, he told the committee, this episode could be the last time, it would be worth the time and money spent in the investigation: "If we succeed in doing to President Clark what we did to Drs. Stubbs and Hendrick, we'll pay for it.... Nobody but an adventurer will care to risk his reputation in a state where reputations are so unsafe."

By 1937 the various pressures on President Clark caused him to have a nervous breakdown. In his history of the university, Hulse locates those pressures in the continuing financial difficulties caused by the depression and hostility on the part of some regents and faculty that came in part from Clark's salary being higher than anyone else's at the school (although when the depression hit, he voluntarily took a $2,500 cut in pay). Hulse notes that "some University-watchers believed he was too ostentatious about his clothes and his automobile during difficult times. ["He was occasionally called a 'bird in a gilded cage.'"] From such petty concerns real hostility can arise, and there were many detractors." And there was constant hostility and obstruction, month after month and year after year, by certain regents. Walter Van Tilburg Clark's son, Robert, recalls that "I grew up knowing that I should hate Silas E. Ross, who, I believe, was a prominent undertaker in

Reno, and forever on the Board of Regents. He seemed to have been W.E.'s main enemy."

When the regents met in December 1937 to consider the resignation that had been submitted by W. E. Clark, Ross would seem to have gained his victory. According to the minutes,

> Chairman Ross said that he thought the Regents should do something for President Clark in appreciation of his services during the past 20 years; it has been the practice of the Board to grant leaves of absence to staff members because of health breaks, to pursue advance work and in recognition of long and faithful service and he submitted the idea that the Regents grant a leave of absence with full pay to President Clark, effective January 1, 1938 and ending with the opening date ... of the fall semester of 1938.

By making this motion, Ross was able to end up looking publicly like a generous spirit on the side of the angels.

By unanimous vote the leave was granted. President Clark thanked the regents and told them

> that he would not leave in January until registration problems properly coming to his office had been in the main disposed of and that he would take care of his part of the copy for the University catalog, the Regents' Biennial Report and the 1938 edition of the Alumni Directory ... before leaving Reno.

His insistence on taking care of these details before leaving, despite his poor health, was typical of his conscientiousness — a conscientiousness that was one of the traits his son inherited from him. Maybe his son took on too much of his father's conscientiousness and his sense of duty, an almost obsessive concern that details be handled just right.

Walter E. Clark's final years came as a sort of shadowy existence, there but not there, the silent presence of a broken man no longer with a mission, no longer even the titular head of the family and the provider. His salary had been reduced to $1,800 a year, and he and his wife moved out of the president's mansion to a modest one-and-a-half-story house in Reno. Robert Clark remembers,

> I knew Grandfather Clark only as a portly, sickly old man shuffling around the Cheney Street house in bedroom slippers, though otherwise I think fully dressed. Maybe wearing a robe sometimes, but over clothes. The grandparents and their house remained fully clothed, Victorian style. There was horrible dark horsehair furniture, and plates under plates when we ate. Grandfather was always there at big family occasions, such as Thanksgiving, which at least once we had out at the Lewers Ranch—a photo to prove it—but later, perhaps as he became sicker and didn't carve the turkey any more—it was always at the 20th Century Club in Reno. All the siblings [V. T. Clark, his brother, and two sisters] plus grandchildren.

Robert Clark remembers his grandfather, after his retirement, with stacks of books, spending much of his time reading. A picture that may remind us of the father in "The Watchful Gods,"—a friendly man, but somewhat reserved and scholarly.

The relationship between W. E. Clark and his son, V. T. Clark, was not warm or openly affectionate. The father cared about his son, helped him when he could, but kept his distance. Robert Clark has said,

> My sense of the relationship of dad to his dad is that the emotional portrait given in *The City* is pretty accurate—that dad was far more attached to his mother than to his father. . . .
> There was also a major personality difference that is reflected in *The City*—W.E. as the practical, duty-demanding Victorian dad, pushing his sons to be worldly successes.

Along these lines it is interesting to note that in the letters V. T. Clark wrote to his wife and others during the 1940s and early 1950s there are a few references to his mother but almost none to his father, and the main correspondence that Clark had during all those early years he was away from Reno was with his mother.

However, Robert Clark has said that he suspects his father "over-dramatized his father's lack of interest in his artistic efforts." W.E. did subsidize his son's first book of poems, and V.T. must have been aware of his father's influence in allowing him to write the first-ever creative writing master's thesis at the University of Nevada. Resentment against the Philistine father, Robert suggests further, probably lasted until the son made something of a success with *Ox-Bow* and

> perhaps [the resentment was] made stronger by the sense of obligation from the help he had accepted (grandfather had much to do with getting that graduate assistantship at Vermont, too, and then [the] teaching job at CCNY that helped to subsidize the idyllic winter in the Essex farmhouse right after marriage).

What V. T. Clark took from his father was conscientiousness, a sense of rectitude, a sense of duty, and a devotion to the work ethic. What he seems to have developed in opposition to his father was his embrace of all forms of art, the less practical the better, and a disdain for wealth and the accumulation of money. While his father insisted on maintaining an upper-class manner of living, Walter Clark loved old, broken-down mining towns and their saloons and enjoyed talking to the characters, sometimes disreputable, that inhabited them. And while W.E. was rather reserved and politically conservative, his son was often voluble and garrulous and was a political liberal. Perhaps the best way to illustrate the difference between father and son is to contrast the fortune made on the stock exchange by the father with what the son did with the money for the movie rights to *Ox-Bow*. He put it in a checking account, refusing to put it into a savings account to earn interest—he stated that he didn't deserve the interest. No wonder, then, that his wife Barbara usually handled the family finances.

Following Walter V. T. Clark's resignation from Nevada, he went on to a writer's conference and then a summer session at the University of Montana in Missoula. Arriving in mid-July, he wrote to his wife:

> There remains now only the apparently much more difficult task of bringing my somnolent mind to bear with some hint of originality and comprehension upon lectures, manuscripts and my own writing.... Maybe it's the heat; maybe it is still too full of splendid mountains; maybe it is at last decently arrived at the ultimate contempt for all contrivances of language; maybe it is just asleep in the low altitude. (To my surprise, having remembered it and thought of it always as high in mountain country, I discover that Missoula is only three thousand feet up.) Maybe it has simply reached a point beyond tolerance for the halls of academe, and is going to leave me sleep-walking all summer —and forevermore in the neighborhood of my classroom. I preach even the Richardson case by rote, which is unfortunate, since there is real concern here, via no few comparable incidents. (7/18/53)

But he did wake up, and his enthusiasm was stirred by a visit to Montana's Virginia City, a restored mining camp in which he saw many similarities to his hometown:

> Bub Dear—
> Back, and partly pulled together, after the Virginia City jaunt, two hundred miles, plus, south and east, and up into the

hills to about home altitude. Six of us went down, and had a
fine time, if a bit short on sleep and crowded on seeing. They
had reservations for us—which was a good thing—for, allowing for the difference in size, they get their weekend tourists
just about as thickly as we do. The Nevins (Alan Nevins,
Columbia, History—friend and collaborator with Commager)
by virtue of years and dignity, were put up in the Fairweather
Hotel (a period replica) and the rest of us slept in a tourist
camp composed of wheelless trailers (very comfortable) down
in Alder Gulch. After dinner Saturday, we took in a variety
show at the summer theatre—with reserved seats, right down
in front. It was a highly amusing, professionally staged, variety
show, all period—the centerpiece being the old Cox and Box
comedy, which I had never seen. There were three or four pros
in the group, the rest college players—all very lively, competent and pleasing—comparing very favorably with our Scarlet
Gulch crew, and averaging much higher in the matter of singing voices and feminine pulchritude. After the show we—and
about two hundred other people, repaired to the Bale of Hay
Saloon—where members of the cast put on another group of
song and dance numbers, and passed a battered spittoon, and
an old and highly authentic mustached bartender, Mike, dis-
pensed the necessary. (Montana, on the whole, mixes its drinks
a good bit tamer than V.C., Nev., but a shot and a short came
and a good deal the same.) After this second show there was a
highly sociable, and liquid, get-together of our gang, the cast
and a few others in the back room. To bed about two. In the
morning I roamed the town alone for a while, peering at this
and that, including complete and well done restorations of a
barber shop, a blacksmith shop, a milliner's, a print shop and
an assay office, all with dummy figures in costume. Looked
only from afar upon visible Boot-Hill, and the larger cemetery
above, where the more Godly went thereafter.... The camp

had about 10,000 in its hey-day, 1863-67, was much shorter lived, in that condition, than ours, and at present has two or three hundred residents in the summer, and fifty or sixty all year round.

Other trips to ghost towns and to Butte were planned, and, he wrote his wife,

I have already given up the idea of getting really rested, but I am certainly keeping interested and busy (which is a good thing, considering how much I miss you) which is just as good or better, and if, in this confusion of new impressions and not at all oppressive must-do's, I can get the writing moving a little, it will all be better than a rest. (7/27/53)

But he was too occupied by being entertained, by weekend trips, and by his conference work. On August 1, he wrote,

Another week gone, and still no writing done; none even begun, excepting occasional transitory flickers in the mind, here an image, there a new glimpse into a personality. The writing classes turned out to be considerably larger than had been expected ... and the daylight hours have nearly all gone to reading manuscripts and conferring. It is a pleasant and eager group, anyway — with one interesting and enjoyable difference from most summer groups I've had. There is about the usual proportion of not so young women, restless or retired school teachers, and mothers whose children have grown up and left, but they are a much more interesting and alert group than any such I've had before, many of them even sufficiently thoughtful in matters of writing so that I don't have nearly the usual sense of trying to talk to two groups at once. And many of them also really have unusual life experiences behind them, instead of a conviction that they can, merely by the possession of spare time, make commonplace lives into good fiction without either thoughtfulness or talent. Or the still more dangerous belief that nothing can be of interest in a story unless it is far away, long ago, Zane Gray and Sabatini—or Gene Stratton Porter, or Grace Livingston Hill. So neither the teaching nor the conferring has been dull, and I have enough—as much as might be expected, or more, at my stage, of that best pleasure of really learning something myself, much about various lives from them, and even new notions about writing from having to answer their questions and peer into their problems. So I am having fun, only I am very tired, because the faculty here is also very sociable, and afraid that I may get either blue (which I do even so, now and then, in just one way, lonesome for you) or dried out if they do not keep asking me places or taking me places in the evening, and filling me with beer and occasional shots of bourbon. So I have been reading and talking all day, and most of the time drinking and talking nearly all night. . . .

I make one more public appearance—this coming Wednesday—and I'm going to give them Julie B. Again. Sometimes I wonder if I'm becoming a kept-man to Julie, but I have discovered she is quite unknown here, and that Montanans are avid for all such western beginnings. So up she comes again.

At the end of the following week, he reported,

All my old ladies are writing like mad, and I'm having so many conferences that my throat has been sore for over a week now, just from talking all the time—the conferences, two hour class, other professors wanting the dope on the Nevada case. (They are really hot and alert at Montana.) And people are still asking me to late drinking bouts, picnics, and have you. And in between, I try to get all the MSS [manuscripts] read, and at least collect my wits before classes, if not really prepare. And the classes grow—instead of shrinking—so that I now have nearly

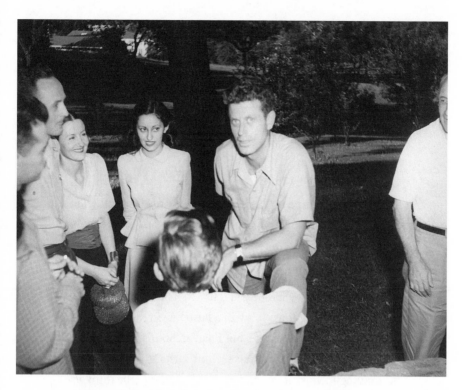

*Walter Clark with students at writers' conference, probably at the
University of Montana, 1953. Courtesy of Robert M. Clark*

as many auditors as writers — coming from Butte, Anaconda,
Helena, even Bozeman — commuting — so that I feel an
uncomfortable responsibility, as if preparing a public talk
instead of a class discussion. . . .

Last night I made my last actual public talk — in the music
hall auditorium . . . I gave them Julie again — and got that same
low feeling afterwards, though everybody was very nice. Sometimes I suspect I must be in love with Julie, and just can't do
anything with her that seems her due — as if I cheated Julie, not
the audience. On the old principle that one must never write
love stories about someone he really loves, because everything
will come out Tin Pan Alley. . . .

How would you like to come to Montana? I suspect there's going to be an opportunity. Out of the frying pan into the fire; Si Ross to Anaconda. It's a very nice bunch in the English department though. If only Virginia City were not so tightly fixed in one place.

Love you—

W. (8/6/53)

Still at the Montana writer's conference on August 13, he found himself confronting once again the question of where he would teach during the following year and the worry that he might end up exclusively a teacher rather than a writer:

The inquiry about whether you'd like to live in Missoula was not altogether facetious. It is still a hush matter, and the dicker in the ways and means stage, but I had an hour's talk about teaching writing in the regular session with Dr. Merriam, and he is trying to work it out on a two quarter basis (the third at Stanford this [school] year, and free thereafter.). . . .

Some pretty good writing coming in from a number of the younger people, and the most earnest and ambitious efforts I have seen yet from the older. But actually I'm getting very tired of talking it all out, and having nothing left to make me even want to write. I feel as if I were getting really old, having to measure the energy (though God knows I haven't been this session) and so as if this might be a crucial period, where I'll have to make my choice whether I'll be a writer doing a little occasional teaching, or a teacher doing a little writing.

⟪ CHAPTER TWELVE ⟫

ALONE IN MISSOULA
AND IN PALO ALTO

BUT HE WASN'T REALLY FREE to choose between a writing life or a teaching life—he had to teach in order to live and support a wife and two children. The alternative was no longer an option. He had been unable to complete a significant part of a manuscript to his own satisfaction and therefore could not even try to get an advance from his publisher. Furthermore, even if he did complete the first segment of a manuscript, he no longer had any confidence that he would be able complete it, and his conscience dictated that he had to have that confidence in order to accept the money.

He was somewhat on the edge, thinking he might have to resort to teaching once again at the Virginia City high school (which he enjoyed but which on a part-time basis really didn't pay enough to support him), when he got the offers from Montana (the University of Montana was called Montana State University in those days) and Stanford. He would spend fall and winter quarters at the one and spring quarter at the other. But once again, since these positions were temporary, it didn't make sense for the family to move to Missoula, and therefore he would have to endure another year, like the year in Iowa, alone.

But the place made all the difference. Around Missoula, he wrote in his autobiographical sketch, "there is some of the handsomest country in all the West." He loved the mountains, but also there was an identification in his mind with Nevada in Montana's old mining towns and ranching culture. He also began to realize that Missoula, like Virginia City, was a small town where everyone knew everyone else, and what he enjoyed most of all (beyond being with his family) was to have a small group of people he could socialize with. Also, true westerners, especially those in the Great Basin and Rocky Mountain areas, *are* different—the hardships of their history and climate have made them so—and Clark found himself at home among Montanans.

What made him especially comfortable with his situation in Missoula was the group of faculty and neighbors he had fallen in with during the summer session. When he returned to Missoula that September 1953, he put himself in the hands of Roy Hinze and his wife, who had volunteered to find him an apartment in the faculty housing, in an area called the Fort because it was former military housing. (Hinze was a theater director-producer for the university and during the following year tried several times to get Clark to accept acting roles in his productions.) The Hinzes showed him an apartment which had an appealing layout of four rooms, but which was a mess. The plaster was peeling in places, and the living room had been painted orange and black—the darkest black, Clark declared, he had ever seen.

He began almost immediately to repaint and clean up. Typically, although friends offered to help, he didn't want to be in debt to anyone: "I find myself—for no good reason I can think of—stubbornly reluctant to take help on my own dirty work. So I'll try it—maybe at night, with the windows open" (9/26/53). However, it became clear that at the slow rate he was going, the painting would never get done, and so despite his qualms, he was grateful when over several evenings the Roy Hinzes and the Walter Browns came by to do much of the work. (Although he did his part, he hated to paint—the smell invariably made him sick for hours afterward.) When it was done and he had bought some second-hand furniture, he decided, "I like the place—and once I am into my routine, I should be able to work well in it" (9/29/53). It was a far cry from the dark and cramped room with army cot that he had had at Iowa.

But when he was invited out or had help, he always felt an obligation and felt called upon to do what he called "squaring his moral debts." At Iowa, he "balanced the books" at the end of each semester by having little parties in his room or, more often, taking out colleagues and students to restaurants. On this occasion, as he wrote his wife,

> I think, if I have odds and ends cleaned up by then, I'll throw
> a little housewarming party—with the whisky you sent and
> some cheese and crackers, for the people who have been so
> helpful—and then gradually, seek my shell—and some
> restoration of the urge—to which loneliness has sometimes
> been a help. I aim to get lonely, if possible. This is such a kind
> and sociable outfit it's not easy. And my teaching program, if
> something less than inspiring this year, is certainly not very
> taxing, far lighter than at Nevada. (9/29/53)

All year from beginning to end, first at Montana and then at Stanford, he continued to express the hope that he would get some writing done. His references to it over and over again in his letters to his wife had become cries of despair, starting with this one at the end of September:

> A day or two of cleaning up corners in the off hours now, and I
> should be able to turn something nearer a whole mind onto the

class work, and even get some writing going. Something has to get written this year, or I'm really going to be serious about some desperation move. I don't even feel like a writer any more, but just like a talker about it. A little more and I'll be feeling like a fake even as a talker. (9/29/53)

In October, at the beginning of the semester, he felt strange, disconnected:

All seems very remote—or I do—as if I were talking to classes, and even individuals, through glass—so that probably they can see my lips moving, but not hear a sound.... I seem to exist in a state of illusion—not really unhappy, like the Iowa one—just not really anything. (10/4/53)

Nevertheless, he had his housewarming, squaring his "moral debts," and afterward declared, "I am feeling very moral—or at least that I must be very moral. Going to cut down on the whiskey and coffee and cigarettes, plan at least six work days out of the week—start reading again—oh, everything" (10/4/53).

As far as his writing was concerned, he was still stuck but now in a somewhat different way. He had taken on the Comstock history (for a series of nonfiction histories to be marketed to teenagers) because he thought it would be easy and help him work into doing the writing he wanted to do. He had taken on the *Holiday* article on Nevada because he thought it would also be easy to do and provide some extra money. Beyond these projects was a historical sketch of Virginia City for a tourist brochure that he had promised to a friend. But now he divided the writing into two parts: "The writing I want to do—with a little heckling going on from the writing I must do, but don't want to—all the v.c. [Virginia City] and Nevada crap." Few novelists would think of doing an occasional article with such scorn. The hackwork he thought might release him from his writing block had become part of that block. He looked forward to the Stanford quarter and its light teaching load to "show something better, and perhaps even restore my soul" (10/9/53).

His sense of disconnection from the world around him continued for several weeks, although in mid-October he told his wife that

> there is a promising if uncomfortable ferment within me, anyhow — so much that I don't sleep — either get restless and go prowling out to see friends — or play the fiddle and prowl around the apartment, then go to bed and lie there awake, staring at stars through the branches outside. (10/13/53)

He was lonely and thought of pictures he might bring back with him at Christmas, mainly prints and paintings by Caples, which if hung in his apartment might break up his vast expanse of gray wall. And a picture of his wife, if standing on the bureau across from his bed, might also serve to ward off "this spooky feeling of being alone the last few years has brought on." He wondered if, when he got home the next time, he would dare touch her at all:

> I sometimes almost believe I will have to sit across the room with my drink, visiting in your house, calling you Mrs. Clark (and wondering who the hell this Clark is — since I never find him home — and really at times, don't seem to know him wherever he is) and talking politely about the weather and the international situation. (10/13/53)

As much as he longed for her, he was shocked and dismayed to find that he had, nevertheless, forgotten their twentieth anniversary. An anniversary card had come to him in a batch of mail that had been delayed in delivery because he had not officially signed himself in onto "Route 3, Missoula." So when the mail was returned to Barbara, she forwarded it to the English Department along with her card. He felt guilty about the forgotten anniversary but felt even worse about not hearing from his wife for several weeks. He wrote her, in his letter of apology, that

> I seem to be in a mood to make the most and the worst of everything. I debated a dozen reasons why you might be done with me—all based on the beginning factor that you had seen so little of me for so long that you didn't really believe I existed any longer.... I am miserable in this matter of dates, I'm afraid.... Despite appearances—I do love you. (10/21/53)

A week later he reported that he was beginning to get some things done beyond the day-to-day routine. He finished writing out his plan for teaching at Stanford and sent it to Wallace Stegner, and he laid out a plan for a new modern novel course for English Department chair H. G. Merriam, a course which he hoped he could teach next quarter instead of one of his freshman writing courses. As far as his own writing was concerned, he reported that

> I'm trying now, along with the routine, to get into the *Holiday* article. I'm as inspired as a sawdust dummy—but it's cash, which we can use, and I'm beginning to believe that my conscience as much as anything, is what is blocking the real writing, and that I won't get it going until all this busy work is out of the way. (11/2/53)

By mid-November he was looking forward to traveling home at Christmas and worried that snow at the passes might delay his trip. While the roads were clear in Missoula, it was snowing heavily in the mountains. He was also concerned to find someone who could look in on his apartment while he was away and keep his oil stoves burning so that his pipes wouldn't freeze. He told his wife that he had become, as in Iowa, something of a "mail box haunter," needing some reassurance in a letter that she wasn't upset that he'd forgotten their anniversary. He planned to take the days off during the Thanksgiving break to get all caught up on his schoolwork and maybe take a slice out of the *Holiday* article. Barbara was working on writing a detective novel (a genre they both enjoyed reading), and he told her that "maybe I can help doctor up your detective story during Christmas vacation. I am now, as Robert [Caples] says, tired enough, and am not likely to over-write on it anyway" (11/19/53). The *Holiday* article continued to haunt him, and he thought if he could just get through it in such a way as not to be ashamed of it, then he wouldn't be bothered if the magazine rejected it and he would be off the hook. He wrote his wife that

the usual diversionary inspirations are setting in; always do as soon as I get started on a duty piece. The long-baffling novel is now repeatedly needling me with new, alive glimpses — tempting me to believe I can write it even in the midst of all. Likewise the novelette I was about a third into a year ago and have not touched since. (11/28/53)

As the fall quarter at the university came to a close, he worried about catching up on his social obligations. Not sure about when he was going to leave for Virginia City, he had purchased tickets for a basketball game between Montana and Indiana that would be the dedication event for the new field house. Clark had planned to take the Walter Browns to the game to pay them back in part for their many kindnesses but changed his plans about going himself, deciding he had to leave before the game in time to get home for a community Christmas party. So he decided to give all the tickets to the Browns as a Christmas present. But

Walter is insisting on buying them from me — which I can't allow. I'm not sure I should have spent the money for them, but the Browns can afford it still less. They have just the prof. salary — I suspect less than I'm making, and very improbably

any more, and they are the most endlessly social and hospitable
people on the faculty — as I know shamefully well. Scarcely an
evening goes by without people dropping in on them — and
getting a drink or something to eat, they have loners, like
myself, in for dinners three or four times a week. . . . I don't
know how they do it. So for a lot of reasons, they mustn't buy
those tickets. (12/6/53)

His close connection to the Browns would continue during the
entire time he taught at the university. Clark's son, Robert, recalls
that his parents

socialized a lot at the Browns, quite a few of the faculty, and
certainly that was Dad's main social outlet for the time he was
there without Mom. He may even have sometimes stopped for
a drink on the way home if he and Walter had some common
schedule. I do suspect that Mackay Brown admired him somewhat, and so gave him the younger female attention that at
other times and places he got from the tennis playing younger
females. There wasn't such in Montana. Once again, I would
be shocked if it went so far as infidelity, mostly because I think
Dad would have been unwilling to be aggressive, and never
wanting (maybe going too much on evidence from *The City*)
to have to feel obligated or responsible. I could be wrong,
obviously, but the folks did a wonderful job of covering it up
if there were any such affairs going on while the family was
together.

About his father's friendships with younger women, Robert
observed further that

the one figure who's always there in each period of his life is
the single female friend. I can't tell you if it's more than that or
less, I don't know. I kind of think not, because it's a pretty public female friend. But there was one back there in Cazenovia

who must have been another teacher.... Then, when he was in Nevada, especially when he was writing, we lived in the Washoe Valley. So he'd write in the mornings, and then had afternoons pretty much free. He did a lot of tennis playing. His usual partner and often his opponent — his partner in mixed doubles in tournaments — was a young woman, Barbara Bradley, the unmarried daughter of a prominent ... physician there in Reno, nice looking.... Then, later on ... is Martha Rising, another tennis [partner] ... from the Mill Valley Tennis Club when Dad taught at San Francisco State.... He's obviously drawing some satisfaction and support from the friendship, or even admiration, of these single, younger women.

But, of course, Mackay Brown was married.

Clark left Missoula on December 20, went back to Nevada for the holidays, and returned on January 3 to take possession of a new office, ready to start winter quarter. His schedule had him teaching five days a week first in the morning and then in the middle of the afternoon, leaving him with a four-hour gap between classes that he vowed to make use of:

> I am bound to make a savage, even a ruthless, try to get some
> writing done this quarter, even to keeping what I loathe at
> least until I see what follows, and have reached a rewrite stage.
> I didn't exactly take an oath; I didn't make a New Year's reso-
> lution. I am sick of making a liar of myself that way. But the
> next thing to it, in hopes it will grow up to something like an
> oath, or better yet into a good habit. It seems to me, sometimes,
> that my will is worn out, that I have ground it down so thin
> with the fruitless efforts of the last few years that there is not
> enough left to move me directly. I teach better than I write now,
> I think, because the natural stimulation of a class, the immedi-
> ate necessity of doing something that does not bore everybody,

serves instead of a will. Yet I must write again; I know that.
Even the flavor of teaching, for me, depends upon that in the
long run. Something within me has always, and still does,
regarded teaching as something very near a substitute activity,
and if ever the writer completely surrenders, the teacher, I suspect, would not be far behind him.... If it stinks, I must still
write, if only in the difficult hope that if I persist, something
real will begin to move again. And it looks as if I must get used
to my office as the place to do at least a good part of it. (1/5/54)

Robert Clark has commented on his father's emotional situation at this point as writer and teacher by saying,

> My notion is that he didn't really have much desire to write
> left in him—he no longer had that compulsion that he had
> when young that also made him want to write, he just began
> to feel he had to do it because he was putting himself forward
> as an expert and authority as to how to do it, and then show-
> ing himself unable to do it. He began to be embarrassed.

During the previous fall quarter he had been offered a permanent position in the English Department, and since he no longer
had hope for Nevada, he had accepted. Charlton Laird had written
to him from Nevada that President Stout and the regents were still
at it, firing and squeezing the faculty in an effort "to establish a dic-
tatorship." As Clark told his wife, they were persisting

> even if it demolishes a university; it is as if they intended to get
> the whole matter beyond repair before any action can be taken.
> At any rate, despite Bob [Gorrell] and Les Gray, it doesn't look
> like a place for us to try to fit into, even if we're invited. I guess
> we'd better try to be Montanans. (1/18/54)

At Montana he would teach literature and creative writing and
further develop a creative writing program at the university. Now,

during January of 1954, he began to plan for his family to move to Missoula in the fall. While the scenery was great and the people he had come to know were agreeable and very welcoming, he had some trouble with the weather in the winter, which he described as "constantly dark, drippy, or wetly snowy." Moving permanently to Montana, away from the place where he was most at home, was a difficult decision, but he was determined not to be separated for a year from his family again. He got Montana license plates for his car and his Montana driver's license. Since they would sell their house in Virginia City, he began looking in the newspaper for a house to rent or buy in Missoula—but with some misgivings: "I keep feeling a kind of finality about buying a place that I am not yet prepared to accept. No doubt that's what we'll wind up with, though, if we can float a down payment" (1/12/54).

Such a decision was tough for a writer so closely connected to his land. Thinking about this, he wrote his wife:

> I think the consideration that keeps a slight flavor of exile in the Montana idea for me is the combination of my age [he was forty-four] and the dimensions of my stake of idea and experience in Nevada. So much that I foresee in novels and stories, nearly all, is Nevada, and I realize increasingly that, despite similarities in history and people, one does not make a shift short of many years, and perhaps, at my age, never, in the full sense. Not that, for most of what I want to do, any particular background is necessary—just western, except that it must really be alive for one, and I wonder how long it will take me to get beyond the superficial recognition here.... Anyway, the Montana plates are on the car, so I feel like the first installment of a citizen, even if I have to think when I look for the car on the street, having no more green license. (1/12/54)

At the beginning of February, although it was still cold, there was something of a thaw—but that produced a dense fog, blanketing everything and contributing further to the darkness. It bothered him that he had run out of money and he not only couldn't pay his bills but had to borrow money from his friends in order to eat. He finally got his paycheck, paid off his debts, and, to counteract his depression, went to a bottle party at the Browns' and then to two basketball games. So, he wrote his wife, "I did all right for a broke hypochondriac" (2/1/54). The pace of his life picked up:

> Tomorrow night bowling, Wednesday night campus theatre—
> Moliere's Imaginary Invalid (which I shall try not to take personally), Thursday evening another book club jaunt, and
> Friday, ah, Friday Dorothy Brown and Jane Dew are throwing
> one of those joint birthday parties . . . at the Chateau, drinks,
> dinner and dance—to which I am invited, and will go with my
> throat open. Saturday basketball—Sunday—a concert. Why
> don't I cut out these extra-curricular activities? Next year,
> I say—always next year. Except, of course, the Friday night
> parties. (2/1/54)

As the winter went on he continued to look for a house, and by mid-February he had found one he liked. The owners were a woman who was secretary to the English Department and her husband, who was being transferred to Seattle. The house was, as Clark described it to his wife, "a small, white, colonial bungalow" with "an astonishing amount of room, since both its full basement and its half second floor are fixed up for living purposes" (2/13/54). He planned to put the children in the two downstairs bedrooms and take the upstairs for his and Barbara's bedroom and a study. He always planned for a study somewhere in whatever house he was occupying but usually ended up writing in the dining room or the kitchen. In addition to describing the financing of the house, he also sent drawings of the outside and floor plans to his wife. The main problem he saw was raising money for a down payment, something they would not be able to do until they sold the Virginia City house.

In the meantime he had been asked on several occasions if he would become chairman of the department on a permanent basis. The request weighed heavily on his conscience, for although he didn't want to take on the position, he was pressured by the hopes of many of his colleagues that he accept and by the sense they conveyed to him that he was needed. At the same time his conscience bothered him because "I realize that the English dept. chairmanship is going to be a test run on the proposed all-university plan of which I approve, and in which I may have had a small, responsible finger" (3/1/54).

The situation was complicated by the fact that he couldn't become chair unless he was an associate professor, and the present chair, H. G. Merriam, voted against his promotion. "Nothing personal," Merriam assured him, it was just that he had not been at Montana long enough to earn promotion in his opinion. Nevertheless, Clark, along with Leslie Fiedler, was recommended for promotion by vote of the department as a whole. Fiedler was, in Clark's words, "the department's prize scholar-critic, with a good many years of service here to his credit." While he understood Fiedler's promotion, he felt a bit conscience stricken about his own, since two of his friends, who had been at the university for three years and were still on the instructor level, had been passed over. Regardless of the promotion, Clark continued to refuse the chairmanship. It would certainly take all his time and block any possibility of writing, but he also felt awkward as a new member of the department. And he wasn't essentially an academic. "I know enough about the footnote routine," he wrote his wife, "so I could get by, but I would have to watch it all the time. I get too bored and impatient with scholars" (2/15/54).

At the beginning of March, his teaching, "schedule of extracurricular activities," and late nights took their toll and he went to bed with a sore throat and fever. He had to miss his classes for a day—unusual for him. Lying in bed, he had time to reflect on his life and wrote his wife:

> Having come closer to idle contemplation while awake than I have in a long time, I have decided that my conscience has got all out of hand—that it is on the way to becoming a dark and monstrous master instead of a useful servant. It does not let me alone about anything—a day's absence from school, a class that does not go as well as it should, a social debt I know the others do not regard as a debt, the possible duty to make myself available for a chairmanship I don't want (and know would be the death of writing for two or three years more— especially with the conscience around) and know a score of good objective reasons for refusing, the amount of time I've been away from you and the kids since we moved to Virginia City, writers' conferences I'm fed up on, correspondence I still answer, though I know the greater part of it is really an imposition, frosh comp. papers I spend six hours on, when I know there aren't results to justify the care, taking the kids away from where they want to be, the perfectional block in the writing (which is really just another aspect of this dictatorship by conscience), worry about not doing enough about the [University of] Nevada situation—when I know that relatively I've done my share and then some, inadequate sympathy to Euphemia [his sister], a sense of deserting the Restoration Campaign and v.c. [Virginia City] when it needs help against the [Lucius] Beebe influence—though I know I couldn't do anything that matters short of an open, all-out fight, and probably not even then; ... Talks around Montana that I hate to make, and feel obliged to, even when I get needled into talking about my own stuff; a haunting sense that I am not adequately

prepared for the Stanford session; most of all and worst of
all, the constantly returning sense that I haven't been what
I should as husband and lover to you—which has, unfortunately, definable substance in act and absence which I can
remember only too well—but which I know your forgiving
and reasonable nature and wonderful personal wholeness do
not hold against me to nearly the degree I hold them against
myself. (3/2/54)

He planned to leave for home on March 18, and as the end of
the quarter approached, he tackled his usual last-minute tasks—
reading manuscripts, giving and reading exams, getting a haircut,
and paying back his social debts. And planning for the future. He
had to move his furniture and pack up the things he would leave
with friends until he returned in June. He gave fifty dollars in
"good faith" money to the owners of the house he and Barbara had
decided to buy, the one he had described to her in some detail a few
weeks earlier.

Plans to purchase that property had become firm as a result of
the sale of the movie rights to *The Track of the Cat.* As a pleasant
surprise, his agent at MCA had given him the news that he had sold
the rights to John Wayne's production company for $7,500. Even
with subtracting the percentages paid to the agency and to Random House, the Clarks would have enough money left over not
only to cover a down payment but to buy new furniture (they
would leave the old furniture in the Stewart Street house). As a result of their windfall, they would not have to wait for the sale of
their Virginia City house, and in fact, decided to sell the house to
friends who couldn't afford a down payment (a deal that later fell
through). Things were going so well that he wrote to his wife,

I am beginning to get a private keep-the-fingers crossed feeling. We have had so many lucky breaks towards what we want

in the last month that I suspect the fates of some hidden malice, some unexpected wallop waiting behind the curtain. So far, however, the luck holds up. (Cross your fingers too. I think the gods probably regard your wisdom more highly than they do mine anyway. They would be more foolish than is probable of gods if they didn't.) (3/6/54)

By the end of April 1954 and after a week at home—almost enough time to get used to being married again—he was at Stanford, living in an apartment in Palo Alto. At Stanford he was teaching in a real creative writing program again, well organized and directed by Richard Scowcroft, who had taken over in Wallace Stegner's absence. Scowcroft remembered Clark as

> an attractive guy, nice guy, and very cooperative—wanted to help as much as he could. The only idiosyncrasy I remember— he never knew when to stop talking. I would schedule him for say 5 o'clock, but we were going to show his movie [*The Ox-Bow Incident*] at 7:30 at night and we scheduled the talk at 5 o'clock, and he went on and on and finally about 6:30 (he was supposed to speak 45 minutes or so) after he had gone on for an hour and a half, I had to get up and say, "Look, we have got to get moving, to get to that movie that is going to be showing." Then another time he did the same thing. He would get going on a speech—he wasn't boring or repetitive—but he just couldn't stop. . . . I liked him. Attractive and bright and very manly. I think that was part of his conscious as well as his unconscious. One of the boys.

The expression of manliness was an important part of Clark's personality. One of his former students, George Bluestone, in looking back on his time with Clark, is not surprised that he never gave any outward indication of the struggle he was having with his inability to write:

It would have been important to Walter *not* to have had a writing block, since tennis and language were two aspects of masculine precision.... An easy competence was the image he always tried to achieve. He was one of those writers who make the difficult look easy.

For the most part, Clark was happy at Stanford. His students, he thought, were excellent, particularly those in the workshop. He told his wife, "The writing of this bunch is very, very good—and they are a pleasant, arguing, interesting group to discuss it with" (4/7/54). For the workshop, Wallace Stegner had developed a program that sidestepped the academic to emphasize writing talent. Applicants to the program were required to compete for places in it on the basis of a writing sample, and while the workshop was technically a graduate seminar, the academic background, sex, race, or age of applicants was deemed irrelevant. In addition, many of the students received full fellowships, thus enabling those without economic means to participate. Clark thoroughly approved of the democracy of the system and liked the fact that the writing instruction was insulated from academic pressures.

However, he also taught an upper-division novel class, and in regard to this part of his job, he wrote his wife,

> I have ... [come] to feel a little ornery about the Stanford program. From the beginning they have put pressures on me—courteously, to be sure, but pressures (as much as to say, "This guy doesn't really know, being a wandering writer and school teacher, what a university is all about") to make the novel course a good deal more academic than I like— with emphasis on a critical reading list, etc. I have a suspicion I'm going to teach that—and everything else—just the way I want to, and leave them ... if I can, with a bunch of stimulated rebels on their hands.... I am going to make [the students] read *the books,* as they have never read them before,

I hope, and think about the books themselves (Ah, revolution. Think, instead of quote — read, instead of gloss). (3/6/54)

He was going to "dish out" a critical reading list long enough to keep the students reading for a year and then, once they had the list, not refer to it again all quarter.

He lived close enough to Virginia City so that he was able to drive home for a couple of weekends. Driving in the Bay Area was quite different from driving in or around Virginia City or Missoula, and he was overwhelmed by the amount of traffic. Coming home one weekend from Nevada, he got to the Bayshore Highway and found traffic was bumper to bumper,

> two lines going each way, without a break in the rows of lights as far as one could see. I sat there waiting for the green light and watched them honk and roar and whiz by — and all of a sudden it struck me funny. This was California, the Golden State, the promised land, enjoying its beauty and its freedom and its wonderful weather. It was so ridiculous — it was so massively, inclusively, appalling frenetic and stupid and pointless — that suddenly one saw that this was not even the mass mind taking over from the individual — it was simply the machine taking over from any mind at all. Nobody driving in all that horde . . . could have been anything but what I had been — two feet, two hands, a pair of ears, and a pair of eyes, all dedicated to the sole purpose of keeping a few hundred dollars worth of shiny metal from being mangled beyond recovery.
>
> It was fantastic . . . imagining how, from the air, every highway in the region must look like this, a brave new world so infinitely more dehumanized than the one Aldous Huxley ironically conceived, as to make his test tube regimentation seem quiet, thoughtful and highly promising. For here was

man already as far below freedom, dignity and decency as his victims of the sterile laboratory, but not, like them, gentle and docile, and dedicated, however mechanically, to their own betterment, but very literally a slave to the inanimate, infinitely more helpless in individual choice, and doubtless of a disposition and intent considerably more savage and dangerous than his remotest apish ancestors. (5/10/54)

On one of his weekends he contracted to go to Mills College in Oakland to give an auditorium lecture and a series of seminars (he decided he much preferred a coed audience to the all-female group at Mills). His hostesses took him to a national flower show being held in Oakland, and while he didn't say anything at the time, he told his wife that he was very depressed by the experience, the plants in that setting—artificial, inside gardens with waterfalls and trees—being in the same sad condition as animals in a zoo, a travesty of the natural world.

On the end of another week, along with a colleague from Stanford who had arranged the trip, he would go down to Carmel to visit Robinson Jeffers. As he planned his trip, he wrote his wife that he "felt a little intrusive about this visit to Jeffers—but it isn't my asking—and it will be a trip to Carmel, another look at the sea. I intend to relax like boiled spaghetti during the whole trip" (5/27/54). Then, when returned, he reported,

> The trip yesterday was very pleasant—though a little awkward in the talk with R. Jeffers—just through lack of any real contact, so the talk stayed remote. He looks very old, tired and frail—but I was relieved, nevertheless, for he also seems tranquil and balanced—very gentle and kind—has obviously adjusted well to Una's absence—and has his son and his son's family with him—baby-sits for them with the three year-old daughter, whom he obviously adores, has taken up his stone work again, enlarging the house for the family and seemed

clearly content with the arrangement. No debilitating spooks of loneliness or neglect. Then we had lunch on the beach, right in the face of a fine, rocky surf, and with hordes of sea-lions and cormorants just off shore, on Point Pinos. A very pleasant day. (5/29/54)

His letters from Stanford to his wife tended to follow much the same pattern as those from Iowa City and Missoula. But as the quarter went on, there was less and less mention of possible writing or even—what had become typical of these last years—self-condemnation for lack of performance mixed with an iron determination for the future, a determination that always rusted away in the weather of ongoing demands. However, after his weekend at Mills College, he came up with yet another idea about his inability to get any writing done:

> I have a newly clear, and depressing, insight into why so much talking kills the writing. It is not only the expenditure of needed energy, but an outward, rather than inward focus of the perceptions, and upon a different kind of response. And I have learned again and again—in different things—basketball, theatre, tennis, bar-room conversation and fruitful conversation, I have to understand the why before my will can act effectively in defense. Well, definitely, with this waking at night at Mills, I have seen more sharply and exactly why the talking, including, I am afraid, the teaching, for in a less costly way ... the same thing happens with each lecture, so presses the writing aside. Whatever writing I have to do to get there, I am convinced I must get outside all the talking and stay there before I will write well, or at least as well as I can, which would be enough, I think, to let one end with a feeling he had not wasted his life, or spent too foolishly whatever he had to spend. There have to be much bigger chunks, at any rate, of writing time without talk. (5/2/54)

Although such contemplations of his writing difficulties became rarer, he did continue to include passages expressing his love and longing for his wife in every letter to her. At the end of May, shortly before the spring quarter would be over, he wrote,

> These long separations must not happen any more. We must make Montana work till the kids are on their own, anyway—and then, if I must wander, we can do it together—or, if I turn out to be a writer again—we can even wander by choice—but together. . . .
>
> I'm not tight—this is just a love letter, I guess. I know I shouldn't do it; I know they embarrass you, but you'll have to allow me one once in a while—in the breaks. I'll clam up and talk facts again (although there are much more important facts—really) when the rush closes in. Anyway—I love you very, very much—and it's only about two weeks now. Walter (5/27/54)

CHAPTER THIRTEEN

THE MOVE TO MONTANA
AND UNCOMPLETED
WRITING PROJECTS

THAT SUMMER OF 1954 THE CLARKS moved to Missoula with the hope that they would now be together permanently. The fact that they didn't rent but purchased their house at 212 Hastings Street suggests some degree of emotional commitment on Clark's part. It was a relatively small house, with a covered little front portico with a slant to the roof, giving the appearance of the front a little idiosyncrasy. It had one and a half stories, with a finished basement below and one big room upstairs with a slanted ceiling that doubled as the Clarks' bedroom and Walter's study.

The Clarks lived half a block from Bonner Park, and there was a grade school another block away. A half-dozen blocks from the house was the university, and you could walk there. In the words of Walter Brown's son, Geoffrey, the situation

> was about as out of the heart of America as you could ever
> want to live. . . . The football games which they all went to,

you would walk down the streets that were lined with maple trees that were turning color. It was a picture of middle America, for whatever value that might have today.

For the children, Bobby and Babs, however, the move was traumatic. Babs, who was a senior in high school at the time, was involved in a romance in Virginia City and objected vociferously. Bobby, a sophomore who was a good student, was apprehensive that he would be exposed in the greater competition as not as good as he had shown himself to be. Clark's son recalls that when he was a freshman at the Virginia City high school, there were 25 students in the whole school, whereas at Missoula "there were some 1,300 kids in a building that looked like a huge stone prison. There were more kids in my homeroom than there had been in the whole high school."

Nevertheless, as resistant or apprehensive as the kids might have been, the parents looked on their move as a new start for the family. In the back of Walter's mind, however, was something of a shadow — a suggestion that he might be entering a university environment like the one he had left in Nevada. In the late spring, Mackay Brown had written to him, as he told his wife, to report on recent events at Montana:

> You remember I told you that a considerable element of the faculty seemed to feel about President McFarland somewhat — if not so definitely — as Nevada feels about Stout? Well — it seems the feeling has suddenly, and with good cause, grown much stronger. He sought the advice of committees concerning a dean for the newly formed Liberal Arts Division, then ignored the advice and simply announced that the dean would be a man no one had wanted, and who is apparently ... disliked by much of the faculty, and despised by enough of it to make him worthless as a dean. (5/2/54)

*Hastings Street house where the Clarks lived in Missoula, Montana,
1954–56. Courtesy of Barbara Clark Salmon*

*Picnic north of Sun Valley, Idaho, on the way to Missoula, July 1954.
Walter, Barbara, and Robert Clark. Courtesy of Robert M. Clark*

Then, affecting Clark more personally, this dean whom no one liked went over to the department to tell some of its members that the president wanted Clark to be the department chair and asked them how they felt about that. "Well," Clark concluded, "no matter how the department felt before, there can't be much doubt how they'll feel now." He was particularly irritated because in a discussion with the president about a new agreement with the faculty, the president seemed to guarantee departmental elections. Mackay Brown had further reported that in an address to some community groups in downtown Missoula, the president had complained that he had been having a terrible time getting things in working order, primarily because of opposition by the faculty. But he also complained about the heritage handed down to him by preceding presidents, and, Clark added, "he included, by name, President Clapp, whose time at Montana, like Dad's at Nevada, is generally regarded as the Golden Age." And thereby, he "alienated most of the rest of such faculty support as he had left" (5/2/54).

This struggle with President McFarland would drag on throughout Clark's stay at Montana, a struggle in which Clark would participate but which he found upsetting and even at times profoundly depressing. Believing strongly in democratic principles and academic freedom, he belonged to both the ACLU (American Civil Liberties Union) and the AAUP (American Association of University Professors). He was a great democrat, and he felt he must stand up for his principles. But there was a conflict in him throughout—he hated school politics and gossip.

Much to his relief, Clark was not further pressured to take the chairmanship of the department. It went to Leslie Fiedler. Martin Bucco in *A Literary History of the American West* describes Fiedler's work, reflecting the attitude toward that work by many of his Western readers:

A masterful stylist, Fiedler finessed a major critical reputation by ruffling "straight" academics with his ingenuity and *chutz-pah*. In the wide wake of Freud and Frye [Northrop Frye who based his literary criticism on archetypes], this pitchman of the archetype can dream, intuit, convert, invert, alter, distort, dissolve, disguise into anything else.

Nevertheless, at least two of his books became required reading for teachers and scholars of American literature during the 1960s and 1970s: *Love and Death in the American Novel* and *The Return of the Vanishing American.*

If Fiedler set out to ruffle the feathers of "straight" academics, he succeeded not only in that, but in irritating a majority of Western critics and writers. In response to an essay, "The Montana Face," that Fiedler first published in 1948, Wallace Stegner, often called the dean of Western writers, has said that Fiedler, after arriving by train in Missoula from the East,

> saw some guy in a big hat, with, as he said, a stern, vacant face, stalking down the platform on high heels, and he thought ... to himself, "Healthy, I thought in contempt." Fiedler seems to me to have left a bad legacy in Missoula. There's a taint of him that lingers, a Mephistophelian smell of sulphur. I don't think he should have been teaching in Missoula, ever.

Still, although Clark's sympathies were with the West and Fiedler's with an eastern point of view (yet Fiedler stayed in Montana for twenty-three years) and there should have been a conflict, there wasn't. They didn't always agree, and they both had large egos, but they seemed to respect each other, perhaps because they were both democrats and each, in his own way, was a rebel. Fiedler, always outspoken — even at times belligerently confrontational — openly fought for his principles, whereas Clark was reticent but quietly steadfast in standing by his. Both were successful writers with national reputations, and although Fiedler wrote as a social and literary critic, his work was imaginative and creative, far from the fussy footnote type of scholarship that Clark disliked so much. While they had different perspectives on many things and certainly different approaches, they seemed to agree, more often than not, about departmental and university issues.

One of the main issues, of course, was McFarland, who, according to Merrel Clubb, a member of the department at the time, was "extremely autocratic and arbitrary, insisting upon what he considered his prerogatives as president." He ran up against a "faculty [that] had long had a strong voice in university affairs and was jealous of its position." That conflict was often the subject of discussion in the Walter Browns' living room.

Clark lived only a block and a half away, and several times a week he and the others from the department gathered there. These gatherings weren't just political occasions. As Brown's son Geoffrey has said, "It is cold, depressing, and dark in Montana, and the way you counteract that is with the conviviality of friendship and conversation and drink over a fireplace." Brown's other son, Mark, remembers Clark during these get-togethers as "reticent, a man who tended to hang back, but all the time smiling at the words and behavior of others. A quiet man, but a presence." Walter Brown recalls that

> we never went to bars together—we used each other's houses. I suppose in an average month, when he was in his prime and Barbara was here and all, Mac and I would be over there or they would be over at our house ... at least six times a week. The only thing that you do when you walk in, you walk to the kitchen, open the liquor cabinet, and hold down some bourbon ... sourmash bourbon. ... I kept the best whiskey I could afford. ... I am a pretty good drinker myself, but Clark was one of the God damndest hollow legged people I have ever met.

Evenings, after they were supposed to be in bed, Geoffrey and Mark Brown would leave the doors of their bedrooms open in order to hear what was going on:

> It was really an intense and impressive time. There was real life in the department. I don't know how to put it into words very well, but that is why my brother and I would leave our doors open. You could pick up on the intensity and the conviviality. . . . Because I was so young, I wasn't able to understand such discussions, but there were a lot of them. They were talking about ideas a whole lot.

As time went by, however, and toward the middle of Clark's second year at Montana, the university political situation became more tense. Geoffrey Brown recalls that the whole department seemed to despise McFarland, who became more and more imperious in his presidency. Brown remembers that

> it was a political world like you've never seen. These guys would park their cars blocks from my Dad's house, and they would meet in his house with the drapes pulled. I am serious. And plan how to get rid of this guy. Ultimately the guy was caught [in a conflict with the regents] and left.

McFarland departed a year after Clark himself had gone. Geoffrey has recalled how Walter Clark struck him:

> I almost want to use the word intensity . . . that isn't quite it— authority is close. . . . He was thoughtful. And you could tell that he was thoughtful and deep and you wanted to know what he was thinking about. . . . [Yet] he always seemed like a Montana man. He was very handsome, and had this deep voice, and had a comfortable rapport with the country, the people and ideas.

A colleague at Montana, Jesse Brier, was struck particularly by Clark's intelligence:

Few creative people are given credit for intelligence as well as talent, but he had that attribute, sometimes using it playfully.... One day, for instance, in a discussion of *Hamlet*, he observed that maybe all the intellectualizing about the play, so arduous and subtle by scholars, could be dismissed by this explanation. Hanging around together, cudgeling their brains about a new play they could offer, the Globe board might have turned to their star playwright and brought up that far-out story set in Denmark. "But it's too goofy," Shakespeare probably said, "too many illogicalities, quirky motivations, straining after effects." They could have answered, maybe Burbage himself, after a moment: "What a challenge — at the height of your powers, Will — to bring it into life enough to make it work, with a big finale. You can do it!" and "By God," the Bard said, "You know, I just might try it, just from the technical angle. All right, I'll see what I can get away with!"

We had a pretty good laugh at this scenario — anti-intellectual, but not dumb. I would say, although I don't want to exaggerate anything or over-generalize the anecdote, that Clark also valued technique highly in his own work, I mean in and of itself, perhaps especially in his short stories. I once asked him ... if he ever discussed current projects of his. He said never, for fear that the pressure at work in him would just be vented and no technique would avail to bring the work to fit conclusion.

Clark's writing, as we saw from his letters to his wife at the time, stuttered and nearly stopped during his year in Iowa. Surviving manuscripts suggest that he did better while he was living in the Fort in Missoula. After his family joined him in Montana, he would seem to have continued to write but at a lesser pace. The evidence for this writing are the stacks of manuscripts and notes deposited in the University of Nevada Library, Special

Collections, which appear to have been produced during these years.

Although he claimed to have frequently destroyed manuscripts, he did not destroy them all — even saving false starts that he apparently had no intention of revisiting. His saving so much material suggests that his "public burnings" may well have been a calculated drama designed to produce dismay or even, perhaps, admiration in his audience. Clark could be a showman and loved an audience. There were times, as has been mentioned, when he simply couldn't let a lecture audience go. The many manuscript pieces that he kept also suggest that he may have looked upon them as seeds, which once planted might, one way or another, one day or another, sprout and grow. He thought, planned, took notes, made outlines and lists, and wrote numerous beginnings, always with the hope that a shower of inspiration would urge one of his seeds into maturity. For one project, he wrote his beginning paragraph some two-dozen times in the hope of getting it right. But "getting it right" was based not so much on whether the paragraph was in itself well-written but on whether the paragraph would act as a spark plug which could fire his imagination and lead to further writing.

The period of 1950 to Clark's death in 1971 has been called his "silent period," and the story of the writer's struggle during this period, which includes his time at Montana, is revealing of both his identity as a person and his role as an artist. Why this writer, so talented and so motivated to write, should fail to publish during the last twenty years of his life is the central mystery of his career. Silent in terms of publication, perhaps, but he was busy writing, off and on, up to nearly the end, working on his fiction until about 1962 and then on a biography and an editing project thereafter. Just what fiction he was working on at any given time is not clear, since few of the manuscript materials are dated.

Whether actually writing or not, he would nearly always be

thinking about what he wanted to write, planning and working out possibilities in his mind. It would seem that at this point in his life he did not find his greatest pleasure in reaching a reading audience but in working out ideas in his mind and letting those ideas flow onto the page. What he seemed to live for was that rush of inspiration, which like a drug was a rush that would carry him off into a domain ruled over by his own imagination. He had, in a sense, become unplugged from his reading audience or for the need for such an audience.

Like Emily Dickinson, he wrote to write; he wrote for himself out of a need to express certain things dear to him, but what made this position especially difficult for him to maintain was that during this period, particularly in the 1950s, his literary reputation was at its zenith. As evidence for that were the offers he continued to get from universities, including Illinois and Texas, to head up creative writing programs at higher pay and with lighter teaching load—but he turned them all down. Texas might be argued to be in the West, but Clark could not bear to leave *his* West.

Clark's son, Robert, after carefully going over the manuscript materials that his father left behind at his death, has detected what he believes to have been his father's overall writing plan during these last decades. He thinks that his father had planned a long-range scheme for developing a Western epic, a series of books that would be based on the progress—or more accurately in Clark's terms, the historical decline—of Nevada. An early book-length manuscript first written in the mid-1930s, "Water," would seem to have served as a foundation, setting out the direction for *Ox-Bow* and *The Cat* as well the works that would follow.

At the heart of the manuscript was the boom-and-bust cycle in Nevada that intrigued Clark and seemed to him the story of the West as a whole. According to a summary by Charlton Laird, we see the "protagonist, Galt Mason, from the time he revolts against grand-parental authority in Maine until he is a beaten old rancher in central Nevada, ca. 1930." Like so many settlers, he comes from the East, sails around the horn, and attempts to make his fortune on the frontier. There, he "has learned about women and small-time crooks, has found out how to survive as a prospector . . . has lost one fortune in cattle and another in sheep." Then, in his seventies, he experiences "a reawakened awareness to something larger than himself."

As Laird points out, however, the manuscript was a good first draft, but "Clark had not yet learned to write." He had come up with the theme that would occupy him for the rest of his life, but in tandem with that discovery he would run into the kind of trouble that would dog him throughout his career. He focused so hard on his theme and expressing his ideas about that theme that the dramatic possibilities of his writing were neglected. As Robert Clark has said in assessing the manuscript, "Its prose is often self-consciously 'poetic.' It suffers from a serious shortage of dialogue and developed scenes, and from an excess of authorial rumination thinly disguised as interior monologue" — all of which tends to make it more like a tract than a novel.

A year or two after the publication of *Ox-Bow,* while he was staying at Indian Springs, Clark wrote another version of "Water." He took out the long introspective passages, enlarged the cast of characters, added subplots in order to enrich his theme, and made the central figure, Galt Mason, the more engaging Jason White. Of particular interest in this version is Clark's use of several characters taken from *Ox-Bow,* including Kinkaid, Farnley, and Drew, linking this incipient novel to his previously published one.

Another long, incomplete manuscript was a new version of the same project. Probably written while he was still in Cazenovia in 1942–43, it was now called "The Dam." This manuscript, tighter in style than its predecessors, was six hundred pages long and was followed sometime later — possibly in 1944 — by another fragment, this time three hundred pages long and also called "The

Dam." It incorporated the changes made in the previous version but broke off after three hundred pages with Jason White still in Maine. Laird speculates that the manuscript broke off because Clark's attention had turned to his latest draft of *The City of Trembling Leaves*. Clark's use of Maine in "Water" and "The Dam" as the departure point for the protagonists in these two early attempts at a western epic would seem to go back to his own experiences in upstate New York and Maine and with his New England in-laws.

Clark would seem to have given up on "The Dam" project first for *The City* and then for *The Watchful Gods*. After finishing the latter in 1950, he turned away from works based largely on his own experience and once again toward the concept of a Western epic. The extant manuscripts for the years after 1950 can, for the most part, be tied to three projected novels with the working titles "Admission Day," "The Man in the Hole," and "Way Station." Robert Clark has suggested that these projects, in this order, had a rough chronology, both in their contents — as related to Nevada history — and in their order of composition. However, his father did not write one draft, go on to the next project, and then to the next, and so on but apparently moved from one to the other, back and forth, so that the chronology is impossible to establish with any certainty.

"Admission Day" is set in Divide City, a town patterned after Virginia City, where Clark was living at the time he wrote the story (1951–52); however, he may have worked on it as late as 1954. Charlton Laird has described the manuscript:

> Like *The Cat*, it was keyed to Nevada history, deliberately planned to be revelational of it: the first day suggests the first Nevada period, the roaring boom times; the second day, the intermediate ranching years, relatively calm and socially decent. In the third period, contemporary and recent, the tourist and the land broker are wrecking the Old West.

We might recall the irritation Clark expressed in his letters for Lucius Beebe and other Virginia City promoters, especially for their using phony imitations of the Old West to attract tourists.

The second projected novel, "The Man in the Hole," was apparently planned and perhaps outlined and started while the author was in Montana, and he worked on various versions of the story up through the early 1960s and perhaps beyond that, while he was at San Francisco State. He worked on it longer than any other project, returning to it again and again. And it was the most complicated of his projects during these years, which would seem to have resulted in repeated tries without any satisfactory resolution of the problems he encountered.

As the title suggests, the story is about a man, Jake Christiansen, who is stuck down in the lower levels of an old mine. He has gone down to find a rich vein of gold that he suspects was overlooked when the mine was shut down. Unfortunately, while dynamiting to expose the vein, he has misplaced a charge, causing a cave-in that has trapped him. Over seven days of frustration, he tries to find a way out, and his predicament and isolation lead him to reflect on his life and speculate on the meaning of life in general.

The complications of the story stem from his taking the three days of "Admission Day" and expanding that symbolic structure to seven days. These are made to parallel the week of Christ's crucifixion and in turn used to reflect the whole of life on earth. Robert Clark has discovered among his father's papers a sheet

> on which he [Clark] had plotted out parallels between the
> seven days of Holy Week and the seven days that this man
> would spend down in the mine. It was worked out in very fine
> detail, so that virtually every small action of the man could be
> lined with an incident in the gospel.

The metaphor of the man in the hole—a man initially motivated by greed and then through his experience led to a religious conversion—obviously had an intense attraction for the author. Nevada was in a hole, so to speak, and mankind was in a hole, but as Clark mentioned in letters, he was also in a hole that his ambitious vision for the project had led him into and that he struggled for years to get out of.

The projected novel had many attempted beginnings and probably a number of trial endings. One such ending has Jake finding his treasure and, after he is rescued, giving it away to his wife and others. Then he devotes himself to following a new, ideal religion that he has developed while buried in the mine, contemplating life. The religion is, according to Laird, "a jumble of Christianity and other cults, oriental and primitive."

The third of the projected trio, "Way Station," is less allegorical than "The Man in the Hole," although the contents suggest that this is a station on the way to disaster—again a period in Nevada history, but also the condition of modern man. The story is a continuation of *The Track of the Cat* and as in that novel is set is a valley north of Reno. The main character is Edna Wheeler, whom Clark describes in a note as "a non-religious kin to the mother in *The Cat*." She runs the old Wheel-R Ranch, and, again according to Clark, is "hard-drinking, hard-talking, and dominating."

Edna believes that she loves the ranch and the land, but according to Clark, in her possessiveness she demonstrates an "emotional greed that WVTC's fictional women often mistake for love" [referring to himself as WVTC]. Greed, which is also Jake's undoing, would seem to be Clark's shorthand for all that he despised in modern society—its materialism, its selfishness, and its lack of concern for history and tradition and for the environment on its own terms rather than on our terms.

Disaster comes to Edna when she can no longer hold on to the ranch, and we last see her defending her beloved land by trying to shoot the sheriff. Clark's son has put the manuscript into the context of his father's overall plan by saying,

While *The Cat* covered the closing of the frontier and the festering of pioneer energies, this novel, a generation later, would depict the collapse of the small rancher, his doom speeded by that same historically factual drought of the 1920s, followed by the Depression, that brought catastrophe in "Water," and put an end to the stable community of the old ranch families.

All three of the projects are tied together by interlocking characters, which suggests that Clark had set out after *The Watchful Gods* on a lifelong exposition of the decay of the West and, by extension, a criticism of the trends in modern civilization. In addition to characters from *Ox-Bow*, "Admission Day" also includes Jake Christiansen and Johnny Braggia from "The Man in the Hole." Harold and Gwen Bridges from *The Cat* come as supporting characters into "Way Station," and the main character for that manuscript was to be Jim Wheeler, "a somewhat footloose young man in 'Admission Day.'" But then Edna Wheeler, another fierce mother as in *The Cat,* would seem to have taken over.

Some clue as to another possible reason for Clark's failure to publish during these years comes out of an examination of these projects, taken together, along with his activities during this period. Charlton Laird has written that

> the commonest guess is that his wandering from one job to another—his occupation with teaching sapped his creativity. So far as I know, nobody who knows Clark and his work will accept that as a complete explanation, but Walter himself gave it some credence.

Clark told his son that his problem was that he had become too much of a perfectionist and told a friend that his writing was "too much from the head."

This leads to the struggle that he had to make his work more dramatic and natural and less overtly symbolic. In a note he wrote to himself, he cautions that he must "learn to incorporate an organized (allegorical) symbolism within a natural context." He was a writer always most concerned with ideas, with theme, and it would seem that theme at last overwhelmed him. Clark's son believes that his father's inability to finish and revise a major work for publication was a result of the material he was working with more than anything else.

This reason for Clark's failure to publish during these years would seem to top all the other possibilities, although all the reasons mentioned above may also have been at work. The projects for this so-called "silent period" would seem to have been extraordinarily ambitious, especially "The Man in the Hole" with its extended allegory. His impulse in these works seems almost messianic, using Nevada history or created incidents set in Nevada history to predict human decay and destruction unless there is some kind of readjustment of values. Looking at his projects in that way, it seems no wonder that he was never satisfied with his progress.

One might add to all these factors the internal split in Clark between the teacher-critic, on the one hand, and the writer-creator, on the other. Here was a man who spent much of his time criticizing the writing of others, judging its shortcomings, and holding up to his students the ideals demonstrated in the achievements of authors like Henry James, Joseph Conrad, and William Faulkner. It would seem that the main reason Clark could not write what he considered publishable work during these last years was that he could not, try as he would, meet the criteria of the critic inside him — that he could not hope to achieve anything close to the writing he so much admired. It was a constant, sad realization.

As to what Clark accomplished during his stay in Montana, Robert Clark has concluded from his study of the manuscript materials that "I don't ... think that anything that was extant was mainly a Montana product. I'm sure it's possible he might have dragged out any or all that he had been tinkering with previously." In his notes on the manuscripts, Robert Clark has written about "Way Station":

> This is the last novel to be attempted, and was probably planned in Montana and worked on sporadically during the years at San Francisco State. There were even more failed beginnings than were preserved.... ["Way Station"] was to be a continuation of the western chronicle, with Hal and Gwen Bridges, though minor characters, establishing a direct connection with the earlier *The Track of the Cat*.

In the meantime, regardless of what writing he was able to accomplish, Clark's life in Montana followed a familiar pattern, although his relationships were somewhat more restricted to faculty friends, by contrast to the connections that he had had with people in his community in Washoe Valley and in Virginia City. This probably came from the fact that in Missoula he no longer frequented local saloons to socialize. Barbara Clark and her daughter, Babs, had become accomplished horsewomen in Nevada, and Barbara even helped out by becoming a cowhand for the roundups on the Lewer's ranch. Babs had her own horse, stabled nearby in Missoula, but her and her mother's riding activities were limited in Montana.

In Washoe Valley, while Clark had tennis friends in Carson City, Barbara was a friend of the landlord and local farmer-rancher there, Henry Heidenreich, and his wife, Minnie. Henry was always doing something, always working, always improving things on the Lewer's place. He might chop a down tree or fix a fence and then have a cup of coffee in the kitchen. Then when the Clarks moved to Virginia City, he would bring apples and other produce up to them. But in Missoula, Barbara's friends were pretty well limited to faculty wives.

When he could do so, Clark played quite a lot of tennis, often with his son. One of Clark's students, Jim Elder, remembers that

> He played in all seasons, and there was one history professor named Jules Carlin, who always ran around in just a polo shirt, no matter how cold it was. He rode his bicycle in the polo shirt and walked into a classroom, threw open the windows, freezing us out. The temperature is inversely proportional to the efficiency of learning. And Walter and Jules were the only ones who would play tennis when it was about 35 degrees and a brisk wind.... He was a very good tennis player. So was Jules, so they were good together.

And while Walter's chess partner was almost always his wife, he did practice things out of chess books—openings and endings. He and the family were fans of football and basketball in season and accompanied faculty families to the games, and Friday evenings were, as before, usually spent at the Browns' house with other faculty celebrating the end of the week.

Mackay Brown was a writer, mostly of short stories for women's magazines, and she wanted to graduate to more literary material. She asked Clark's help, and he read several of her manuscripts. In order to get her to think in terms of a deeper investigation of human nature, he recommended that she read the stories of Henry James. Mackay did but became very frustrated—she didn't take to James at all and couldn't figure out what Clark wanted her to discover in his work.

On the other hand, she was very grateful to Clark for his help on another occasion. Her husband, Walter Brown, recalls Clark's kindness, particularly in a situation involving his wife:

> When you discovered you exist in another person's mind, it is an act of great kindness on his part. It gives you a sense of being, you are alive, you are sort of worth something. And

Clark gave that certainly to me. He did many little things. When my wife, driving up to the university in the wintertime, in the old Studie [Studebaker] pointy-nosed convertible, she got in the wrong tracks of snow and piled head on into another car. They called me out of class and said your wife is critically injured. I was terrified at first. But I got down there and found out, nothing at all.... Without hesitation Clark appeared and said, "Now hold it Mac, I would like you to take my car. Our car is a '48 Pontiac." Barbara and her daughter both loved it, and they called it "Old Ponty." He just let us use that until we got another car—about a month or so, which I appreciated very much. An act of generosity, totally uncalled for.

Another incident involving Clark in Missoula was observed by Robert, impressing him with his father's physical courage. There was a club called the Short Circuits Club, which was a social organization primarily for the young people "from the wrong side of the tracks." One of Robert's high-school friends, who lived near the Clarks, had joined the club because they periodically had dances, and he talked Robert into joining also. Parents of the members were asked to be chaperones and guardians of the entrance—only members or their guests could get in, and the member had to show his card. The dances were held on the second floor of a late nineteenth-century business building in a hall provided by the Masonic Lodge and Knights Templar, since, as Robert remembers, there was ceremonial paraphernalia on the walls—flags, plumed hats, and swords. A small band provided live music.

For a dance one evening, Clark and his wife had volunteered to chaperone. Some large teenagers, members of the formidable Missoula County High School football team, tried to crash the party—three or four of them. They were turned away at the door by Clark, and then, when they began to give him a little lip, they backed down and went away when he got angry. Robert remembers that he called the leader "chum" at that point, which was a favorite diminishing/derogatory label.... My most vivid memory is of my own apprehensions, not to say fear, that here I was going to have to throw myself into the brawl that Dad's telling these drunken adolescent studs they had to get out there was going to cause. I didn't think we would win. But there was no brawl.... Dad was six foot tall ... and at that time was not in the best of condition, but his 190–200 pounds was fairly firm. But I think it was the sensed fierceness of his anger rather than his physical size that intimidated them.

In 1955, while Clark was at Missoula, his daughter married her boyfriend from Virginia City and moved with him to Sparks, Nevada. Her husband, Ross Salmon, was the son of Clint and Nell Salmon, who had been close friends of the Clarks for years. And then, on May 1 of that year, Clark's father, Walter Ernest Clark, died at age eighty-one. In an obituary, the *Reno Evening Gazette* praised his accomplishments at the university, the several buildings he was responsible for, and the many educational improvements he effected during his tenure. Just after the funeral, Clark wrote to his editor at Random House, Saxe Commins,

Dear Saxe—

Thanks so much for your note about Dad. His death was unexpected in the immediate sense, and so, since we're a close family, something of a jolt to us all. But in the larger sense it was not unexpected. He hadn't been well for a number of years, and he had seen a long and full life. It was perhaps even good this way, coming quickly and easily. We had been much afraid, both for him and for mother, that he would fall into a lingering helplessness. I only wish, in a way, that he might have died sooner, before he had to watch the university, which was the main work of his life, torn apart by fools and worse.

As for us—we live a good enough life here. My teaching is interesting. The kids profit by the larger and better school and like it. Only the writing does not move at all. I am too tired, and too used up by *talking* about writing all the time. Against my will I come closer and closer to the conclusion that if I am to write (except for the waste basket—I keep filling that) I must get myself free of the teaching. But since that means writing myself free, I arrive at a kind of impasse. There is plenty of grist for the mill, but the mill does not grind. And I teach again this summer, at San Francisco State. Another year I promise myself. I will take time off—three or four months. And I struggle to do better even within the schedule. I have, I think, a kind of almost destructional perfectionism as my work enemy.

Love and blessings to all the Commins,

Walter

P.S. Spoke with Wm. Faulkner while he was here. He quite evidently shares my fondness and esteem for you—and promised to say hello.

And we are in the process of selling the Virginia City house. It seems a little like selling out a life, though I know it isn't. (5/17/55)

Clark, with the help of Jesse Brier and others, had taken over the Montana Writers Conference and had the enthusiastic support of Leslie Fiedler. Not all the gatherings of the department were at Walter Brown's. As Merrel Clubb recalls,

Fiedler hosted many gatherings, often including prominent writers [who had been invited to the Writers Conference], Nelson Algren, Auden, Faulkner, for example. The last was especially interesting, for his public talk was plain lousy, but when he was asked to read from his own work at Fiedler's (I don't remember what now), he was spellbinding.

Clark and Fiedler were getting along fine. Clark really admired Fiedler's rebellion against academic orthodoxy. He wrote to Saxe Commins:

> Item — there comes your way — to lecture at Princeton next year, in [R. P.] Blackmur's stead, I believe, Leslie Fiedler of the department here. A brilliant lecturer, and enormously read. You would find him interesting, I think, though hard to reach where he lives. (6/9/56)

At Montana one of Clark's most remarkable students was Jim Elder — remarkable because he was almost not one of Clark's students at the outset, even though he would later in life become an accomplished writer of articles for various magazines and journals. But in those days, as he has testified, he was "as green as could be" as he enrolled in Clark's creative writing class. He remembers,

> We turned in a few sample things the first week or two, and then he called me aside one day after class, and he said, "Jim," in a very kind way, "your fiction stinks. You might have a chance in nonfiction. I love your sense of humor. And nonfiction certainly needs some humor, and a sense of irony, but you are not ready for this class. But you know, we are not going to be in this classroom much longer. Why don't you drop the course while you can still get credit on your tuition" (because we were paying by the credit hour). He said, "Drop the class, but then stick around, because you are a good critic and you are a good devil's advocate."
>
> To me, that was remarkable because most professors, you know, consider it an insult to their ego to have people drop. You like to have your classes full, but he didn't care. He wanted really serious, contributing students in his classes. People he thought he could help. And he wasn't counting numbers on enrollment — it wasn't a popularity contest with Walter. So I

did. I dropped the class, but kept going, and after a couple of weeks, the classes were no longer at the university. They were at his house or some student's house.... These were what I guess we all thought of in our minds as the real Camelot of university education—getting together, sometimes all-nighters, sitting around maybe with a jug of wine (Barbara would always bring a jug of wine) and just discuss ideas and writing.... Sometimes we would be wrapping it up by midnight, or sometimes it would go to 2 or 3 in the morning, sitting around on the floor, on pillows, or whatever furniture there was.

Elder recalled the time when he and his wife, Lee, and the Clarks went to a writers' seminar up in Coalville. Leslie Fiedler was also there, and during the discussion he went on and on about the Freudian symbol of the bolt in a revolver. And as Elder tells it,

Walter looked at me and I looked at him, and Walter just kind of smiled. I wasn't as tolerant as Walter, and I said, "Dr. Fiedler, the revolver doesn't have a goddamn bolt." And he said, "Well, whatever." Later that evening, Walter said something like "He had that coming."

Elder also recalls that although Clark tended to dislike writers' conferences, he was expected to participate in them from time to time [in fact, toward the end of his tenure at Montana, he was put in charge of them]. Although he had a lot of patience, he couldn't deal very happily with the wannabes that wasted his time. At such conferences, he would like to get off in a corner one-on-one with someone who he thought really had some potential or had a problem that he might help to solve. But in the open seminars, you could see his attention beginning to wander.

During one of those writing conference seminars, a woman raised her hand, and Clark acknowledged her. She said, "Mr. Clark, should I use a synonym?" He very politely asked, "What do you mean by a synonym?" And she said, "Well, you know, to protect my privacy and my identity." Without cracking a smile or embarrassing her, he asked, "Well, have you written anything?" She said, "No, but I am going to. Do you think I should use a synonym?" And he said, "Well, maybe later if you change your writing style or if you get onto a controversial subject, you might consider a synonym or even a pseudonym." Elder, who tells this story, adds,

> He would never be unkind. If he had some serious things to
> hash over with a student, it would always be in private. He
> would never humiliate anyone in public. Even in private he
> was gentle, even though he didn't pull his punches. He always
> respected your own sense of worth.

CHAPTER FOURTEEN

ON TO MILL VALLEY
AND TO TEACHING AT
SAN FRANCISCO STATE

JIM ELDER WAS CLOSE TO CLARK during the period when Hollywood was trying to get the rights to *The Track of the Cat*. He recalls that Clark initially refused, saying, "No, because it is an introspective novel. It is not visual — it won't work." But every two or three months he would get a call or letter telling him that the studio really wanted to make a movie of the novel. Finally, he thought that he could put the would-be producers off by insisting that the only way he would consider the project would be if Bill Wellman would direct it. Wellman, who had directed *The Ox-Bow Incident*, was said to be on the verge of retirement. But one month after that, Hollywood called back and said that Wellman would direct if Clark would let them have the rights. So he was stuck. He refused to do the screenplay, saying, "I am not a screenwriter, but I do trust Billy."

Elder continues the story:

> So they do the film and they are going to have a sneak preview in Missoula. Barbara and Walter and Lee and I go to the the-

ater, and we park several blocks away and kind of go in after the movie had started ... [so he could] kind of sneak in and be anonymous about it.... So, we watch the film, and he was very interested and pretty caught up in the way it was handled ... But toward the end he started to get real nervous. He was fidgeting in his seat and then the climax came, and Walter just hung his head clear down to his chest. The film was over, and we left. We were walking back through the streets of Missoula in the cold toward my car, got in the car, and he didn't say a word. Drove over to his place, and he still hadn't said a word. Ordinarily, he would have said come in, or Barbara would have said there is a little bit of wine. But Walter just got out of the car, and he said, "Damn. They had to show the damn cat." And he turned and walked in. He was really crushed.

The movie had brought the two cats together, "the real and kill-able" and the other, the "invention of the primitive mind—and everlasting." For Clark, by killing the "combined cat" at the end the movie had erased the essence of his story, cancelled the symbol that was the heart and soul of his work.

As a footnote to the Elder story, according to Clark's son there may well have been a public showing at a later date at which Clark "made a few remarks in response to a request from the local theatre manager to do so, as was to be expected in a small town." In light of Clark's disappointment, it is difficult to imagine what those remarks may have been.

Then one evening Clark told Elder a story of a strange occurrence while he and Caples were up hiking and camping around Pyramid Lake. They hiked onto the area north of the lake on an Indian reservation, trying to find some petroglyphs and peculiar rock formations. In their search, they wandered about and finally became lost. Elder adds that "Walter wasn't the kind of person who got lost easily—he was a good outdoorsman." Finally they thought they were on the trail of where they wanted to go, perhaps responding to some Indian legends they had heard.

They camped for the night, and the next morning they found moccasin footprints all around their campsite. There were two or three sets of them, around their sleeping bags and around the remains of their campfire, and a very crude arrow stuck in a little leftover piece of their dinner. And during the night they hadn't heard a thing. Clark said that on several other occasions he tried to find the place, but he never could. He felt that he wasn't supposed to.

An odd thing happened that concerned Clark while he was still in Montana. A colleague from the University of Nevada sent him a paperback book, *Ramrod* by George Appell, which was published by Lion Books. The colleague had underlined a number of passages that had been taken word-for-word from *Ox-Bow*. Such a gross plagiarism was very upsetting, and Clark wrote to his editor, Saxe Commins, who answered that the case for plagiarism was clear, but that because it was hard to prove and expensive to go to court, it was unlikely that Random House would take any action. Clark wrote back:

> Yes, there isn't much question about the "Appell" Lion *Ramrod* plagiarism from Ox-Bow. Whole gobs of it in four chapters, with only a word here and there changed. I am taking the matter up, advisory-wise, with M.C.A. [his agents], and action if they think proper. But they say they cannot undertake the direct legal action, if such becomes necessary. (I've told them I'd prefer to settle for withdrawal of the book and payment of any profits it may have brought him or "Appell.") (4/15/56)

Clark had discovered that "George Appell" was a pseudonym and that there was already a book called *Ramrod* by Luke Short. After further investigation, Clark found that not only was his book raided, but Luke Short's was also—passages from the two being intermixed in the plagiarized text. Lion Books claimed that their book was a parody, a common defense for plagiarism, but they did agree to withdraw the book from the market. According Clark's son, his father had a strong suspicion that "Appell" was a pseudonym used by a creative writing professor, a colleague of his during the year he was at Iowa — a man whom Clark intensely disliked.

Clark taught for the 1955 summer session at San Francisco State College (now University). The school, which had a tradition of offering classes in creative writing, wanted to establish a formal program and had invited Clark for the summer in order to get acquainted and possibly hire him for the job. That fall, after he had returned to Montana, they did make him an offer. Clark had been happy in Montana, but his situation there had some disadvantages, and the job offer was very tempting.

One of the things that bothered him at Montana was the intradepartmental wrangling over one thing or another. At the end of his last semester at Montana, he wrote to his editor:

> Yesterday, the hectic, largely pointless politics of academia
> drew me into one more controversy where I might (I doubt it)
> be useful to the department. Just between you and me there has
> been no cessation since I came here of this constant, ridiculous
> bickering, jockeying, stirring up of feelings, nearly always, it
> seems to me, about nothing of importance, and always, cer-
> tainly, about nothing that is helped by the stirring up. (6/9/56)

Like most such departments, this one was divided between the traditionalists and the academic liberals. In connection with that split, Clark was disturbed about academic elitism, not only in Montana but in universities generally. As someone who had taught for twelve years in high schools, he mourned the lack of what he called "continuity" and thought, from what he had heard, that San Francisco State had the kind of close ties to local high schools and junior colleges that he had always advocated.

In writing to his editor, Saxe Commins, Clark stated that in his experience, colleges and universities did very little to establish connection and continuity between educational institutions at various levels. They were perpetuating themselves in a sterile round of the academic and condescending to the secondary schools in a way that

> perpetrates the unfortunate cleavage, and with unjustified certainty of superiority, as if the mere accumulation of information and degrees somehow made one a more intelligent and worthwhile being. I have seen enough of both sides to know better—better than a dozen years in each. And while I am aware that there is still a lot of theoretical nonsense in education curricula, I am also even more heavily aware that there is at least as much "scholarly" nonsense in the other, though the basic error being the same, the application of something faintly resembling the scientific method to an area where real scientific method is, and always will be, inapplicable. And, at least, the educational group remains willing to learn and change, and have a major concern that I can go along with—doing something for human beings. I am, frankly, sick of being surrounded by the academic attitude, which, in English, at least, amounts to the most sterile of all conditions of the mind and spirit, the devotion to "knowledge" (as if there were any) for its own sake—and most of that at second hand. ("Never mind Chaucer; what have the forty thousand scholars said about him?") (5/13/56)

But the continuity between educational institutions was not his only concern. There was another continuity that throughout his life he argued for and that he demonstrated throughout his fiction. He was passionate about what he considered to be the false separation between body and mind, a doctrine he felt was too often maintained, destructively, by the intellectual elitism so often found in universities. In a letter to his editor, he wrote,

> I submit, wearily, that, not only should no one be allowed
> to teach in a college who has not taught for a few years in a
> school, but that no one who has not played some form of com-
> petitive athletics along the way — and learned its usefulness
> in the reductions of ego, venom, and ambition — should be
> accepted either. So many places I have found the same thing
> — that the "intellectuals" most ferociously contemptuous of
> sports, of any life of the body ... as "brutal and evilly competi-
> tive" are the most brutally dogmatic with their students and
> competitive among their colleagues.... And how, intelligent,
> however withdrawn and fearful people, can go on drawing this
> medieval distinction between the body and the soul ... I don't
> know. (6/9/56)

He and Barbara took spring break to drive to the Bay Area to scout out where they might want to live. He had already, when he was there earlier, decided on the area of Mill Valley, north of San Francisco, across the Golden Gate Bridge. Accompanied by a professor from the college, Art Foff, who lived in Mill Valley, they looked at a number of houses and found one — but lost it because they weren't ready yet to move. Walter also took Barbara across the bridge to the city to see the college, which a few years earlier had moved from downtown to a new campus in the Sunset district, on the west side of the city near Lake Merced. All the buildings were relatively new, except that the offices for the Language Arts Division were still in World War II temporary buildings. But Clark had seen that before.

Clark's colleague at Montana, Walter Brown, recalls,

By and large people liked him here a great deal. They wanted
him to stay.... He was ... a damn good nose-on-nose teacher.
He was terribly interesting, curious, and he asked questions of
young people. They flocked around him pretty much. He was
very popular.... [And] he was a damn good administrator. We
wanted him as chairman of the department and to stay here.

On the other hand, Clark's son remembers that while his father
was usually very agreeable in public, he would often come home
and blow off steam about problems within the department. Walter
Brown was close enough to Clark to be aware of this side of him
also. He recalls that privately they would call him "the great stone
face." He and others who knew him well would tease him by call-
ing him "Van Tilbury ... [or] Tillsbury Clark—he didn't appreciate the joke though." He recalls also that Clark always had something to be indignant about. Because it was actually the corollary
of his general philosophy—the people around him were all a
bunch of boob humans, who were always making mistakes. And
he didn't like it.

One of his hopes for his new school was that it might provide
relief from the wrangling. As he told his editor,

The last and one of the ugliest of the pointless involvements
only confirms me in my hope that the bigger school and the
narrower and more isolated schedule it permits, will not only
give me more time for writing, but a kind of anonymity and
separation that will leave that time freer in mind and spirit
also. (6/9/56)

He wasn't getting much writing done, and he had gotten the idea
that he couldn't write if he wasn't in Nevada. In the fall of 1955,
he wrote to Ray B. West, editor of the *Western Review,* who was
teaching at San Francisco State at the time:

Montana as a school is doing very well. To Montana—or Missoula, specifically—as a climate and state of being, the Clarks don't seem to be adapting so well. Bred to the desert is used to the desert, I guess. Here, even when the sun is out, it doesn't seem to us to really shine, and from the end of September to the end of June, it is seldom out, and the days shorten up. I remember the Iowa City argument for that perpetual grayness—food for the creative state of mind, induces useful inversion, etc. But if one has the desert soul, there are limits to the usefulness of this inversion—a point where it seems to produce a collective misanthropy. (11/9/55)

Barring a return to his desert, which seemed impossible, the best remedy he could find would be to go somewhere to teach from which he could easily drive to Nevada.

Clark also felt that in Montana he was at a dead end in his teaching career—the university had one of the lowest pay scales in the country, and his chances of being promoted there without a Ph.D. seemed dim. By contrast, the opportunities at San Francisco State seemed to him golden. He wrote to Saxe Commins:

They are being very generous to me in many ways—grouping all my classes and consultation hours in three straight days, giving me two straight days at home, for my own writing, and waiving the academic degree requirement to put me on the scale as a full professor. Increasingly, I have become aware that the chief difficulty in writing, in my program heretofore, has been distractions and the sapping of energy in mostly the same time. If any teaching program can remedy this, the one S.F.S. is giving me should do it. If it doesn't go now, the fault will certainly be in me, not in my job. As it is chiefly, anyway, of course. But at least I will have a chance to quit battling to give my young writers an opportunity to use their imaginations and experience instead of just their memories and the library. And that should be a great saving of energy.

San Francisco State is bigger by some than my ideal college — nearly eleven thousand — but I am forced to confess, far as that seems to me from the ideal for an undergraduate, that the very size is what promises me my relative freedom. And of all cities San Francisco is the only one I love — that really excites me instead of depressing me — that has everything — beauty and freshness, crotchety originality, theatre, music, eating places, drinking places, waterfront and sea, terraced lights, fog and brilliant sun — and it is only a few hours over the Sierra hump to the beloved desert. Sea and desert! They have ever been my chief mentors and awakeners and awakeness. And many people there that I am fond of — some new, and many date back and back, even to my childhood. (5/13/56)

As he went on from Missoula to Mill Valley and began to teach at San Francisco State (1956–62), Clark's reputation continued to thrive even though he had no new publications to speak of. That reputation led him to a lot of what his son has called "literary side business," and as he has summarized that business, it included: "Talking at luncheons, writers' clubs, teacher's associations, universities, judging fiction contests, writing recommendations for grants and fellowships, and blurbs on advance copies of novels."

One of the letters he wrote to a publisher, in answer to a request for a blurb, was about the novel *Go in Beauty* by William Eastlake. The letter is revealing of Clark's attitude toward Native Americans, an attitude of support for their way of life that he shared with other western writers such as Wallace Stegner and A. B. Guthrie Jr.:

There is so much in the book with which I find myself wholly in sympathy that I wish I could praise without reservation. The theme, for instance, of the durable values of the Navajo way of life, deeply rooted in place, as compared with the shifting values or total lack of values of so much of the white man's life, and the strong implication that such values can have force for the white man, too, if he will only let them. . . . And the author's evident and often moving love of the stark grandeur of Indian country. And his true, but relatively rare, perception of the fact that Navajos are as various and individual as any other people, and often perfectly able to see the worth of their life as compared with that of the "outside world," not merely because they don't know the outside world. (7/27/56)

For the first part of the summer of 1956, Clark taught at the Montana Writers Conference, and before and after it he went to Mill Valley to look for a house to rent. The Clarks had been on the realtor's rental list for several months. In the meantime, Robert Caples had come back to Dayton, Nevada, to paint and wrote to Clark about having a reunion at Pyramid Lake. Clark replied,

> Still there is no Mill Valley house. So there may be a sojourn
> at mother's house for Barbara and Bobby while I go scouting
> again in the peninsula hills [which he was thinking of as an
> alternative to Mill Valley] and Mayflower charges storage and
> time dwindles.
>
> Nevertheless—we will not surrender until September. You
> may live another year, but I feel less and less likely to. I popped
> a ligament and after two days in the hospital and under the
> heavy hands of physio-therapists, have continued to float upon
> two kinds of pills all through a week of writer's conference. I
> am older than Methuselah. I tremble (bourbon) and peer at the
> sun (temp. 96) through filmy eyes (MSS) and hobble (massage)
> into the back yard to sweat out language and liquor in a steamy
> silence. All else aside, if I were to go to Pyramid now, I would
> never make it back. The idea is attractive. (7/23/56)

But on his next trip to Mill Valley in early August, he found a place right away, telling Saxe Commins that he

arrived at 10:30 A.M. and had the place by 11:00. It was a
big, old, homey frame house, of the kind we love, right
down in a sun-splashed glade among the redwoods, only
a couple of blocks from the shopping center of the village,
yet with entire woodland privacy.... Only one big question
remains for me—how damp it gets during the winter rains
—for our desert beings don't thrive too well in the too wet.
(8/7/56)

Despite the confusion of the move and the imminent start of
fall semester, Clark and Caples still were trying to work out a
meeting. Clark wrote to him,

> So—for about a week? (San Francisco State begins to press
> upon my conscience on the other end.) About the middle of
> next week? And I will have to bring work to keep my con-
> science doped. But as I recall—it seems another life—our
> former sojourns, a little work to play with daily—made the
> real purposes, the sun, food, drink, talk, star-gazing, all the
> more palatable. I shouldn't come at all, but we must do it.
> Pyramid, say the busy, human boys planning their next irri-
> gation project, will be dried up in another thirty years. It's
> been almost that since the last time. We can't risk it.
>
> Love to Rosemary—if she hasn't gone already. And see
> you in four or five days. We must get there before the Pyra-
> mid is out of water.

His trip to Nevada gave him not only the opportunity to see
Caples but also to pick up his wife and son at his mother's house.
After his return, he settled into a routine of teaching and commuting and promptly joined the Mill Valley Tennis Club. His work at
San Francisco State was more demanding than he had expected—
the creative writing program had two hundred students, and Clark
was immediately involved in reshaping the program. As a result,

he was not able to do much with his own writing, and he confessed to his editor that only now and then was he able "to get back to the six or seven thousandth version of the first chapter [presumably of "Way Station"]." Still, by overcoming his constant preoccupation with "technical considerations," he felt he was beginning to bring an increasing sense of life to his characters.

He went on to report that

> the teaching has been interesting in itself, as always. We've bought a Volkswagon convertible in which I commute — a change most beneficial to the pocket-book, as compared with the appetite of the previous Olds 88, but good in better ways too. Top down, I sidetrack from the direct line when time per-mits and look at the Pacific and the gulls and the ships going out and in, and listen to the surf. And we have explored far up the still quite wild north shore and among the hills — and have even been over the Sierra into the desert twice. All of it much more alive and close in this little, low-slung car with the top down. Not quite as real as walking, but look at the distances we make — and so much more alive than through the glass of the usual travelling hearses. And we are still playing tennis, of course — which helps. Bobby [son Robert] quite happy over his game — having, despite the big jump from Montana to Califor-nia tennis, made a number three singles berth and a letter in a victorious Mill Valley school team.
>
> Trickles of life beginning to move in many arteries, some of which I had even feared closed — mine, and Bobby's.
>
> Love to you all, Saxe —
>
> Walter (11/15/56)

Clark's colleagues in the creative writing program at San Fran-cisco were mostly from the Iowa Writers' Workshop — oddly enough, considering how unhappy Clark was at Iowa. One was Irving Halperin. He recalls,

Walter was the first one I know of in our English department
to do without a tie. That was kind of considered sort of unconventional back in the late fifties. But nobody questioned Walter, because he was Walter Clark. The administration was
very glad to have him. If it had been any of the rest of us, they
wouldn't have fired us, but there would have been some eye-
brows raised. He just wouldn't wear a tie—he was a westerner
or he saw himself as a westerner and that's it, take it or leave it
and we took it. That was one thing I noticed about Walter, and
the other thing was he was kind of a man's man. When we
went to parties, he could down a whiskey and a beer and whatever else and be perfectly sober and walk out of the door and
remember everything—and he really could. But he wasn't an
alcoholic, for God's sake, but he could hold his own. And the
other thing I noticed, the women in the department—the faculty members—they thought of him as a man's man ... they
were just aware of him as an unusual male, put it that way. He
was a damn good tennis player, I remember that. I played
against him and was beaten badly.... I remember that Walter
told me where to hike in the Sierras. And that was the Desola-
tion Wilderness. That was his favorite, and I did take him up
on it. And I did hike there, and I can see why he was so ecstatic
about it.

There was, Halperin recalls, a close threesome in the department—Walter with Ray West and Herbert Wilner, both from
Iowa. Clark was particularly close to Wilner, who had been a student of his at Iowa, and he was so impressed with him, he brought
him to San Francisco to help him develop the creative writing program. Giving Wilner particular status in Clark's eyes was the fact
that he was an athlete—he had been quarterback on the Brooklyn
College football team. Very close to Clark, he wrote a memoir of

his friend, "Walter Clark: Complicated Simplicity," which is one of the most perceptive commentaries on the man. In it Wilner recalls an image:

> I once saw Clark at a service station as I was driving by. He was standing at the side of the pump while his convertible Volkswagen was being filled. The attendant was nearby, there were cars around, and in the close distance the high redwoods of the San Francisco suburb in which Clark then lived must have broken the plane of the horizon he was looking toward. He was staring into the distance. He was wearing a tan raincoat, his hands in the pockets, and with the added inches of the cement platform of the gas pumps he appeared quite tall and somewhat lean. His face was unsmiling, but quite cheerful. He was quite alert, not at all daydreaming, and yet he seemed to be looking at something that someone standing at his shoulder would not have seen. As I drove on and he fell out of my sight—all this was a matter of seconds and he had not seen me—I knew I had taken an impression that would last. It has. That was fifteen years ago. In that crowded and ordinary spot Clark seemed to have been surrounded by space. It seemed both an ambience he gave off and one that came to him.

Wilner goes on to describe his relationship to Clark:

> My "conversations" with him often took the form of listening to his monologues, which were filled with anecdotes—what might more technically be called yarns. His voice was deep, resonating, and it impressed with how much more power it kept in reserve than it used.... He was a natural at stories, and they were sometimes, it seemed to me, full of natural stretchers.... I remember after-dinner times when these tales carried

us to one, two, and sometimes three o'clock in the morning. In the beginning of my knowing him, I often wondered what kept him at it. Whence came the need for it? Then I began to understand the storytelling—if it is not excessively subtle to think so—as the other side of the need for silence. The silence and storytelling derived from the same part of the recognizably unified temperament. He was, I decided, an essentially silent man.... But when people got together, especially friends, the necessary silences and solitudes had to be broken, or what did they get together for? ... I decided the storytelling for Clark was very much his way of making contribution to communion as well as community. In short, a ritual.

And yet there was almost always the impenetrable ultimate space.... [At a faculty party] a small circle of people crowd in on him, and he is sometimes listening to one or another of them, and sometimes telling one of his own stories. I see him from a distance across the room. He is eminently cheerful, very much with the party; and yet he is also for me rather prominently walled off by that air of space, so that he is simultaneously in touch and remote.

This quality of spatial enclosure had an effect on me in different and unaccountable ways. It gave him a sense of formidability mixed with shyness, of great dignity mixed with vulnerability.

On the basis of testimony from many colleagues and students, there is little doubt that Clark was a gifted and extremely effective teacher. And as several of his colleagues have pointed out, he gave so much time, effort, and thought to his teaching that, combined with his highly developed sense of duty, it would be easy to see why he wasn't able to get very far with his writing. Or as colleague Irving Halperin has quoted Clark, "It is difficult to serve two masters." And he told Halperin that he had "come to terms with a writing regimen which was limited to the summer vacations and the winter spring breaks."

At the start of his teaching career, Halperin, who was dissatisfied with his own performance, sought out Clark for advice. Clark told the beginning teacher not to be so hard on himself and to be patient—it would take time. Halperin asked him, "How do I reach students? How do I reach them so that they can experience the feeling of having learned something worthwhile?" Clark talked to him at some length and then later sent him a letter in which he tried to answer those questions:

> I don't believe there's any such thing as conversion, for either the teacher or student, in the slow, specific strengthening of the strengths and weakening of the weaknesses. I feel sure the best happens between teacher and student not by means of the direct attack, but only indirectly, by way of the "thing between," the poem, story, what-have-you. A mutual concentration coming as close to self-forgetfulness as possible. Only I'd call the thing between the attachment, the means by which teacher and student get to know each other, as they never would by a direct approach. I know more of my friend from watching him watch a bird flying than from looking into his eyes. I will know still more if we both watch the bird flying, and then take the same length of time to begin moving again when the bird has vanished. Which might not be too far from the rationale that understanding, both intellectual and emotional, can grow only gradually, by way of the little things, the particulars, and only by way of the thing between.
> (6/12/00)

Charles Brashear, novelist and editor, recalls his classes with Clark at San Francisco State:

We were a pack of graduate students at San Francisco State in the late 50's, early 60's, wolfing up Walter's classes. In analyzing a piece of fiction or in drawing our insights into the creative act, he was superb, and our admiration for him was little short of idolatry. Among ourselves, we called him "The Younger Brother of God."

He liked 5 x 7 or half-sheets of paper and usually came to class with several of them stuffed into a frayed textbook. He could get a discussion, an honest to God discussion, going in a group of 60 or more students. We often marveled at that, even then, when 60 was a common enrollment in the Fundamentals of Creative Writing and the Craft of Writing courses.... Reading all that written work must have been Gargantuan. I still have an essay I wrote for Walter in one of those classes. It's 27 pages long; he wrote a comment on it, 1500 words long, in his difficult left-handed scribble.

In class, he would call our attention to a particular section of a story and talk about it for a few minutes, drawing comparisons and corollaries to just about everything in creation; then he'd ask us to juxtapose that passage against some other passage and comment on what the author was up to in theme or technique. He often called on individuals by name. Typically, that student's answer was clarified, built on briefly, and directed to another student. Pretty soon, the first student found himself talking across the room with two or three others.

Not everyone could participate in that sort of discussion, but listening was often a heady experience. "They also learn, who only sit and listen," we told one another. Walter's rephrasing of our answers gave direction to our unorganized gropings and, usually, at the end of the period, he would spend five minutes drawing the discussion together. As we left, we felt brilliant—felt we had grappled with a story's essence and pinned it to the backsides of our foreheads.

Clark seldom talked at length to these classes, sometimes ten or fifteen minutes at the beginning of a period to get the discussion going. And unlike earlier in his teaching career, he did not tell stories out of his own experience or of the West. The one exception that Brashear remembers was the story of how *Ox-Bow* came to be published. According to the story as Clark told it some twenty years after the fact, in the late 1930s he was going through a series of periodic depressions. He had become very discouraged because he was not getting any interest in his work by publishers. He told the class that he had started burning manuscripts just to get rid of them—he was going to give up completely. Then, while he was in the middle of his burning, he got a letter from an agent who had read one of his manuscripts while at one agency and was going out to set up an agency of her own. She asked if he had anything that he thought might be publishable he could send to her. He stopped burning, started to read through the remaining manuscripts, and found two that he thought were not as bad as the others—the story "Hook" and the novel *Ox-Bow*. It was a piece of personal history he gave the class to help them banish the evil spirits of discouragement.

Brashear goes on to recall,

> We knew he wasn't writing much then, and we felt guilty. It had been almost ten years since his splurge of publishing. We saw that he was giving all his creative energies to teaching us, but it was so very good, and we were so very selfish. Our greed was greater than our guilt, so we devoured him, like vultures.

Brashear also remembers that in those days, Clark

> always wore a colored T-shirt [usually dark green or dark blue] and a floppy old corduroy sport coat. Years later, when I was on the Hopwood Committee at the University of Michigan, I suggested Walter would make a great Hopwood Lecturer. One

member of the committee snorted, "But do you think you can get him to put on a tie?" and that was the end of that suggestion.

During his last semester at San Francisco State, Brashear took his whole program with Clark: Advanced Craft of Fiction, two tutorials, and master's thesis. According to Brashear,

> When I had finished my thesis and got through the orals and everything was set, I was gone. I went around to his [Clark's] office just to say thank you and good-bye. I thought we would do a handshake and that would be it. But he closed up his office and said let's go for a little walk. So we went out to Holloway —a boulevard near there—and we sat down on a couple of concrete benches out there and chatted. He was asking what I was going to do next, and was talking about his tennis game and a little about Barbara—he was kind of worried about her. Just a real friendly, outgoing, sharing kind of person. I saw him one time after that. It was at the party that they always have for the graduating students at Herb Wilner's apartment in San Francisco.

Sometime during the middle of Brashear's last year, Clark suggested over a cup of coffee that he go on to a school that offered a doctorate, and so he applied, was accepted, and went on to the University of Denver, where he got his Ph.D. At Denver, he met Alan Swallow, an old friend of Clark's, who published Brashear's first book—two novellas from his M.A. thesis.

Clark's ex-creative writing students testify to his interest in imagery, symbolism, and myth—particularly myth. He liked the close examination of text, and sometimes he would come to class prepared to discuss a single passage for the entire period. One student remembers that there was a story by Flaubert, "A Simple Heart," that Clark loved and spent a lot of time on:

For him, it demonstrated something he wanted us to understand which was that deeply spiritual things, interior things in
a character could be developed entirely by exterior action.
[The story is about] a simple French girl who at the end has
this enormous spiritual revelation, and it is achieved entirely
by exterior handling, and in my recollection, we spent days
talking about that, but we also discussed Stephen Crane's
"The Open Boat."

Another student recalls that "one of the things that he liked so
much about [Hemingway's] 'A Clean, Well-Lighted Place' is that
nothing happens. But the meaning of that story is really quite
rich."

While Charles Brashear was a graduate student in the creative
writing program, John Christgau was an undergraduate taking
writing courses from Clark. One of his most distinct memories is
of Clark's handwriting, which

was probably his identifying signature at San Francisco
State — everybody talked about it who had him for any of
the numerous courses he taught. And it was a discussion
item because nobody could read it. It was really instrumental
in forming friendships in classes, some of which were huge. . . .
First course I had was Introduction to Creative Writing. It was
about one hundred and fifty students, and we had about three
or four weeks for our story to turn in. And when we got them
back, he kept three or four to discuss with the whole class.
Then when you got your story back, it would be folded length-
wise and then he would write in blue pencil that must have had
a point on it like a carpenter's pencil . . . a broad pencil tip so
that writing was flat and very small and almost completely
unreadable. So three or four students would kind of gather
outside in the corridor, in the hallway, and would have conferences trying to figure out what the hell he said. And if we

hadn't cared, if you did not know that buried in that inscrutable writing there was enormous technical wisdom about story writing, we would have let it go. But he was so thoughtful in his remarks and he took such time with each student and each story that it was really hard to understand that he could put that much time and effort into evaluating 100 to 150 stories, three or four times in a semester. To this day, I don't know, having taught English myself for thirty years, I don't know how he did it.

What brought Christgau into a special relationship with his professor was that he was first string on the Golden Gator basketball varsity. He recalls that

the first basketball game I played at State, the first home game in the gym, I was warming up before the game, at the layup lines, and I came back toward the bleachers and there he sits. He sort of twirled his fingers at me because by that time I met him in his office, and I was stunned to see him, and then the next time I go to see him all he wants to do is talk basketball. That relationship lasted for two years. I don't think he missed a single one of our games and all of the conversations when we discussed basketball were not personal, except once. I asked him what his basketball experience was and he told me, I think, that he had played semi-professional basketball—in upstate New York.

When Christgau went to have conferences with Clark about his writing, he hoped that he could get advice about his program but ended up, because Clark was such a fan, talking about basketball. "I always walked away," he remembers, "with very little understanding about what the hell I was doing right and wrong as a writer. But I had great knowledge about what I should be doing as a basketball player" (6/1/00).

One day, Christgau, who was a radio-TV minor, was presenting a noontime DJ program in front of the student union. He called
his program "The Music You Like ... Whether You Like It or
Not," and it included classic jazz performers like Benny Goodman,
Artie Shaw, and Eddie Condon. As Christgau was standing by his
turntable talking to his girlfriend,

> WVTC strolled by, spotted me, and asked me what the hell I
> was doing. I answered that I was a radio-TV minor, and I was
> trying to get experience. He listened to the music and my pat-
> ter for a second, gave me a very tiny smile, and told me some-
> thing like, "Stick to writing."

During the 1957–58 basketball season, the Gators went to Reno
to play Nevada on a Friday and Saturday night. Christgau recalls
that they had a player on their team by the name of Willy Brewer
"who was one of the best passing guards I have ever seen." He was
spectacular, but at the same time he was aggressive and provoca-
tive on the court. Opposition fans would get on him vociferously,
and he would taunt them in turn. On a Friday night, the San Francisco State team was in a nip-and-tuck game with the University
of Nevada, and the Nevada rooters were all sitting, wearing white
shirts, right behind the San Francisco bench in a rooting section.
They started to get on Willy at one point, and he went up to the
rooting section and spit a big gob on the floor right in front of all
those rooters. Christgau recalls,

> It damn near precipitated a riot. People came out of the stands
> and it was just horrible. Afterward, after I showered, I came
> out of the locker room, and I was standing around, and there
> was Walter Van Tilburg Clark. And guys were passing around
> the scorebook, and we made small talk for a minute or two. I
> don't even remember what about, other than, too bad you lost
> or something to that effect. But I remember his distinctly look-

ing at the scorebook and point[ing] to Willy Brewer ... and he said, "You will never win a championship with this guy on your team"—meaning that he was so eccentric and personal that he lacked the unselfishness to mold the team. Sure enough, he didn't play the next year, and we won the championship.

CHAPTER FIFTEEN

BACK TO NEVADA AND BECOMING ALF DOTEN

STARTING IN THE SUMMER OF 1957, the city of San Francisco prosecuted Lawrence Ferlinghetti on the charge of disseminating obscenity by publishing Allen Ginsberg's *Howl and Other Poems* in the City Lights Pocket Poets Series. It was a landmark case in civil rights law. J. (Jake) W. Ehrlich, with two other attorneys, handled the defense on behalf of the ACLU and called as one of his witnesses Walter Van Tilburg Clark. Clark joined several other professors from San Francisco State as well as Mark Schorer from the University of California, Berkeley, and the poet Kenneth Rexroth.

During the trial, Lawrence Speiser, for the defense, asked Clark what opinion he had formed about the literary merit of the publication. Clark replied,

> They seem to me, all of the poems in the volume, to be the work of a thoroughly honest poet, who is also a highly competent technician. I have no reason to question in my own mind

the feelings, Mr. Ginsberg's sincerity in anything that he has said or the seriousness of his purpose in saying it.

[Speiser:] In forming your opinion as to the literary merit of the publication, have you considered some of the phrases and words about which Mr. McIntosh [the deputy district attorney] questioned other witnesses prior to your taking the stand?

[Clark:] Yes, when I knew that I might appear and have to offer an opinion, I examined the poem not only in a general way, but specifically for the purpose of determining my reaction to what I believe might be expressions or passages in question. I found none anywhere in any of the poems that seemed to me irrelevant to Mr. Ginsberg's purpose, and it seemed to me also that there is even aesthetically a sound defense to be made for each use of what might be considered a questionable term in the way of the tone desired for the whole volume, particularly for the title poem, the tension, the sense of destruction, the sense — even if we wish that — of depravity that he wished to produce.

The deputy district attorney began his cross-examination by asking in a sarcastic tone: "What is your definition of literary merit, anyway?" His back up, Clark replied,

It's very hard to define. I don't know if this is getting outside of my purview, but I don't know exactly why we have to define literary merit in this particular case.

This answer prompted the judge, Clayton W. Horn, to admonish him:

Mr. Clark, we appreciate your coming here, but you're a witness, not to lecture the prosecution. We will have the question read. If you can't answer the question you may say so, but we're not interested in anything but your answer to the question.

After some further back-and-forth between the judge and Clark, Clark answered by stating that the final test of literary merit is the power to endure, which cannot be applied to a recent work. He went on to say,

> Aside from this test of durability, I think the test of literary merit must be, to my mind, first, the sincerity of the writer. I would be willing, I think, even to add the seriousness of purpose of the writer, if we do not by that leave out the fact that a writer can have a fundamental serious purpose and make a humorous approach to it.

After several others testified for the defense, the trial was concluded in October of 1957 when Judge Clayton Horn ruled that *Howl* did have redeeming social value. It was an amazing performance on Clark's part, since he did not particularly like the San Francisco beat poets and thought that Jack Kerouac, Ginsberg's mentor, was a real phony. He thought that, without much regard for others, Kerouac sought out titillating experiences for their own sake rather than having trying experiences from need. However, Ginsberg did express reactions to contemporary society that Clark could share. Also, as a member of the ACLU, Clark believed strongly in the artist's right to express himself—no matter who he was and what the mode of expression. It was for him a matter of principle rather than taste.

During this period, Clark became a grandfather when his daughter, Babs, had a daughter. Babs became secretary to the English Department, while her husband, Ross, delayed by service in the air force during the Korean War, finally was able to finish his degree at Nevada. Their son, Bobby, after the move from Montana, finished high school at Tamalpais Union High in Marin County and then, on an Alfred P. Sloan Fellowship, went to Stanford.

In March of 1957 Clark flew to New York to appear on the NBC

Walter Clark on the campus of San Francisco State, 1957,
in his teaching "uniform," blue T-shirt and corduroy jacket.
Courtesy of Robert M. Clark. Photo by Harry Redl

television program "The American Scene" in conjunction with the presentation of an animated version of "Hook." In the East, he stayed with Saxe and Dorothy Commins in Princeton, New Jersey, and wrote a thank-you letter to them at the end of the month. He told them that his stay with them was

> a human and believable substance out of what seems otherwise a kind of busy hallucination. Not that everybody wasn't very nice on the program—and more—going out of their way to make it easy for me—but we were all so locked into the inhuman compulsions of clocks, angles and lights that I suspect we all saw each other as parts of something that was not really any of us. . . .

Saxe—I feel dangerous stirrings. As if I might be going to write again. There are, of course, a couple of large piles of ms. to contradict me, but the stirrings persist. Out of our visit, I suspect, and Bennett's promise to send you out when I have a book. I will make it a ms. in which not a word needs changing—but it should take at least a week, sitting in the sun with beer, and looking at the hills, to be sure that is so.

Love to you all—Walter (3/30/57)

Both Saxe Commins and Bennett Cerf at Random House were very concerned about Clark's continuing inability to produce a finished manuscript. They both liked and respected him and were impressed by his talent, and Saxe, particularly, seemed almost as frustrated and hurt by his dry spell as Clark himself. It was difficult to understand—how Clark could do so much writing, as he would periodically report he had done, and yet produce so little. They had never encountered a writer with so persistent a block. And both had seen the roots of greatness in *The Ox-Bow Incident* and *The Track of the Cat* (neither Commins nor Cerf much liked *The City of Trembling Leaves* or "The Watchful Gods" [the novelette]—which may have been part of Clark's problem).

At one point, Cerf told Clark to send to him some of those ten-, twenty-, thirty-page "beginnings" to read. Cerf thought if he could endorse one or another of them with praise, he could get his friend going to finish a novel manuscript. The editors' concern was not just commercial, it was personal and touched with a deep sadness for a lost talent. These were the days when publishers were as much concerned with literary merit as financial gain. It was a gentleman's game—not always a bad thing.

In an almost desperate strategy to get the writing going, Clark returned to Nevada to spend two months alone in Virginia City during the summer of 1957. He drove to his mother's house in

Reno in early July and then went up to Virginia City to spread the word that he was looking for a place to stay. A week later he reported to his wife,

> Tuesday I drove up here and parked the v in the only hole remaining on C Street, right in front of the P.O., and before I could even get out, here comes Florence Edwards under full sail, convoyed by her dog and freighted with mail. She bore down upon me, arm and voice outstretched. "Mr. Clark," she informed the town, "you're just the man I've been looking for. I have just the place you want." And once I had sufficiently recovered from the attack and the publicity to understand what she was saying, it seemed a fact. So I have been extravagant and committed myself for July and August at seventy bucks a month. "The place" is the little red house down behind the priest's house.

He would fall in love with this little red house and return to it later in life. At this point it was somewhat empty, with most of the furniture in storage in the basement of the Silver Dollar. But Florence got him a bed and loaned him sheets and blankets. He had an easy chair and footstool, reading lamps, a stove and refrigerator, two tables that he could work on—all he would need. He told his wife,

> I have already eaten my first four meals here, and thrown away my first dozen pages—so everything is proceeding normally. And the house is far enough off C Street so very few tourists came down this far. Very quiet. Baring some housecleaning, I've spent nearly the whole of two days now scribbling away, but I plan to stop that unless something really gets moving— to work only until noon, then do some roaming around in the hills, getting sun at least, and perhaps playing tennis, if the arm will work and I can find a victim. (7/4/57)

He felt right at home. A lot of people asked him out to dinner, including Bob and Joyce Laxalt, his daughter, Babs, and her husband, Ross (they spent weekends and vacations in Virginia City), and Robert and Rosemary Caples, and he went on picnics with the Caples. He volunteered to act as swimming instructor for the children at a local swimming pool and worked out with Rosemary's son on the tennis courts in Carson City twice a week. He "socialized on the street" in the evenings and spent afternoons walking and driving around the area, walking down the Six-Mile and up around the surrounding mountains. While walking, he often carried a large rock to strengthen his tennis arm. One day he drove over to the flats below Silver City and then up into the hills west of the flats until the dirt road petered out. From there he walked to the quarry — a pit with no beach, just rocks and a sheer drop to the water. He wanted to go swimming, but there were tourists there, including a woman, and they wouldn't go away.

He acted as if his convertible vw was a jeep and drove down the canyon below Silver City, up the mountains north of Sun Mountain, and down on the Carson River in Brunswick Canyon. He followed the power-line road from the summit out to the Chalk Hills and planned to go to Pyramid Lake, to the Walker River, to Topaz Lake and Mono Lake. All his exposure to the country he loved helped him, as he said, to "break up the dismals." He occasionally overestimated the jeep qualities of his car. Up on the side of Sun Mountain above the top of the town, he thought he could simply drive down across vacant land rather than go back around. He got a few feet down the mountain and realized it was a foolhardy idea, but he couldn't go back. So he had to risk his neck by slowly and carefully wheeling down the slope until he could make it to a street. As he reported to his friends later, he had been trapped, and it really scared the hell out of him.

But the "dismals" were creeping up on him. After three weeks away from Mill Valley, he wrote to his wife,

In Virginia City, ca. 1957. From the left, top row: Joyce Harper, Marian Gladding, Barbara Clark, Walter Clark, Clint Andreasen, Gordon Lane. From the left, bottom row: Bill Harper, Tex Gladding, Nell Salmon, Ole Hart, Clint Salmon. Courtesy of Gordon Lane

I put in the daily shift—but finish nothing. However, I have variety, at least—which is some change. I now have beginnings to eight stories. Sometimes they even get mixed up. The mysticism-western desert variety—of an old man at Pyramid lake has moved over into an Indian medicine man in Hamilton (Nevada). (7/23/57)

But by a week later, he was so discouraged that he considered coming home earlier than he had planned, and Barbara became so alarmed by the tone of his letters that she suggested to him that maybe she should join him. He told her,

> Whatever you decide about coming to v.c., please make it all your choice. My aura of gloom, I'm afraid, is no smaller—and the writing no better. If you can stand me, you will not be interrupting anything. Actually, I have been thinking of giving one will-power try more to the piece I'm on now—and then, if I can't bull it through—a draft anyway, coming back down, by the middle of the month [August] or earlier. I'm squandering our substance to no good end, and I know it. If I were getting something done it would be different. Since I don't, I might better get back with my books and at least try to get into a state of mind that will work for the teaching.
>
> I'm sorry this sounds so grim—but I must write you something—and this is the fifth try. The habit is spreading into letters too. (8/1/57)

Ten days later, he told his wife that he wanted to stay another week so that he could see his brother, Dave, and his sister-in-law, Marge, who were coming up from Albuquerque and would be staying at his mother's in Reno. But again, he apologized for the tone of his last letter:

> I'm sorry I made that note so depressed. I should have skipped it until I came to the top again. Which I always do—so far.

The writing still is not going. It's a funny state; I don't quite understand it. There are plenty of ideas; sometimes I think only too many. I've even added half a dozen notes for novels and stories, new ones, to the notebook. And in the matter of particulars, images, good lines, a voice in the dialogue, etc., I think I'm writing as well as I ever did, perhaps, in many ways better. Indeed, if there is any trouble in that department it is over-fertility—so many ideas, images, insights that I can't keep them in order, or am likely to take an old Indian sitting under a piñon, a minor figure of a passing phase, and explore his soul to the length of twelve pages before I can quit. So he is all out of proportion and the story has not begun to move, and I have to throw him away. But that is the hitch; again and again the big thing, the life of the story itself doesn't happen. And my distaste for the fragments from which I cannot readily move on, keeps me throwing away. However—though I begin to feel time pinching badly, I still have hopes of getting one piece—it doesn't much matter now which one—going. I've written a couple of exploratory poems, quite long ones, all the way through. They weren't good, as poems, so I have had to throw them out too, but at least I did finish them, give them a shape and a completed statement of a sort, and experience a little of the old satisfaction of the completed. So I think I will stay on another week or two.

He continued to be invited out to dinners, parties, barbeques. He was so frequently entertained that he suspected there might have been a conspiracy, a plan to boost his morale. Among the events was a birthday party, on August 3, put on by his mother at Wally's Hot Springs. Included were his daughter and her husband, his sister, Miriam, and her husband, John Chism, and the Caples. He was also invited to a dinner with his close friends from the Nevada English Department—the Gorrells, Lairds, and Humes.

The conversation, Clark reported to his wife, was "very diplomatic": How did he like S.F. State? And Bob Gorrell, once again chair of the department, asked him, if in the next year or two things changed sufficiently at the school, whether he would be interested in coming back? He of course would be interested in at least considering an offer, but he doubted that Nevada could match the deal he was getting in San Francisco. (8/10/57)

As the end of his time in Virginia City approached, he made a last visit to Robert Caples in Dayton, signed out of the "teach the kids to swim program," and put the Silver Dollar linen in the laundry. He wrote his wife that he hadn't

> even tried to write a word in the last week, I have been partying so much it will take till school starts to dry out.... By the time I get home and get the whiskey out of my blood, I should be ready to make one more little try before school starts....
> I'm almost afraid to break up your peace and security again, but I'll be glad to get home. (8/20/57)

In early 1958 Clark mentioned in a letter that he would like a photo of his editor, and Saxe Commins sent one, inscribed. Clark wrote a letter of thanks and told him that he would get the photo framed and put it up on the mantel in the living room. It would be the only photograph in the house aside from those of his children on his wife's desk. He added,

> If it makes you feel uneasy and too conspicuous to be on the mantel (beside my very favorite painting, one by Robert Caples — the Lawrence Black of the *City* — showing a mountain in a lighted and moving cloud), I assure you that nothing is too conspicuous in that living room, even when there is sunlight outside, which hasn't happened more than two or three times in the last three months. We live down in a little clearing among towering redwoods. There is a huge "picture" window

on the north side, but almost no light sneaks in it, and when you look out through it, you meet, at close range, only the trunks of three big redwoods. The light within, save in the evening, when the cave is lit, is one great green and aqueous shadow. Even Robert's lighted cloud makes but a faint soft glow, and you, I fear, become a little more than a shadow yourself. There is someone there—that is all anybody else would know. But I know it is you—and like to look up from my foolish, unceasing reading and think: "How are you, Saxe, my beloved friend? The distance does not matter, I know you know." You are definitely a presence, and all to the good; no interference.... I keep writing, first paragraphs and first chapters, but they keep dying under the insidious pressure of the critical self at my elbow, and the more decent demands of student Mss and the lapses of time and breaks of continuity they bring about.

I have at least one long, perhaps very long, story and one novel, that burn to be out, and one of each that have fire enough to blow on, besides more than I will ever last to do that lie there like wood that might take fire, sure, but by other light than their own, piled behind one another back into the shadows, a dozen at least.... [I have not] moved from one to another of them in the last few years in hopes I may find the urge somewhere ... two long short stories, even novelettes, perhaps, called, just between you and me, *The Serpent in the Sky* and *Admission Day,* and two novels, *Way Station* and *The Man in the Hole.* They should come; everything is ready but the most important thing—the true, undiverted energy. (2/15/58)

Apparently, he still had hope for projects that he had been hammering on for years. And it may be that he thought the presence of

Saxe Commins. Courtesy of Robert M. Clark

the photo of Saxe Commins on his mantel, reminding him of the love and regard that Commins had for him, would inspire him to complete something. In the fact of the photo there would seem to have been an expectation.

In June of 1958 Walter and Barbara traveled east in order for him to receive an honorary doctorate from Colgate. He wrote to Saxe that it was really an excuse for him to visit Saxe and to introduce Barbara to him and to his wife, Dorothy. But it also gave Barbara the opportunity to see her sister in Essex and for Walter to visit with old friends in Cazenovia, which was near Colgate.

He returned to San Francisco State. It was a good job, but some things began to bother him. When colleague Art Foff published

a novel and sent a copy to Clark for a blurb, Walter could not en-
thusiastically endorse it but could only wish Foff well. Clark had
to stand by his critical standards, but he felt guilty — the Foffs had
been the ones who had welcomed him to the Bay Area, shown him
around, and repeatedly invited him to dinner during the summer
when he was there alone. Thus began a period of strained feelings
between the two — difficult, since they saw each other several times
a week.

Then, when Walter Brown visited from Montana, Clark complained of the dampness — Mill Valley could have coastal fogs or
low clouds for weeks at a time. And it was dark where he was living among the trees. The world seemed dim and drippy. Brown recalls Clark's telling him that he would

> get up and walk out toward the Volkswagen brushing the fog
> out of his hair and his eyes to get to the car. Brushing the fog
> off the windshield, climb into his car, had no idea what direc-
> tion of the road was . . . [and just said to himself] "Keep
> going." [Muttering to himself], "God damn miserable place."

His desert soul was suffering. When he was fed up with the damp
among the redwoods, he and Barbara moved to a sunnier location
at 552 Northern Avenue, south and a little west of Mill Valley.

But there are other snapshots from Mill Valley and environs and
from San Francisco State. Colleague Thurston Womach remembers that when he moved into his new house, built on a steep hillside with about fifty steps up to the front door, Clark volunteered
to help him move furniture, including a big, old refrigerator up
those steps. They sat in the shade afterwards, drinking a beer and
reflecting on how tough, even dangerous, the job had been.

> At the end of a party one night, Womach started playing
> records, and when one selection came on, Clark turned to Bar-

*552 Northern Avenue, Mill Valley, California, where the Clarks lived
from August 1958 to August 1960 (Walter and son, Robert, on steps).
Courtesy of Robert M. Clark*

bara and said, "We can do the Charleston to that" and they
did. Thinking back on that, Womach reflected, "He could be
a lot of fun."

Another colleague, Irving Halperin, remembers an incident at
school:

> A tough, ex-gang member, said to be quick with a knife, sub-
> mitted a very pornographic story to the college literary maga-
> zine. Clark, who was the advisory editor, turned it down. He
> said, "I am not rejecting it on the grounds it's obscene, or
> pornographic. I am objecting to it on the grounds that it isn't
> well written."

In 1960 he and Barbara traveled east once again, this time to stay
for the academic year. Although Clark would never have applied

for a fellowship, having to ask other people to write recommendations for him when it was offered to him, he did accept a resident grant from the Center for Advanced Studies at Wesleyan University. It was one more chance to work on his fiction without the demands of teaching. The grant was designed to subsidize creativity, and Wesleyan provided a place to live and a stipend for living expenses, only requiring that he give one or two public lectures.

During that fall of 1960 Clark's son, Robert, was flown to New York to attend a cocktail party and dinner for Alfred P. Sloan fellows. Afterwards, he took the train north to Middletown, Connecticut, in order to visit his parents. When he got to his parents' apartment, provided by the university, it was a bit of a shock. "It was all done in modern furniture, minimalist, and, in the living room, I remember, all black and white, so different from the seedy, comfy, academic, eclectic furnishings that were the Clarks at home."

Even though they had a bit of inherited income and some continuing royalties from *Ox-Bow*, the Clarks lived very modestly throughout these years. Rather than shopping at a furniture store or a men's or women's clothing store, they were far more likely to go to Montgomery Ward or Sears or a variety store.

During that fall Walter Clark, from Middletown, wrote to Robert Caples, who was in New Preston, also in Connecticut:

> I have wasted this rare autumn for us. We had planned trips to the Adirondacks and to Maine to look at the leaves, and have actually driven fifteen or twenty miles from Middletown a couple of times and bought vegetables at the roadside stands, while I used all the rest of the time on the San Francisco correspondence, and then, with no better results than heretofore, on the Virginia City book. The former, I trust, is now done with—long letters anyway. The latter, finally having become gray-

Walter, Barbara, and Robert Caples at Turtle Hill,
the restored barn turned into a studio in Connecticut, 1960, while
the Clarks were at Wesleyan. Courtesy of Robert M. Clark

faced, underweight, smoke-filled and red-eyed without getting
out of the first chapter—I abandoned formally. Some nice useful money down the drain, but since it seemed to be developing
into a choice between that and insanity, I decided to try for the
latter. As you know too, this kind of failure, throwing away,
wasting of time, seems more disastrous with each year that
passes. I have been having comparable woes with the stories
I want to work on, but at least they seem a better place to pour
the blood.

So now I am starting a few days of restoring, or at least

testing — the sanity. When the record in my brain stops playing, "It does seem to me, however, that since the new department, however constituted, is going to be unwieldy, etc." and,
"In the far-western part of what is now the U.S. between the
western most ramparts of the Great Rocky Mt. complex on the
east, and the high barrier of the Sierra Madres on the west, lies
a vast, desolate region — etc." (I have, in fact, several albums
of just such records, which keep playing themselves) and I can
sleep again, and am smoking less than three packs a day, I trust
that some of my own little men will begin to move in the imagination — at least enough to slump a little farther down in the
chair and turn the shot glass a quarter of an inch. (10/22/60)

"This new department" refers, of course, of Clark's task of setting
up the creative writing program at San Francisco State, a task that,
when he was there, because of continuing meetings and the never-
ending planning memorandums, had become onerous and too demanding of his time.

By the end of the fall semester at Wesleyan, his year off, his opportunity, seemed to be simply evaporating in frustration. He was
unable to get anywhere with his writing. He had even tried, exasperated with repeated failures at fiction, to return to the Landmark history (as he noted in the letter above), but that, too, failed
to jell. His conscience began to bother him, prompting him to offer
to teach a creative writing class at Wesleyan in the spring, and the
offer was accepted.

For the speeches he was required to give as part of his Wesleyan contract, he spoke twice about Julia Bulette in Virginia City.
And then on another occasion he stayed up all night rewriting his
story "Why Don't You Look Where You're Going?" to use in a
speech at the Faculty Club. In her diary that she began about this
time, Clark's wife noted that they had dinner a couple of times
with Robert Penn Warren, had dinner with John Cage, and met

Evan Hunter, author of *The Blackboard Jungle,* all of whom were also visiting fellows.

On the way back from Connecticut, the Clarks stopped in Reno and then spent a few days at the Clark cabin at Lake Tahoe. The cabin had originally been leased from the Forest Service and then been purchased by Clark's father. Clark's son has noted that the cabin "is pretty accurately described in *The City,* where it is the locale for the writing honeymoon of Tim and Mary — Dad seems to have taken some operational details from their winter in the Essex house and transposed them to the Clark Tahoe cabin."

After returning to the Bay Area in late June of 1961, the Clarks had the task of finding a house to rent and looked once again in Marin County. There was nothing in Mill Valley, so they went on to nearby Larkspur, where they found another large old house on an expansive lot. The advertisement said "no children and no pets," but Clark, writing to Caples, stated with mock seriousness that Bobby, twenty-one, was certainly no child and that "three small turtles in a bowl certainly did not constitute, in the implied defensive sense, pets."

The living room, Clark wrote, was large enough to be a boccie-ball court, with sixteen-foot ceilings and ten-foot-high windows. Their furniture would barely make a small island in the center of the room, but the landlady graciously left her furniture for their use. As they moved things around, they found that they

could make no arrangement which did not come out like a Victorian hotel lobby with a touch, perhaps of the reading room at the Harvard Club. So having done our best, we are thinking of completing the effect with brass cuspidors, such large and admirable bar-room paintings as Budweiser's well-known *Custer's Last Stand* and Cyrus Noble's dim and smoky *Faro Bank and Roulette,* and maybe even, finally a potted palm and an aspidistra or two.

He felt, sitting in the wing chair next to a gilded floor lamp (with an onyx base which lit up), that he should "tighten and straighten a non-existent necktie and to breathe a little heavily while looking around for the Wall Street Journal and the waiter with the sherry" (7/10/61).

Clark resumed his duties as professor at San Francisco State and director of the incipient creative writing program. However, in January of 1962 he was offered and accepted an eighteen-month contract, to begin the following summer, at the University of Nevada, Reno, to write a biography based on the journals of Alfred Doten. In the meantime, Professor Russell Elliot, of the university history department, was signed up to edit the journals. Doten, as Clark has described him, was a "California 49er and rancher, Nevada silver miner and long-time Comstock (Virginia City and neighboring Gold Hill) newspaper reporter and editor."

The seventy-nine volumes of journals and miscellaneous other materials had been acquired by the university with funding from the state legislature and the Fleischmann Foundation, and the plan was to have the biography published as part of the Nevada centennial, to be celebrated in 1964. The Doten materials, as described by Clark, included the

> almost unbelievable journals ... (missing not twenty days
> between March, 1849, when he left his native Plymouth, Mass,
> to sail around Cape Horn, to Nov. 1903, when he died in Car-
> son City, Nevada) and thousands of manuscripts, newspaper
> clippings, letters and pictures which he kept with them.

While still at San Francisco State, the Clarks went to a book party in the city for Mark Schorer, whose biography, *Sinclair Lewis: An American Life*, had just been published in October of 1961. Then, in the spring, they had Wright Morris to dinner in Larkspur, and they also hosted a "creative writing party," inviting not only San Francisco State professors, but the George Stewarts, Wallace

Stegners, Richard Scowcrofts, and Paul Horgans from "outside." A week later they had dinner at the Ray Wests, along with the Malcolm Cowleys. In June, in preparation for the move back to Reno, Clark spent several days going over and burning old manuscripts and notebooks.

Clark was delighted with the offer and the opportunity to move back to the University of Nevada, even though there was nothing very permanent about his new job. The Clarks moved into his brother Dave's old house on the edge of the city, overlooking the Truckee River. As Clark wrote to Caples, the house was on a hill, west of the city

> under Welsh's milk farm and in the midst of Manuel Costa's irrigation, cows, and dogs and Wm. Smith's too enterprising goats and sheep. [It has] a new bedroom downstairs in place of two garage spaces, everything surrounded by what the moving van left just yesterday and several small mountains of what the builders and previous incumbents left. (7/19/62)

Not only was there a lot of cleanup to do, but there was a large yard, about an acre, that had been neglected for years — a bedraggled lawn to be reseeded, the garden spaded, the tumbleweed to be hoed out, the fence repaired, olive trees pruned, a drainage ditch to be cleaned out, and the driveway graded. On top of that, as he wrote Caples,

> Alf Doten left 46 more journals [beyond what he had already read] and over 2000 newspaper clippings, letters, unpublished mss., which I must read forthwith. Nevertheless, all is beautiful, the view and the sky are huge, it is only five quiet minutes to the campus instead of forty rat-race minutes.

The house was known as Old Gallery, because when Walter and Dave were youngsters in Reno, there was a ranch on that lo-

Old Gallery in Reno, where the Clarks lived from 1961 to 1968.
Courtesy of Barbara Clark Salmon

cation by that name. It was a small house, as Dave and Marge had no children (this was before the era of trophy homes), and they had left it when Dave, a surgeon, moved his practice to Albuquerque. Constructed of wood painted a redwood color, it had a shed roof with the face pointing east. On that face was a large picture window that overlooked a deck and beyond that looked out across the Truckee Meadows and the town of Reno. There was one large room upstairs, with a kitchen on the south end and a living room and dining room on the north. On the north end of the room there was a stone fireplace, and Clark worked at a Formica-topped dining-room table that was set at right angles to the picture window. Downstairs, on the ground floor, was the bedroom and bath.

Clark was home again. He and Barbara had great joy in sitting out on the deck and having a drink at twilight, enjoying the changes of sunlight on the Virginia Mountains before the dreaded lights came on down below at Harold's Club and the Mapes Hotel (7/19/62).

In returning to Reno, Clark returned to an extended family. His mother had died the previous September while he was still in Larkspur, and his son was away in the air force. But in addition to his daughter, Babs, in nearby Sparks, in Reno he had a sister, Miriam, whom he was close to, and also had her family—her husband and four children. Her husband, John Chism, was on the Reno City Council from 1960 to 1972 and served his last term as mayor. Clark's other sister, Euphemia, was also in Reno. Her husband, Jim Santini, had died in 1955, leaving her with two sons, James David (J.D., as he was called) and Clark. J.D. grew up to serve four terms as a Nevada congressman from 1975 to 1983.

Family get-togethers—birthdays and holidays—were usually at the Chism home on West 2nd Street—a large old Victorian-style frame house. Occasionally, on hot summer afternoons, Walter had the Chisms and Santinis with all their children over for barbecues at Old Gallery up on the hill. Sometimes the gatherings included his daughter and son-in-law and occasionally his brother, Dave, and his wife, who would fly up in their private plane from Albuquerque. Barbecues seemed to have been Walter's favorite mode of entertaining, using the large brick barbecue out on the lawn that had been built by his brother. He had a unique method of outdoor cooking. He would put a steel plate down on the coals, let it get hot, and then sear his steaks (his favorite food) on both sides on the plate. He tended to cook his meat well—only easterners wanted their steaks rare. Cowboys remembered only too well where the meat came from.

In many ways it was an ideal situation, but the location did have its drawbacks. For one thing, whenever it rained hard (and Reno can have fierce thunderstorms), the downstairs flooded. No matter how they tried to fix the roof, sheets of water would run down the west wall. For another, the plumbing often plugged up and the pump used to bring water up into the garden often failed. Barbara was a gardener who loved planting and caring for flowers and vegetables. But, as another ongoing problem, the neighboring goats, cows, and calves, which had never been contained, came in periodically to devastate what she had just planted, striping the trees and shrubs, digging up the bulbs, and devouring the vegetables. The Clarks repaired the fence and added to it; they put in gates; and they even put in a cattle guard just beyond the gate. But nothing seemed to prevent the livestock from finding a way through, under, or over whatever barriers they put up, and they got little cooperation from the owners of the animals. It was a constant battle that occupied them all during their stay in the house.

Clark continued to give lectures on Western literature and creative writing and was able to make some extra money by reading manuscripts, acting as a judge for a Dell novel contest. He wrote prefaces to several Western books, including his own *The Ox-Bow Incident*. The Alf Doten project changed in its form and objectives several times over the next months and years. The most immediate change was that Clark decided to use all the journals, which covered 1849 to 1903, not just those relevant to Nevada. The first book was tentatively titled *The Pilgrim on the Mountain*, and when that was abandoned in favor of using all the materials, it was to be called *The Delegation from Spunkville*. Clark thought of it as "a kind of speculative autobiography-biography." In June of 1962 his wife wrote in her journal that her husband had become very discouraged about the Doten project—the sheer size of it alone was intimidating. In her entry for September 4, 1962, Barbara wrote: "Walter collected rest of Doten journals—these the original handscript. Miriam up with the mail in afternoon. Listened to election returns and Giant & Dodger baseball game."

When the Clarks listened to the radio or watched TV, they usually tuned in to sports, even to the local high-school games, and as time went on in the 1960s, they listened or watched more and more sports, sometimes every day or evening. But they had not yet been entirely captured by the emerging electronic age. They continued to play chess occasionally, but in their evening routine, they turned to cribbage or two-handed pinochle with drinks and snacks at cocktail hour. When members of the family came to dinner (daughter, Babs, and son-in-law, Ross, were frequent guests), they might spend the evening playing whist, dominoes, bridge, or pinochle. Outside, Walter put in horseshoe pits, made a dirt boccie-ball court, and continued, although not quite as frequently, to play tennis (usually with Bob Gorrell and son Bobby when he was home). Aside from actually attending football and basketball games — from high school, through college, to professional — the Clarks went out periodically to local little-theater productions. Barbara spent some of her afternoons at the Little Theatre working as a volunteer in the box office.

By the end of September 1962, Walter had finished a preliminary reading of all the Doten journals. He told Caples something that he would repeat over and over again during the years that followed as he struggled with the journals: "I have become Alf Doten." And in his letter to Caples he claimed that he "had to think twice in order not to head this note, 'Austin, Lauder County, Nevada, September 24, 1882 — or some such.'" As Doten, he had been

spending my evenings so steadily drinking and reading the newspaper in the lobby (which Clark also knew) of the Arlington House in Carson — the papers I couldn't afford to buy — that the confusion has become well-nigh inextricable. Last night, however, or today — it is uncertain which, for the body was not discovered until exactly now — two o'clock — I, Alfred, died alone, a bitter 74 years of age and probably drunk — in a stone rooming house called the Alta — near the Arlington — November 12, 1903. So returning the last of the

journals, and with them, I hope, Alf, not Walter, to the vault
[of the university library]. . . . [Then he would turn to] the hundreds of clippings and mss.—and the struggle to see the shape
of the book in it all. Alf has certainly done his part in the col-
laboration. (9/28/62)

Also, at the end of September 1962, he made the first of several
searches in graveyards for Alf Doten's grave.

Three months later, he wrote to Caples to report, along the
same lines, that

I am not living my own life. Even the quality and substance of
my dreams have gone 49er, and when I have too many boiler-
makers, I am seventy-two and tumble down a long flight of
stone stairs in Carson and have to be picked up by others
because my knees have failed and because, although I am only
5′ 7″ tall, my last pair of pants—ordered from a new mail-order
firm called Sears-Roebuck, and duly entered in my journal,
measurements, material, price, and all, have a 32″ inseam and
a 42″ waist. I check over all my letters before sealing the enve-
lopes to make sure they are not dated 1862 or signed Alf Doten.

These chicken scratches are the result . . . of the passing of
the last of the fine old cannon-sized, free-writing fountain
pens. Every time I try to set down a period with it, it makes
a blot the size of my thumb nail. So I have fallen to a ballpoint
also. I am not happy with it. I have to hold it vertically in order
to make a mark. It is so small that I keep losing it in my hand,
and I suffer increasingly from a conviction that it is cramping
my imagination and my language as well as my handwriting
—I know it is cramping my hand. After four hours of taking
notes on Alf, I walk around for another hour as if I were looking for a wall to make a bird's head shadow on [referring to his
chicken scratches], except that my bird cannot speak.

The Clarks had gone to two shops in Reno to view several of Caples's paintings. In his letter, Walter reacted to them by telling Robert that

> every one [is] splendid and all its own. They are alive, Robert, wonderfully alive. All those years in the back studio with the austere shapes have paid off with the new dimension. I do not yet understand how one paints time—hell, I do not even understand how one writes time, though I have been trying for it in forty ways, and it *should* be more readily accessible to my linear, progressing and discursive medium. So I know this has been a good year for you and that wishes for another are all but superfluous. I even take personal encouragement from your emergence. I was beginning to think that maybe there was just an age and a specific measure of bourbon which made it impossible to come out again with anything that was alive in any terms, let alone in the changed terms which are all that can justify troubling the work further. Also, I think I am learning something new about time, something that may even get into writing—though I cannot yet—if ever—it is like what your Irish castles won't tell—from poor Alf. There is something about being able in months, to live more than fifty years, day by day, in another era and another soul—well, never mind. You give me new hope. [Robert, with his wife, Rosemary, had just returned from a working trip to Ireland]. (12/24/62)

In September of 1962 Caples sent to Clark a copy of *Ishi in Two Worlds* by Theodora Kroeber. He was certain that his friend would become as fond of the book as he was. The book is about a Native American who was thought to be the last of his tribe, the Yahi, a subgroup of the Yana Indians of the upper Sacramento Valley in California. Not only was Ishi possibly the last of his tribe, but it was believed that he might have been the last Indian to have lived in a completely wild environment without any knowledge of white civilization, its culture or material goods.

Ishi had suddenly appeared out of the hills on August 29, 1911, outside a slaughterhouse near Oroville, California. He was at first put in the Butte County jail by a sheriff who wanted to protect him and didn't know what to do with someone with whom he couldn't communicate. Then, hearing of him, two University of California anthropologists, Alfred Kroeber and Thomas Talbot Waterman, took him into custody, befriended him, and sheltered him in the university anthropology museum, where he lived for most of the rest of his life. Ishi was free to return to his homelands, but he chose to stay at the museum, providing insights into his language and culture to the anthropologists and giving demonstrations of his arrow-making skill to visitors.

Although he was obviously unusually adaptable and although he was treated with kindness and respect, there was, nevertheless, something very sad about Ishi's story that both Clark and Caples found touching and symbolic. Aside from his giving up his life to live in strange circumstances among strangers, Ishi lived only five more years. He had no resistance to white man's diseases and died of what was thought to be tuberculosis.

CHAPTER SIXTEEN

TEACHING AND TELLING
STORIES IN RENO

IT WASN'T UNTIL FEBRUARY OF 1963 that Clark finished the
Ishi book and reported to Caples:

> I have now met Ishi full length—though passage by passage
> between longer passages of Alf Doten. A disturbed kind of
> reading—yet, a most telling juxtaposition. Alf's five years on
> the Mother (who did that occur to, I wonder?) Lode includes
> the vanishing of only too many Ishi's, though never, I am glad
> to say, at Alf's hands or with his approval. And yes—like you,
> I grew very fond of Ishi. Such courage, such good values walk-
> ing quietly contained in the midst of a city which contradicted
> them all, and such superior superstitions, as compared with
> those of his captor-survivors. Inevitable and more fitting as it
> was, however, I could not help but feel very sorry for an Ishi
> spending his last days in a museum. Yet that made another and,
> for me, very present bond between us, though again I had to
> bow to his superior realism and superstition. He would not stay

in the room with the remnants of the dead. I find that I too
would much rather not, but, like his professors, I am enlight-
ened, and am, therefore, spending a good deal of time in that
clean, well-lighted, windowless mausoleum in the U of N
library which is called the "Special Collections" room, where
Alf lies entombed in all his fragments in seven drawers. Ah,
well, perhaps I can bring him out of there, as Mrs. Kroeber
brought Ishi out. He is no Ishi, God knows. Quite the con-
trary....

Back to something much closer to Ishi—the photo of the
Pyramid which comes herewith. You can see whence it was
taken, from the top of the rise to the north, where the road goes
over that used to arrive at the old copper camp. Of course, the
camera was very old, over fifty years old, and the film is also
now obsolete, and neither Barbara nor I is much with a camera,
and we were facing into the sun. But I can't really feel that even
the total of those practical shortcomings explains what happened, and certainly there was no deliberate contrivance. And
we took two pictures from the same spot, and there was no
difference, save that in the other, the mourning, even pre-Ishi
face to the right of the sacred lozenge was a little more distinct,
a little farther down toward the horizon and distinctly pre-
pre-Ishi. In face, I think it was the great-grandfather of Jack-
rabbit. Ah, well, I'll enclose them both. The manifestation was
purposeful. I am convinced—though beyond my comprehen-
sion. All that I can feel was present: my new acquaintance with
Ishi, my growing sadness and dismay over Alf, and, of course
my intention in taking the picture, to send you the dark word
that the Pyramid is not longer an island....

Somehow it all ties together. Alf, Ishi, floods, sandstorms,
the supernatural snapshot. I can't say just how—but feel it
does. I feel it in my middle. Perhaps the face behind the Lozenge is really emerging, not receding. Perhaps it is *hungry* not

sad. When it has rained again, we will take the old camera out behind the Pyramid once more, and also listen. Nobody said anything last time, but it was very, very quiet—the kind of quiet you will remember, which before Charley Mapes took all the fish out of the lake—would make the jumping of a trout between the Pyramid and this little island echo like a gun-shot. Something wanted to say something, and the whole place was all ears. Perhaps next time.

Barbara also says love to you and Rosemary—and I add— may the day-star and the octagon hang about Turtle Hill too.

Walter (2/6/63)

Clark's letters to Robert Caples often ended with a benediction that involved a reference to a turtle, something like "I raised a glass to all at Turtle Hill" or "May the day-star and the octagon hang about Turtle Hill." The turtle would seem to have been something like an animal totem, a symbol that Clark and Caples shared and one that would seem to have had a mystical connection to Pyramid Lake, their experiences there together, and perhaps to Indian myth. Caples's ranch in Connecticut became Turtle Hill and Clark's residence in Nevada became Lizard Hall, the lizard having been another shared totem.

We might recall the turtles that are modeled out of clay at Pyramid in the early part of *The City of Trembling Leaves* when Tim meets Lawrence Black. There is also the turtle drawing in the same novel that is left on a wall of a motel where Lawrence had stayed briefly—this during the episode in which Tim is tracking Lawrence to Death Valley. Having renounced his wife's wealth and manner of living, Lawrence is seen as a sort of holy man who makes a pilgrimage into the barren wilderness to find some kind of spiritual redemption and renewal by stripping away all his non-essentials—and even beyond that, risking death when he deprives himself of water, food, and shelter. The sign of the turtle on the

motel would seem to have been "a kind of a blessing on the place
... or thank you, for it having been a good place"

Clark's son recalls that

> Robert Caples was always impressively oracular. He spoke
> very slowly, in a deep voice, with statements that often seemed
> to have been distilled down to the essence. Reminiscent of the
> Transcendentalists, sort of, and often about equally fuzzy as to
> any precise meaning, but also invariably struck me, as child
> and teenager, as deep, too deep for me to grasp.... Robert's
> correspondence was like that, too. He seldom, maybe never,
> wrote a regular letter. It was more often a little drawing with
> a saying, or sometimes just a card with one of those oracular
> sayings. Of his own creation, I think, always.

On one card sent by Caples, he wrote, "I incline to think that
the heart's image is the truer image, that those things 'heard with
the blood' are nearer to the center of things than those things
more carefully handsomed-up by the 'educated' eye." At one
point Clark wrote to Caples in response to a gift card: "Thank
you for the Lizard [drawing]. He too—and needless to say he is
full of implications which reach way back—shall have a place of
honor.... The color makes a great difference. He was very handsome" (1/11/66).

Clark also sometimes included drawings with letters and
manuscripts, something he did even before he met Caples, and it
was another thing that the two had in common—a way of making
a connection visually that might be deeper than that achieved ver-
bally. Robert Clark goes on to comment on the connection between the two men:

> I do think Robert's manner inspired, even coerced, a kind of
> emulation out of Dad. He would try to be oracularly profound
> also. But I would say, too, it was also part of the way they reas-

sured one another of the other's friendship and feeling of kin-
dredship, not quite "baby talk," not quite "jargon," but a way
of speaking they had created and used with each other. But not
entirely that, either. Dad had a certain, I don't know what to
call it, affectionate mock epic diction and way of phrasing that
he used with friends in writing—not talking, that I know of.

In addition to the university sponsorship of the biography of
Doten that Clark was supposed to write to celebrate the state centennial, the university also planned an exhibition of Caples's
paintings and drawings. The university museum officials knew
Caples well enough to know that he would resist. So they got
Clark's sister, Miriam Chism, to write him and try to talk him into
it. Then Clark wrote him to tell him that he had agreed to do an introduction to the exhibition catalog-portfolio. Typically, as someone who shunned publicity and fame and who would prefer they
not have the show at all, Caples had a list of works that he didn't
want to be shown. One such painting was entitled *Job at His Com-
forters*. But Clark told him,

> Resign yourself, Robert, whatever your feelings and reserva-
> tions, Job has been living a life of his own for thirty years now,
> and he belongs to the lookers. You can't tear up your own past
> ideas—it's been so much a part of others for so long. (4/8/63)

In the spring of 1963, Clark still intended to start on the biography even though it might be published too late for the centennial. However, by the spring of the following year, his earlier suspicion became a certainty—he just didn't seem to be able to write
a life of Doten. He had worked hard on the materials, religiously
going to the library and copying out entries from the journals by
hand into bound ledgers. And deeply immersing himself, living
Alf's life, as he would say so often. Clark's son, who from the beginning was skeptical of the biography as a fitting project for his

father, suggests that his father found that there simply wasn't enough breadth of material, enough sources beyond the journals and newspaper clippings. He did a compensatory piece for the Special Centennial Issue of the state highway magazine, *Nevada Highways and Parks,* entitled "Alf Doten in Como."

Robert Clark finds the article instructive

> in that editor switched to smaller print for the late pages to manage to fit the text in, suggesting to me that Dad had overshot the expected wordage considerably.... [It shows] how little auxiliary material besides the journals there was ... it is really just extrapolations from the journals with some summarizing and characterizing by Dad, and not something sustainable for a whole biography.

Some time after he decided he wouldn't be able to write a biography, he turned to the idea of doing a novel based on Doten's life as revealed in the journals. But that, too, he found impossible. He told his colleague at Nevada, Bob Gorrell, that he had written nine beginnings to such a novel but had to throw all of them away as unsatisfactory. Although Clark gave up first on a biography and then on writing a novel (though out of his stern sense of duty he went back to trying to start on a biography two years later), the university fortunately stepped in, in October of 1963, to offer him an extended contract with the title of Writer-in-Residence. He would edit the journals for publication (the historian had given up on the job), and in addition, starting in the fall of 1964, he would teach creative writing courses half time, every other semester. Robert Clark thinks that "in part he took on the editing to justify the payments from the university he had been getting, to pay off what he saw as a debt the failure to write the biography had created."

In January of 1963 Clark was talked into giving a speech to English teachers in Las Vegas. The conference topic was Mark

Twain, and so Clark decided to do it on Twain and Alf Doten in Virginia City. He spent all day and part of the night typing up his notes and left, in his car "Mr. Bangs" (a Corvair), with three colleagues, at 7:30 the next morning. The following month, he gave his talk in Virginia City to a general audience at a Mark Twain festival. He did not just give speeches to teachers and professors. In June of 1964 he gave the commencement address to the graduates of Virginia City High School—four boys and two girls.

As he began to teach again in the fall of 1964, he encountered as a graduate student Tom Massey, a student he had had as an undergraduate years earlier. Massey had been at Nevada on a football scholarship and took some English classes because he liked to read. Included in these were a short story class and creative writing classes from Clark. Massey went on to become a high-school football coach, but after several years he found that unsatisfactory. He returned to the university, largely due to Clark's earlier influence, to get his Ph.D. in English and found that his professor had returned. Massey remembers that when he was an undergraduate on the football team, Clark

would come to the games, and we would talk about the games. He was just the kind of guy that would get someone like me interested in literature. He was the one who made me change from a PE major to an English major.... In none of the classes I took did he read his own stuff. He read ours and talked about ours like they were very important literary documents.... He was really an all-out teacher. He served on my Ph.D. committee, and I did my dissertation on Faulkner. I would send in three or four chapters, and I would get it back, and most of the comments were his. The other guys read it, but Clark always wrote a lot of comments on it which I would follow, because he is one of the best critical literary minds I have ever seen....

The faculty there was so small, and our graduate school was so small, we could have parties and have all the English faculty in. That was usually in one place—I had probably the biggest house of any of the graduate students, so we had quite a few of the parties at my house. Clark never missed one. He would always talk and sit around and bullshit with everybody. . . . We would try to drink our way through a keg of beer.

Over these years, as Clark worked on the Doten materials in order to prepare for a biography and, then, to edit the journals, his belief that he would get back to his own writing gradually weakened. His failure even to get into a Doten novel confirmed his suspicion. He mentioned the possibility occasionally in his letters, but the dim hope in those brief mentions became rarer and rarer as time went on. At the end of 1963 in a letter to Caples, he contemplated his work on Doten and his own writing—one of the few times during these years that he reveals a really strong regret:

> I wonder, sometimes, though only vaguely now—how I
> got into this [the Doten project]. More often—and not at all
> vaguely—I wonder how I am going to get out of it—by what
> name, at what age—etc.—short of Mt. View, I mean. [Mt.
> View was the cemetery where he had already picked out places
> for himself and his wife in the family plot.] One thing, how-
> ever, something of my own—a short novel, two or three little
> stories—a murder, something, becomes increasingly neces-
> sary. I thirst for such; I hunger for such; I dream of such,
> though God knows the dreams are not children of anything
> I have ever written before—or Thank God—anything Alf
> ever wrote either. (12/31/63)

Nevertheless, consciously or unconsciously, the work on Doten that he so often mocks or complains of would seem to have given him "cover," or an excuse for not getting back to his creative work.

He had a ready answer when asked that dreaded question, "What have you being doing lately?" He planned to teach for two weeks at a writers' conference at the University of Utah and four at a writers' workshop at the University of Montana during the summer of 1964. And as already noted, in the fall he would begin his half-time assignment teaching creative writing at the University of Nevada. He felt that he was now home for good and that his future was " 'planned' farther ahead than it ever has been before—all but out to the old folks home or Sparks—whichever proves advisable when we—or I—get there" (12/31/63).

After the Clarks moved to Reno in 1962 and during the following years, they often went to Virginia City to see old friends and "do the street." Sometimes, as on New Year's Eve in 1963, they stayed overnight rather than to risk navigating the grade down to Reno after an evening of partying. Then, early in 1964, they completed arrangements to purchase the "little red house" down the hill in Virginia City, two blocks below the Catholic church. It was the house Walter had rented when living in Virginia City in 1957. They wouldn't move in right away, although they might use it on weekends occasionally.

He had more work on Doten to do that would keep him in Reno, and the house needed extensive repairs—a new roof, rejuvenated plumbing and heating, insulation, and painting inside and out. But the most drastic repairs involved a new foundation. Actually, like most older houses in Virginia City, the Clarks' house didn't have a real foundation but was set, unsecured, on a base of leveled stones. The town was honeycombed beneath the surface with old mine shafts and tunnels, and cave-ins caused many of the houses to sag, tip, or sink. (Back in 1957, when living there, Clark told his students that he came out of his house one morning to discover that the front yard "was gone.") So the house needed to be raised up, a foundation poured, and then a sheet of copper placed between the concrete and the wood framing to protect the wood from bugs and rot. One reason Clark wanted to teach at Utah and Montana that summer was to help pay for all the work that needed to be done. He wrote of his plans to Caples:

> Chiefly I think of it as a stake against our old age. You know— only a couple of blocks and mild incline up to the grocery store and the Sazarac and a nice, sunny back-porch to smoke our corn-cobs on. More literally, we hope to move up in three or four years and have it all fixed when we do. Now trying to buy the lot alongside, too—to make a bigger playground for Barbara and her green thumb. (2/19/64)

He wrote to Ray and Lou West that he was particularly excited about his first built-to-order study

> with day and night life for the left-handed, a desk with both sit down and stand up working sections for the relief of authors with fused vertebrae from youthful athletic mishaps, and a floor to ceiling bookcase from which the books are never to be removed again save one at a time for immediate purposes. Special bookcase over the desk too, for reference works, MSS etc. in use, and a built in typewriter place. Why I'll be so happy in a place like that I may even stop working [on] Barbara's kitchen table. (Going to put in a hot plate for a coffee pot beside the desk too.) Only question, will we ever be able to get all that into such a small room—really just a king-sized walk-in closet with one window. (8/18/65)

The man in Virginia City whom they hired to do the work on the little red house sometimes worked on it and sometimes, for weeks, did nothing. It was very frustrating for the Clarks, even though they had not planned on moving in right away. They would periodically go up to Virginia City to check on progress, and the contractor was nowhere to be found and no progress was visible. Eventually, they hired on a workman to help who really took the project over, but it took four years to get the house ready and cost them over thirty thousand dollars.

In the fall of 1964, Clark went to Oklahoma to give a talk on Doten at the annual meeting of the Western History Association. He and Barbara drove to Norman, stopping by to see Walter's brother, Dave, in Albuquerque on the way. In her diary Barbara noted the occasion of the meeting: "Walter had interview with newspaper man and worked on speech. Cocktail party at the Inn ... Walter on to 'banquet' and speech made to 12 or 1500 people in a rotunda—half the audience in back" (10/30/64).

However, this speech was an exception—as mentioned earlier, he began to turn down most invitations to lecture, except locally for colleagues and occasionally for friends elsewhere. Colleague Robert Harvey, who became chairman of the department at the end of the 1960s, remembers introducing Clark on one occasion. He was to lecture as part of a series of lectures for a general audience of several hundred people. The series included talks on the Nevada cowboy, the Nevada gambler, and the Nevada miner, and Clark took the cowboy.

Harvey recalls that the idea was

to meet at 7:30 P.M. and talk for forty minutes or so and then everybody would be edified and then could go down into the casinos for the rest of the evening. I don't know whether you know the stories about Walter once he got started. But he lectured for three hours. Nobody left. Nobody left and it is a crime that we did not tape that. ... I sat there and said to myself—not a note, good sentences, and every 15 minutes or so, he would pause, and if he had been Mark Twain, he would have puffed on his cigar and walked a couple steps each way, and then come back to start over again. And I began to wonder whether Walter knew where he was going because there was this, and then there was that, and then ... by God, when he got to the last 15 minutes, it all came together. It was a magnificent lecture, but it just went on and on and on.

[Robert Harvey continues] *The Track of the Cat* is set near Markleville at the south end of the Carson Valley. One of the things that he talked about in this lecture that I have retained was about a ranch that was up the other way, in the mountains.... It was out toward Beckworth, in the Sierras, that he talked about a cowboy who had a line cabin. This was an enormous ranch that was sort of a big square, like maybe three miles on each side, and so he would ride the fences and repair them in the winter. And he had a line cabin at the far corner, and the line cabin was in case of a Sierra snowfall, and he needed shelter. And so he [Clark] talks about what it was like for this cowboy, living alone, to ride that line and have to stay in that cabin. On one occasion, he was snowed in for a week or so, and he was living on shoe leather and coffee, and the coffee was in a big pot, yea high, and so on. He went on and on with his lecture and even the possibility of having a smoke or a boilermaker downstairs at the bar could not sway him from his course.

Bob Gorrell tells a similar story:

He was an excellent speaker, but he talked forever. I remember one time we were together at a teachers' meeting at Las Vegas, and I guess I was chairman or president of the thing and I got Walter down to speak to them, and we were speaking in a room in the university. It was a cold day, and the heat had gone off, and he had a large audience. And we started at 2 o'clock and the room was full of people in overcoats and galoshes and beating on their hands, and Walter started talking, and he was supposed to talk 40 minutes, and at an hour and a half, he was still going strong and nobody had left. He was mostly telling stories — he was a wonderful storyteller —

telling stories about the days of Nevada he remembered as a young man. At two hours I got up and stood in front of him and waved, time to sit down, and about 2 hours and fifteen minutes I wrote out our plane schedule on a piece of paper and stuck it front of him, and at 5 minutes more I grabbed his coat, and we made our airplane. He loved to tell stories.

All his life he was a collector of stories, and it is impossible to know where or from whom he heard them. Several of his favorites were about Mark Twain in Virginia City. One of his Nevada students recalled two of them:

> He told his version of how Sam Clemens came by the moniker Mark Twain [a version that contradicts the usual Mississippi River story of the call "Mark Twain!" as a plumb line that was used to measure the depth of the river]. Clemens never really did fit in with the rest of the crew on the *Territorial Enterprise,* most of whom had cut their journalistic teeth on the Mother Lode. He was a latecomer. Also, he had some personal peculiarities that got him the reputation of being an odd duck. One of them was his tight-fistedness. He was cheap—in an expansive era when "drinks for the house!" was a customary celebratory gesture. But young Sam would order one for himself, and if there was no way he could get out of buying for whomever he was with, he would put it on his running tab, tell the bartender to "Mark twain!" on the blackboard. Of course, when you got paid and paid off your tab, you were starting over with a clean slate. [But he hardly ever went for more than two at a time.] ...
>
> And I think it was Clark who told us another Twain anecdote.... I am sure I heard this one from Clark.... Twain was an inveterate practical joker, sometimes to an obnoxious degree. And he had a knack for making enemies—no wonder he was the target of some practical jokes himself. Once upon a

time, the Divide [a roadhouse] between Virginia City and
Gold Hill was built up. It has all long since burned down, of
course. One cold, dark, windy night, Twain and a companion
were walking back from the Divide. They had come to a dark,
open place, and a voice came out of the dark, "Freeze! This is
a stick-up! Put up your hands!" Twain raised his hands. Then
another voice, "Drop your trousers!" He reached down to
undo his belt and suspenders. Then the first voice again,
"I said keep those hands up!"

This went on, back and forth, for some time until he was
thoroughly frightened and confused. Then he was told to toss
his wallet out into the dark toward the voices. Then his watch.
Then his notebook. Then his pencils. Finally, he was told to
stay there and not move for a full half hour and someone would
stay behind to shoot him if he did move. Finally, after what
seemed like an appropriate interval, he looked around to his
companion, who was nowhere to be seen. Not too long after
that, on the morning he was leaving Virginia City for good,
a bundle was tossed through the window of the stagecoach.
His watch and wallet were intact. All written-on pages had
been torn out of his notebook, and his pencils were broken
in half.

Walter Clark loved to tell stories—told them constantly—but
what was sad was that he could not tell them on paper to his own
satisfaction. Perhaps this was because he could not connect the stories he loved to the abstract themes that had motivated him to write
in the first place.

Sometimes the stories he told were about his own writing, usually in response to a question from the audience. He was proud of
what he had written and seemed to enjoy talking about his work.
Bob Gorrell has said, "He was one of the best people I ever knew
at telling how he did the writing and going into background."

One of the stories that he often told about the background of his work would come in response to questions about the origins of the characters in *Ox-Bow*. He got the idea for Ma Greer years before he wrote the novel, while he was driving through Nevada. He got thirsty and stopped for a beer at one of those little, broken-down roadside bars that are still all around the state. The woman who was running the place was huge, and she was standing by watching while two older, rather pathetic men were trying to help her close down the place. Walter remembered that the men tugged and pulled, trying to load a cookstove into a wagon. Finally, the woman came, put her knee under the stove, and hoisted it up and into the cart. Her size and strength, particularly as compared to the men, came to the author as he was writing the novel. She was obviously as strong minded as she was physically strong. It was an example of how one should be aware of the slightest incident in one's life and of how fiction writing is produced out of the accumulation of such small impressions. One piece of advice Clark sometimes gave to very young students was to give up fiction for the time being and live, with awareness of people and surroundings, so that they would have something to write about.

After one more summer, in 1964, teaching at Utah and Montana, Clark avoided going out of state but continued to attend conferences during summers at his own university. He often contributed to those which involved teachers, since he continued to be concerned with the quality of high-school teaching and he wanted to strengthen the connection between such teachers and the university. During successive summers in 1965–67, he took part in Nevada's NDEA (National Departments of English Association) Institutes in English. At one such conference, one of the speakers, following the fashion at that time of linguistic analysis, read from Clark's short story "Hook" and then analyzed the metaphors and discussed syntactic relationships between them. Afterwards, someone in the audience asked Clark if, when he was writing the story, he thought about all those things. Clark said, "No, all I wanted to do, I just wanted to make that hawk fly."

While Clark was almost invariably kind, both in response to students in class and in his written comments on their fiction, Robert Harvey observed him one time when he jumped on a student. He had come in to Harvey's class as a guest lecturer, and a middle-aged woman, by her accent obviously from the South, asked, "Why is the bad guy in *Ox-Bow* made a Confederate officer?" Clark replied, "That's easily answered." He went on to talk about the Confederates and their defense of slavery. "Those sons-of-bitches lost the war, and they had nothing to do. They couldn't make any more trouble because they were occupied by the Union army which had freed the slaves." And, according to Harvey, Clark went on to attack the whole notion of flying the Confederate flag over the South Carolina capitol. Then, again according to Harvey, Clark went on for a fifteen-minute lecture on why it was that Ulysses S. Grant, but not Jefferson Davis, was given the freedom of the city of Dublin.

What Clark did not mention was that he had intended *Ox-Bow* to be a parody of the pulp Western, going back to its origins in *The Virginian*. Nevada, as well as most of the West, was on the Union side, and he did not like the fact that so many Western pulp novels had southerners, displaced "gentlemen," as their heroes rather than rough-hewn cowboys or miners.

Early in 1965 Robert Clark wrote to his father with a series of questions about his future. He would have the opportunity of getting an early discharge from the air force, since the service had decided it had too many junior officers — this was just before the Vietnam War began to crank up. After an early out, he thought he would go back to school, get an M.A. and perhaps a Ph.D. But he was primarily concerned about developing himself as a writer and supporting himself while writing. The thought occurred to him that he might do his writing while staying in the air force for his twenty years and then retire with his retirement pay as some security for the future. Perhaps at that point, if he hadn't been able to get published, he could start on a second career.

In response, Clark wrote a long letter (eight pages in small handwriting) in which he gave advice, commenting on literature and the writing life. (He liked to call his son during this period "Lieutenant," and the son has said that "I think ... my being in the service made him feel a bit more comfortable about his not managing to get into W.W. II.") Parts of that letter follow:

Dear Loot—
I've made two long, circuitous passes at replying to your letter, so circuitous that "I came back out where in at first I went," and you, I fear, could not even have found the out. You know: sentences as long as Faulkner's longest—excepting, of course, that one in "The Bear," a chapter long, where the heir apparent to the plantation looks through the record book in the expectation of discovering, which, at last he does, that he is not the only heir, and that the other one is not the same color—and more parenthetical than James's most parenthetical, (with actual parenthesis, each set enclosing five to ten lines put in at three or four places, in order to make it possible for the reader to find, with sufficient care and numerous readings, the fragments of the main clause, because they were all that were not enclosed) that sort of thing. In an effort to let you know how I felt about the numerous questions the unexpected time-squeeze has brought up for you, without seeming to be trying to make decisions for you that only you can make, it being your future at stake, and only you knowing how you really feel about the various elements involved.... I'm not trying to lay down the law, but only to make it possible for you to discover what I do feel. With that lengthy preface as an example of what I'm trying to avoid:

Twenty years, or even another short hitch, if that comes into the question, is too much of a life to give to any activity to which one is not naturally and wholly dedicated, and that goes double for any of the services, since their way of life and the kind of obligations they entail are so special. It is *not* true that one can start on another and entirely different career as easily at 45 as he can at 25. A lot more than time goes by the board in those years, and no amount of money, let alone the minimum security of retirement pay, can make up for it. Also it is *not* true, even if you come by enough time and privacy, that you can write in the service, not in the full sense, at least. That I can say on the authority of scores of ex-service students I've worked with whose terms of service and degrees of responsibility ran all the way from buck privates doing a draft hitch in the occupation troops, through marine sergeants and lieutenants in the Korean War, to a retired Major General and a retired Rear Admiral, both in their sixties. Most of them had plenty to say, but they hadn't been able to say it in the service. The obligations of a service man and the obligations of a writer are too constantly at odds — even down to the kind of language they should use. *Must* use. (Quoting the Rear Admiral, a worthy Virginian and a semantics scholar, whose occasional bits of profanity had the power to astonish, coming as they did in the midst of precise sentences and in the same delightfully soft half-drawl: "It's not, Dr. Clark, that I am idiot enough to believe that I can become a writer starting at this late date. It is merely that I have had a great many experiences which I would like to be able to relate effectively, personal experiences, not official ones, and that, try as I will, everything I write continues to come out sounding like a fucking Admiralty report.") So I'd say, as far as the Air Force is concerned, *take the earliest out Uncle will give you,* and don't

let any of the typical twinges of the Puritanical family conscience deter you just because you feel you've been marking
time since you were moved west. You didn't ask for *in,* you've
put in your stint, and well, and it isn't your fault they weren't
ready for what you were supposed to do.

(Too long again, but at least I believe the sentences are
comprehensible.)

As for the writing—if I read you correctly that is where
you *do* feel an urge—it shouldn't even enter the question
except insofar as further study is concerned—writing is not
an occupation, it is a way of life, in a sense not altogether
unlike that of a religious devotion. It is a means of discerning
what one feels and believes about life even more importantly
than it is a means of expressing the feelings and beliefs discovered. Only a fool, or a propagandist in the worst sense, someone who hasn't the faintest understanding of what the personal
discipline of writing really means, especially if he is, like yourself, still serving his apprenticeship, his novitiate, feels that he
has a unique and burning message for the world. And it is
beyond question that when he has delivered himself of that
message, which he will do quickly and painlessly, like an elephant dropping a mouse, (apologies to Mohammed—not
Ali—and others) it will prove to be something which has
already been said at least 10,000 times, and which probably
was not greatly worth the saying the last 9,999 of those times,
though it was almost certainly said better than he has said it
all the way. There are no new truths, in that simple sense. It
is only that old truths take on new strength and meaning in
changed circumstances when they have been rediscovered
honestly and expensively out of one's own experience, that
experience including, very much including, the sustained
and repeated effort to write one's way into that truth as clearly,

vitally and un-dogmatically as possible—the effort, in short, to *prove* that truth, not preach it, by compelling the reader to experience it himself. Which the boy with the burning message never does. Witness the scores of little self-appointed savior, beatnik "poets" and "fiction" writers in S.F. and elsewhere, from the author of "On the Road"—I forget his name—and so does everybody else, on down, if it *is* down. (That book, and by exactly that title, was written twice before that particular fool was born—once by Jack London about the turn of the century, and again in the 1920s by a guy whose name also slips me at the moment—and this time it shouldn't. But anyway— he was an honest to God circus roustabout, hobo train-rider, itinerant, tank-town prize fighter. And both books were much better than this last bit of fakery, not only because both authors really were "on the road," out of need, and really had some tough and important experiences they didn't deliberately cook up, but also because neither of them thought he was a savior, or that getting drunk, taking dope and gang-banging little also drunk, doped wenches was the way to truth and salvation, and because both of them tried to tell what had happened to them just as vividly and clearly as they could—while the third on the roader, almost without fail from start to finish, alternated lengthy, exhausting, incoherent essays on the profundity of his perceptions, with renditions of his calculated "experiences" which invariably read very much like this: "In Denver there were seven of us in this place in a basement, and for three days it was big, very big, we flew, and then the three of us who had come there from this place in the basement in Chicago rode the rods to Kansas City and found this place in a basement where there were already four other who knew, really knew, two of them floozies, and we had it big, really big, we flew.") Well, finally—out of those parentheses. Anyway—you know the stuff I mean. All the little self-appointed Christs and Buddhas mouthing shoddy paraphrases of their ancient masters with an air of ultimate discovery (while it may be well for them, since they make it abundantly clear that they have never bothered to really read, to try to understand, Christ or Buddha) and really revealing only their own pretentiousness, ignorance, blind egotism, bottomless self-pity and, of course, the fact that they have never taken the trouble to learn to write, or even to read, because no one who "really knows" is going to extinguish the God-given brilliance of his unique illumination by "making like a professor."

So — I'm as bad as ever — to get to the point — don't worry because you don't feel that you have anything important to say. Of course you don't — and the fact that you *know* you don't, makes it certain that you *will* have if you keep trying to write as well as you can about *particular actualities* that interest and move you, trying to discover as you write, why they interest and move you, until you find, in the true Jamesian sense, your "subject" — or rather, for that is what really happens — until your subject finds you. Which does not mean that all between now and then must go in the waste-basket. Plenty of good and publishable writing — writing well-worth the reading, comes of any honest quest. Read Faulkner's first air-force and army stories, and even his *Sartoris,* when he is beginning to find his home. They can't sit for a minute beside *The Sound and the Fury,* or *Light in August,* or *The Bear.* But they are a damn sight better in many ways, than anything O'Hara has written, just for instance, and even O'Hara is better than Sartre. Or compare the first stories of Henry James, or even *The American* and *Daisy Miller* with the masterpiece *The Ambassadors,* or Conrad's *Victory* with *The Heart of Darkness.* They don't look good in the comparison. They are very much still in the quest stage. But they are alive, very much alive, and they deserve to be. But who now reads Upton Sinclair—the crown prince of American message bearers? Or H.G. Wells (except his scientific horror stories) the king of English message bearers? Yet both of them were at least *real* message bearers, not Sartres, let alone third "on the roaders." They don't stink of self-pity. In fact they keep themselves out of it altogether. And they took the pains to look objectively at the world, and to make themselves enormously well informed on their subjects, and they *had* subjects, and their opinions rose logically, inevitably, out of their experience and knowledge and were expressed with unmistakable sincerity and clarity. The one fatal thing they didn't take the pains to do was to learn to write fiction, to make their truths arise unstated out of rendered experience.

So—I labor the point again, in spite of my vow to be brief because I guess that the writing is centrally important to you—to the statement: *Don't dream of giving the writing an all-out fling for a year at S.F. State or anywhere else, and deciding, on the strength of that year, whether you'll keep on writing or not.* It's not the kind of thing that one can make decisions about. And even if you never published, whether out of too modest misgivings, belated learning and perfectionism like your old man's, or whatever, the writing would be well worth keeping up the rest of your life, because of what you keep discovering by way of it about yourself and about everything else. I regret having *had* to throw away so much of what I have written, but I don't regret having written it. I learned much while I wrote even the worst of it.

So, finally—to the practical point, what after the air-force? What to do *while* you write? I'd say get your degrees and teach. It's not only that I'm sure you'd make an excellent teacher, and so do well at something more worth doing than most, and enjoy yourself and continue to learn meanwhile. It's also that teaching, on every level from the kindergarten to grad school, furnishes the most decent and variously interesting human environment the world affords, the best chance to think and to try to tell the truth, and, of no small consequence to one who wants to write—by long odds the most and most usable vacations.

Clark goes on to suggest to his son that he apply to Nevada to start on an M.A. in English, live at home, and work on his writing on the side with him:

> And despite initial embarrassments out of mutual concern, I can at least promise you honest readings and opinions if you feel you can take them from the old man. I have an incurable *habit* of doing that. And there'd be no trouble at all about making conference appointments.

He adds that there would be "no board and room, no heat and light, no liquor bill to pay, and my minimum tuition fees" plus the possibility of a graduate instructorship, and

> If you can stand having Alf Doten around all the time (I'm getting pretty tired of him myself, though he's coming along much better now) it seems to me a pretty workable and unpressing proposition, and one susceptible of many variations and improvisations.
>
> And besides [he tells his son] your mother heartily approves of the idea.

He ended his letter by describing his little dog's activities:

> Dogette is very well, and kills more voles and pocket gophers than all the hawks, falcons (we've had one, a beauty) and owls

(we've had them too, three of them, big brutes with flat, white, heart-shaped faces) and cats about here, and eats them all too. She sends her love, as we do too.

Dad

P.S. Long as I tried not to make it; hopeless. But at least my reactions and suggestions. (2/14/65)

CHAPTER SEVENTEEN

THE DOTEN JOURNALS
AND DECLINING HEALTH

WALTER CLARK HAD A RELATIVELY productive year in 1964, writing and publishing several pieces of nonfiction, including the article "Alf Doten in Como," a foreword to a new collection of Bret Harte's stories, an introduction to a new edition of A. B. Guthrie Jr.'s *The Big Sky,* and a foreword to a catalog for a retrospective exhibition of Robert Cole Caples's paintings and drawings. In addition Clark contributed to a written symposium on the Western novel, appearing along with Frederick Manfred, Frank Waters, Vardis Fisher, Harvey Fergusson, Forrester Blake, Paul Horgan, and Michael Straight. The contributions were in the form of questions—the same ones asked of all the contributors—and answers by each author. Clark's answers to the first two questions are revealing of his literary stance:

1. Are you conscious of being a western writer, and how does this affect your writing?

Yes, I am conscious of being a western writer, in the sense that, since the American west is the world I know best and care most about, it is also the world from which most of my stories have emerged. I can't see, however that this means anything in terms of my purposes, or those of anyone trying to write well about the west (certainly it shouldn't, anyhow) that it wouldn't to a writer from any other region. No story is without a world. Every world has its individual characteristics which furnish certain problems for the writer. But the effort of any writer must always be to make the actualities of his world say something of more than local and passing validity.

2. What are the characteristics of the American West, especially the chief motivating force on fiction?

The only important difference between the west and any other American region — if we are talking country — seems to me to be still what it has always been, that it is a vast land with relatively small population, so that other aspects of nature than man must count for more than they usually do elsewhere. Nature, we might say, must become actor, not backdrop.

But by the next year, 1965, Clark had gotten to the point where he not only had trouble writing his fiction — indeed, he would seem to have just about given up trying — but writing other things as well. Successive entries in Barbara's diary during November and December of 1965 suggest the depth of his frustration:

11/11/65 Walter working on piece for *Rotarian*—What the West Means to Me.

12/2/65 Walter still working on article for *Rotarian*.

12/8/65 Walter depressed about writing, so suggested trip to Pyramid [Lake]. Were too late to take a picture of all the water coming in from river [to send to Caples].

12/12/65 Finished Christmas cards. Walter very depressed about article for *Rotarian*. Snow on ground in morning.

12/14/65 W. still working on article.

Apparently he gave up—the article was never published.

Because no new Clark fiction had been published for years, his fame began to fade; however, it must be said that *Ox-Bow* was still alive in paperback and his stories were still being included in anthologies, especially the "big four"—"Hook," "The Wind and the Snow of Winter," "The Indian Well," and "The Portable Phonograph." Nevertheless, invitations to write reviews, prefaces, and articles were now coming less often to him. And what jobs he did take on usually caused him to struggle. In 1967 he accepted a *New York Times* invitation to write a review, which he worked on day and night for three weeks and finally had to send off airmail special delivery in order to meet his deadline. In June of 1968 he struggled with and finally wrote an introduction (to *Lady in Boomtown*) but had to give up in September, in frustration, on another introduction to a book by a friend. Thus it was that his writing life seemed to fade away, just as his own life began to fade away. But Alf Doten was with him until the end.

In almost every extant letter from these years, Clark notes his ongoing work on the Doten journals. His editor, Saxe Commins, died in 1958, but Clark continued to write to his widow, Dorothy. In 1966 he wrote to her,

> It was good to hear from you and decidedly good to know that you've been able to keep working on the lullabies [Mrs. Commins had published a book of lullabies]. We look forward to seeing them, and who knows, they may even be the melodies, if they have pleased babies long and in many places, that will even tempt me into getting out my violin again after some twenty years of silence, so that I can hear them too.

(Some time when Barbara and the dog are out shopping, so I can imagine how the melodies should sound without inflicting my actual rendition on anyone else.)....

Life doesn't change much with us. We sit on our green hill, surrounded by pastures full of cows, horses, sheep and goats (the latter, with their invincible outwitting skill in gates and fences, keep us stirred up just enough as defenders of our trees and flowers and Barbara's little vegetable garden) much the greater part of the time, while I get on slowly with the seemingly endless task of editing the journals of one Alfred Doten, native of Plymouth, Mass., descendent of Mayflower compact signers, California 49er and rancher and longtime boom day newspaper man in Nevada—the job which brought me back up here. Even now, when I've been at him for four years, I can't really believe how much of him there is. It's like the figures astronomers use. They may represent an actuality, but they simply are not really comprehensible to anyone endowed with no more than his native abacus of ten fingers and ten toes. There are 79 journals, containing daily entries from March 1849 into November 1903, some two and a half or three million words, and something like twice as much in accompanying MSS, papers, news clippings, etc. But my progress begins to be visible. I'll finish the main task, cutting the journals themselves, some time this winter. I think then I'm going on half time, get back to some writing of my own in the mornings and trudge along with Alf during the afternoons and evenings ... (Alf was quite exciting for a while—he was everything and into everything in those wild gold rush and silver boom days —miner, horse breaker, line rider, musician, store keeper, rancher, teamster, correspondent reporter, editor, story writer, politician, sailor, fisherman, hunter, vigilante—the works— but I know him so well now that he's become a bit of a chore.) (9/9/66)

Clark's chore was to select from the material that which should be included in a printed version and occasionally to summarize or explain in order to make the narrative coherent. He ended up cutting the journals to a little over half of the original — an amazing job, considering that the final product was three very large printed volumes of close to 750 pages each (containing the journals plus an appendix of 107 pages and an incredible index of 95 pages).

While the chore may have eventually become onerous, Clark still saw the record as doing a "unique and really important" thing, as he declared in an informal progress report to the University of Nevada Press. That is, he explained,

> it presents in graphic and often moving detail the tragic course
> of single representative life through the violent transforma-
> tions enforced by the predatory and essentially amoral life of
> the California Gold Rush and the Nevada Silver Rush. I know
> of no other account of the kind, or fiction either, for that mat-
> ter, which even begins to do this as fully and memorably as
> Alf's journals. He becomes a kind of epitome of the individual
> course through the times, the rarely touched decline as well as
> the rise, and that in the person of a man of considerably greater
> initial integrity, and considerably more intelligence, literacy,
> general awareness, courage and human worth and loyalty than
> the average.

It is important to offer some sense of the journals themselves, since work on the journals took up the last decade of Clark's life. Most of the passages are brief, some are lengthy, and some are graphic; others are routine, even banal, sometimes rather vague. The lack of specificity was apparently caused by Doten's worry that his journals might be stolen, and, in the case of controversy, what he had written might be held against him and put him in danger. In his preface to the published journals, Clark's son has noted that Doten "had to keep the diaries in shanties, saddlebags, boarding houses with muslin partitions, and crowded newspaper offices, and he never went back over material to put in what had been risky at the time." He even used a letter-substitution code in a few passages to hide his affair with a married woman.

The excerpts from early journals that follow report on everyday happenings in the California gold-rush scene and then go on to describe a very dramatic and violent series of events. After sailing around the horn from Plymouth, Massachusetts, and landing in San Francisco, Doten made his way to Stockton, California, and then up to the Woods Creek area "diggings." In January of 1850, he recorded the following entries:

> JAN. 1 New Year's Day — Rainy — morning George Bradford & myself went down to the Woodsville camp for pork, beef and other provisions — After we got down it rained so hard that we couldn't get back again so we staid all night — evening had a fine time at the store below; music, dancing &c —

> JAN. 3 Clear — worked both cradles [a placer-mining tool that rocked back and forth to separate out the gold from the gravel] all day & got about 2 oz — A Mexican dug a large piece of gold weighing just 22 pounds & 9 ounces, and smaller one which weighed 3 pounds & 9 ounces, and a smaller one which weighed three pounds — He got them out of an old hole in the creek, just below the Sonorian camp....

At this point, Clark inserts an editorial note in brackets explaining why some entries have been omitted:

> JAN. 4 through 31 [Short entries, almost entirely routine — Much rain & snow, work in the diggings, trips to Woods Creek camp for supplies, cards & music in the evenings — Of interest:]

> JAN. 10 ... E Rogers, E Morton, Gifford & Everson have all got the scurvy —

JAN 12 Shaw's ... Evening we went to the Sonorian tent below & got 10 pounds of fresh beef for 50 cents per pound—

JAN 14 ... Evening played cards to see who should have the first three days cooking to do & and it fell to me—Heavy snow storm during the night—

JAN 20 ... The President & Swinbourne went down to Woodsville; they stopped at the Sonorian camp & sent us up a piece of sheet iron for sieves—12 pounds for 3 dollars a pound, 36 dollars ...

"The President" refers to the elected head of the Pilgrim Mining Company. Typically for this time and place the miners had joined together to form a company—just a group of men—which shared both expenses and returns from whatever gold they were able to mine together. The journal continues:

JAN. 23 Snowed all day—snow from 6 to 8 inches deep on level ...

FEB. 1 Weighed our gold—had 3½ pounds—A large number of frenchmen have been passing and repassing here the last 2 or 3 days, loaded with tools, cradles, baggage, provisions &c. They have been driven from the Mormon Gulch—They were very numerous there and infringed considerable on the rights of the Yankees, and as they were the strongest party they were pretty saucy, defying the power of the Alcalde &c—At length the Alcalde [another company] went to some neighboring diggins & procured an armed force of some 100 men who marched up and the French were given but 5 minutes to leave in, otherwise their tools tents & all would be sold at auction—

As Clark explains in a headnote to the section, books 3 to 12, Doten leaves the goldfields in July of 1851, trying other jobs such as storekeeping and freight hauling. He goes back in November of that year but avoids the members of his old company and finds various partners to work at placer mining. Clark notes that "his small-town eastern values erode, as he necessarily gets involved in the frequent trouble with other races." As noted in regard to the infringement by the "Frenchmen," conflicts between ethnic and racial groups were common. Working at Rich Gulch in Calaveras County, California, in December of 1851, Doten becomes involved in an incident involving a group of Mexican miners.

As Doten tells it, a group of his acquaintances went to a saloon set up in a tent. They made their way toward the bar, but some Mexicans who were talking together stood in the way. One of the Americans, Alex McDonald, asked them to step aside if they weren't going to drink, but the nearest Mexican replied, "No sabe." So Alex gently moved him aside, whereupon the Mexican and his partner left the tent, coming back a few moments later armed with swords and pistols.

What followed, as Doten writes, was that one of the Mexicans

attacked Chinn and the other one Alex with their swords. Alex tried fend the sword off with his hands, as he was entirely unarmed, and in so doing got an awful gash on his left arm, near the wrist. He said to Chinn "shoot him Jake" as Chinn had a revolver, but Chinn was hot pressed by the other one, who backed him right through the side of the tent before he could get his pistol out. He then followed him up, striking him, till he nearly backed him into the chapparal, when Chinn fired at him a second time and wounded him on the hip and he fell and at the same moment another pistol was fired and Alex fell just outside of the tent door, saying, "Oh God!!! I'm shot!! I'm shot!!!" The Mexican who was cutting at Alex followed him up till he got out of the door, when he fell backwards over a log and just as he was about to run him through the body, Mr.

Dixon took him by the shoulders from behind and threw him backwards. Just as he regained his feet he was shot by someone from behind, when he again fell. All of this occupied a very short space of time, when the lights were put out and all was darkness—It seems that Old Uncle Jimmy was just outside of the door, and just as Alex fell the Mexican came at him and purely because he was a white man he commenced cutting at him. Uncle Jimmy held up his hands to fend off and he got three of his fingers cut off from his left hand and a gash on his right wrist. He then received a cut on the left side of his head which felled him senseless. After he fell the Mexican cut him again so that he had two cuts on the left side of his head some six inches in length—The Mexicans then fled. When Alex fell and the lights were put out, Mr Chinn and James Flynn ran down and alarmed our village.

Doten tries to raise a party to go after the Mexicans, "arguing the case and talking on the subject some time, and daring two men of them to go with me, I managed to get some half a dozen to go with me." They search in several camps for the Mexicans and then learn that Alex has died. They finally find the two men they are looking for and put them under guard at the local store. Alex's partner arrives on horseback, dismounts, pulls out his gun, and rushes toward the store to kill the prisoners. Doten and others, however, stand between the partner and the door of the store, preventing him from entering. Eventually, a jury of six of the miners is convened, find the Mexicans guilty of murder, and they are hanged. In his headnotes, Clark, with some justification, calls this a "lynching," although Doten claimed that the most violent of the two "was a desperate villain and a noted highway robber and murderer in México."

Doten goes on from California to spend the rest of his years on the Comstock in Nevada, where he has little success as a miner and turns to journalism. He does achieve some prominence as owner of the *Gold Hill Evening News* and, at least in his own mind, as a mining speculator. But as the Comstock begins to fail he loses the whole thing through further speculation, and his social drinking turns into "grim, unhappy alcoholism, wherein his honesty fails him too." He is alienated from his family and his journalistic connections and, according to Clark,

> winds up a bitter, touchy, backward-looking, pan-handling, lonely old bar-fly, town drunk and figure of fun in Carson [City], occupied chiefly with dreams which would mend all ... following closely the similar and often even more disastrous ends of other old men of his generation. It [Doten's story] is so perfectly the whole, inevitable rise and fall, that even in form, within the journals themselves, it practically assumes the structure of classical tragedy. Even with violent, elemental accompaniments.

If not tragedy, Doten's life and fate were certainly sad—a decline in fortune, in social standing, and, most of all, in character. Clark saw him as an archetype of the easterner who comes to the West to seek his fortune, coming out of a constrained environment, both physically and socially, to one that is wide open. The story was the story of the westward movement that started with the gold rush and continues to this day. What happens to a man when almost all constraints are taken away? How deeply rooted in us is our civilization? Doten's story was to a large extent for Clark *the* story of the West—man dropped into the center of nature, having to cope not only with raw, untamed nature but with his own nature. But it was the story not just of the Dotens, the unlucky prospectors and unsuccessful speculators, but of the successful ones as well, the Stanfords, Mackays, and Huntingtons. They gained their wealth by dubious means in a permissive environment, though they were able to die with the respectability that Doten had so badly wanted but lost.

In January of 1966 Clark's work on the Doten journals was suspended while he took time to write an article on the teaching of creative writing for the university magazine. As he wrote Caples,

"Oh, sure," I said, off hand, when the editor asked me. (I always say "Oh, sure." The last time I said it was when I was asked to talk about *Language in the Arts,* for a semantics conference at San Francisco. That one cost me six weeks of despairing labor and three weeks of painful revision for a printing. I am nearly 58 years of age. I must learn to think better about time. I act as if I were still eighteen, when there is no end.) Thinking: I could cook up 5000 words on any one of fifty angles for that. After all, I've been teaching it under that name for fifteen years and under various disguises for thirty, which, of course, was just the trouble. How do you write a short article, about everything in your life? So, after nearly a month, I am still throwing it away. And whatever I get done at last will be a sad, small portion.

Clark goes on to report to Caples that

a man by the name of David Myers, who does very good documentary and educational films and a couple of my erstwhile poet colleagues from SFS [San Francisco State], talked me into being the talking presence for a film on Robinson Jeffers (the poems will [be] read in his own voice from library and Congress recordings) which they are hoping will help to revive his poetry. I couldn't very well say no, though I've been very uncomfortable, sort of half phony feeling in several TV appearances about writers and writing and teaching. I feel at least as strongly as they do that his poetry should be revived, and they were giving their time to the project, and making the trip here to do it, too. So I said, "Oh, sure." (1/11/66)

Clark's son, whom they called "Bobby," was home in Reno from his time at San Francisco State, taking the year to try to write some stories that in his words "could at least stand up to the public exposure of Kay Boyle's creative writing seminar at San Francisco State." He never managed to write the stories, and he never returned to San Francisco State. In her diary for February 13, 1966, Barbara notes, "Bobby working on a story downstairs, Walter editing upstairs." The diary also notes that in June Walter finished editing the last Doten journal (a preliminary editing), in July her husband taught once again for the institute for English teachers, and on July 28, "Walter up until 4:00 AM doing papers." And again in August, "W doing papers all day and on into the evening so did not see the Unidentified Flying Object on TV. Went to bed to read" (8/2/66). Clark then started to take his lunch to Special Collections at the library, presumably working on further editing. At the beginning of December he was quoted in the newspaper on his objections to a death sentence for a black rapist.

At the end of 1966, in a Christmas letter, he congratulated Caples on the manuscript of "The Potter," telling him it was a "beautiful job" and that he would send the manuscript on to his agent, Phyllis Jackson. Although she had many connections and would do her best, Clark was afraid that "such a book with drawings and all, is ... an expensive and hazardous undertaking these days." He suggested that as a last resort, Caples might think about a private publication. "We must get 'The Potter' out."

He concluded by talking about his own situation:

> I'm going to start trying to recount some myself before
> very long. Must, for I am so much the walking dust of Alf
> Doten now that I fear even high breezes will dispel me. I have
> now completed the cutting piecing of 74½ of his 79 journals.
> When I get through the 79 I'm going to start *really* doing him

in the half time I've nominally been on for more than two years, and start trying to do something of my own in the mornings. (12/25/66)

On the evening of April 19, 1967, Clark gave a reading and discussion of "The Indian Well." Clark's nephew, David Chism, remembers the occasion:

> This would be the Art Festival ... at the University of Nevada, and it is the only time that I remember that he ever allowed [himself] to do anything very public. And he said, "Well, I will come and read one of my stories." It was very well done. It was at the Engineering Auditorium which held maybe 600 people total and 800 people showed up.... And so his contribution to this art festival was to have ... to explain what his thoughts were in one of his short stories and at the end of about 15 minutes discussing what brought him around. He just opened up the book and read it. And he had this wonderful baritone, booming voice that ... I always think of Charles Laughton, who made a living off just speaking, that speaking voice.
>
> When he did this little talk ... the first thing [he said] he thought about was the interaction ... the sort of graphic thing of the mule and the mountain lion getting into a scrap and him saving it, but he said he didn't know what to do with the well. What was drawn to this well? And then he had things like a '49 Fort Station Wagon full of drunken Indians coming up to this well. That was one thought. He worked around and finally it ended up being this prospector, this old, old man and this animal and that rapport. So he used the well as a center of thought, and thought about various possibilities....
>
> [His stories] always seem to center around the animal having equal status ... even being more noble when you get to the

hawk, with the blood. I think his whole concept was to sort
of glorify the simple existence of man, again which gets back
to being animal. He was very observant—the lizard doing
pushups on a rock, the shadows of the trees coming through
and loving it and watching that and thinking that that was as
important as anything. If you analyze some of the things he has
written and I love, I really do, like *The Watchful Gods,* the little
collection of short stories that he did. They are, as somebody
pointed out, sort of painting pictures with words more than
telling a story.

Although Clark's nephew remembers only this one public occasion at the art festival, Clark did similar readings and discussions
on several occasions over the next year and a half. Usually he read
"The Indian Well" or "The Wind and the Snow of Winter," as
when he read the latter story in October for the Friends of the Library. That summer of 1967 he taught at the institute again, and
once again his wife notes that he was up all night reading papers
and writing his lengthy comments. Early in 1967 Robert Caples
had a serious operation and had recovered nicely. Clark wrote him,

> Now I know you've not only escaped Charon's ferry, but
> really turned Phoenix. I'm considering asking Fred Anderson
> [Clark's doctor] if he'll remove part of me, preferably whatever
> part most resembles Alf Doten's counterpart, excepting only
> his incredible alcoholic tolerance. (1/30/67)

But at the end of the year, the Clarks got word that Caples had
been in the hospital in Athens for five weeks. At about the same
time Clark had the first signs of serious illness himself, with pains
in his back and leg, the cause of which his doctors had difficulty di-
agnosing. He wrote to Caples:

> A bit fuzzy headed remote and off in all directions, today,
> though not far in any. In part due to Christmas dinner and

*Thanksgiving in Old Gallery, 1967. Front row, Robert Clark,
Barbara, and Walter. Daughter, Barbara, is just behind Walter.
Courtesy of Robert M. Clark*

cheer with all the tribe at Bab's [his daughter's] house last
night, both items fully indulged in and the effects thereof
doubled after three weeks of an austerity program with pills
established for me by the docs — which I now more or less
resume — and must, shudder-shudder, submit to in every
particular after the holidays. (Nothing specific or serious.
Just nothing quite the way it ought to be either. Sort of a
one-horse shay conclusion remotely threatened). . . .

In short, I am suddenly getting very old in both the flesh
and the head [he was 58]. I would rather fry a couple of steaks
(one for you) behind the Pyramid, if there is a bit of winter
sun (all fried foods forbidden) or sit up an Austin bar with
cigarettes and beers (tobacco and alcohol also tabu), but then
so is *spinach* of all things, so I don't know. (12/26/67)

In January of 1968 Clark agreed to contribute to a documentary on Robinson Jeffers produced by National Educational TV. In March he reported that the little red house should be ready for them to move in the coming summer and that his son would take over Old Gallery while he finished his Ph.D. But as he also reported to Caples,

> My lunch still consists of one small tin of water packed tuna
> and one half tin saltless tomatoes. If austerity still demanded
> in your case, come summer, easy to support you. But hope
> for beer and vin ordinaire. Buttermilk is no help to conversa-
> tion. (3/17/68)

In April Clark read and commented on "The Wind and the Snow of Winter" for a Library Association dinner. A friend sang "The Sweet Promised Land of Nevada," the poem near the end of *The City of Trembling Leaves* put to music, which was often sung by Clark after two or three boilermakers and sometimes sung together with his friends at picnics and get-togethers. (When interviewed for this book, Clark's colleagues at Nevada Bob Gorrell and Bob Storey were both able to recite this rather long poem from memory.)

At the beginning of June 1968, Clark began to work on his last publication, an introduction to *Lady in Boomtown: Miners and Manners on the Nevada Frontier*. The book was a memoir by Mrs. Hugh Brown of her life in Tonopah, a boomtown in the middle of the Nevada desert. Tonopah was established after a gold strike in 1900 (the area also went on to mine silver, and, in the same region, Ely mined copper), and Mrs. Brown moved there in 1904, when she was a bride of nineteen, married to a San Francisco lawyer whose firm had decided to open an office in the mining town. She left a refined and genteel atmosphere to enter the rough-and-ready environment of miners, speculators, opportunistic businessmen, and all the hangers-on attracted by the promise of sudden wealth. In the beginning, her story is one of shock and adjustment, but it goes on to recount in vivid detail the day-to-day occurrences among the miners and their families in one of the richest of twentieth-century mining towns. Although she might be termed an "amateur," the book is well written — vivid and engaging.

For someone who had spent years reading and editing the day-to-day journals of an easterner thrust into a similar environment in Virginia City, writing the introduction to Mrs. Brown's reminiscences would seem a job made to order. But Clark struggled with this one as he had with every other writing assignment during this period. The final product is a bit odd in some ways. He spends some time comparing the northern mining area, including Virginia City, with the southern area, including Tonopah. In doing so he reveals an extensive knowledge of Nevada history and spends more time on that than on talking about the actual contents of the book, its virtues, and its author. His argument seems to be that Virginia City has been more famous than Tonopah, and justifiably so, although the latter deserves more recognition than it has gotten and this book is likely to help provide that. Clark asks, "How can Tonopah or Goldfield compete" [with Virginia City]? He answers, "The fact is, given half a chance, they can: known, they reveal their own picturesque color." In a strange way, however, his essay is almost more a paean to the place he loved, Virginia City, than an introduction to someone else's book.

On August 12, 1968, the moving van came to Old Gallery, on the hill at the edge of Reno, to take the Clark furniture and belongings to the little red house in Virginia City. With new cabinets, appliances, and shelving for Clark's study and a new paint job inside and out, it was, after several years of work and many delays, ready for occupancy. It was a dream fulfilled. David Chism remembers the house as a "little jewel." The stairway going up inside was unbelievable … [it] went up about ten feet to the second floor, and I swear to God it was maybe five feet [in span] so … it might as well have been a ladder, but it actually had a railing, and you went up, and he had a little study up there.

However, a few weeks after moving in, Clark was hit with more severe pain than he had had before. It was so bad that he realized it was a serious problem, and on September 4, he pulled out of teaching for that fall semester. His doctor prescribed sulfa pills, suspecting some kind of internal infection. Two weeks later, his doctor, puzzled, decided on an exploratory operation. Clark went into surgery at 8:30 A.M. on September 17 and didn't get out until 2:30 that afternoon. Shortly thereafter he was notified that the lab reported prostate cancer, and he went in for a second operation on September 21.

The final authority whom Clark consulted on his health was his brother, David, with whom he had a very loving, trusting relationship. Yet they held diametrically opposed political views— David was an ultraconservative, while in many ways Walter was an ultraliberal. In her diary, Barbara notes several occasions when David was visiting from Albuquerque that he and Walter would stay up until 2:00 A.M. disputing various political topics. Walter's nephew has said,

> I think they lived apart from each other almost because they
> were diametrically opposed. I don't understand, you know, my
> Uncle David, who always thought the world was going to hell
> in a hand basket, but the world treated him very well. He lived
> as a very respected doctor.

He would send John Birch Society literature to all his relatives. When a health decision had to be made by the family, David, perhaps because he was a surgeon, tended to recommend surgery.

While Walter was still in the hospital, Barbara was helping to

*Walter Clark with Dogette in front of the
"little red house," 1968. Courtesy of Robert M. Clark*

prepare for her son's marriage. And a couple of weeks after Walter came home on the 24th, one of the Clarks' dogs, Jocko, who had been adopted a couple of years earlier, got hit and killed by a car. The Clarks didn't know for a week, because his collar had been torn off in the impact and his body tossed up against the fence outside the school. There were no fences around the Clark home in Virginia City, and the following spring their other dog, Dogette, was also hit by a car although not killed. Their new location presented other dangers. The winters in the mountains were much colder, and there was a lot more snow. During the winter of early 1969, Walter slipped on the ice, spraining his wrist, and Barbara slipped and sprained an ankle. And Walter had to make his way through the snow on a plowed but icy, narrow highway in order to get to the library to work on the Doten papers. Much of the highway, with no shoulder, had a sheer drop off one side with a long fall to disaster.

Barbara Clark in side yard of Stewart Street house in Virginia City
with Dogette and Jocko. Courtesy of Barbara Clark Salmon

Nevertheless, he and Barbara had a busy social life and were pleased to be in Virginia City. Frequent notes in Barbara's diary refer to evenings, two or three times a week, when they might have their son and his wife, their daughter and her husband, or their daughter's in-laws (the Salmons, who had owned the grocery store in Virginia City) to dinner or they might go up to the Sharon House. They also dined with friends such as the Laxalts, the Gorrells, and, occasionally, ex-students or other writers who were passing through for the evening. Evenings, with discussion and drinks, often lasted until two, three, or even four in the morning. On one occasion at a faculty party in Reno, Barbara notes that it wasn't a very good party—everyone left by 2:30 A.M.

In June of 1969 Walter was awarded an honorary doctorate by the University of Nevada, and in August he wrote Robert Caples to report on Virginia City and his own activities, beginning his letter by playfully taking on the identity of Alf Doten. Then he assumed the voice of a tourist confronting Alf, who was now the "hundred year-old man":

So now I have come to the "old age, ribald, coarse and bloody." I will speak my mind. I will never not speak my mind, or anybody else's if I choose. I will sit in the sun on the C Street benches with Speed Hessey (who has become the town's new Charley Addis [Virginia City's old town drunk], though a bit more physical. Swamps out and shovels snow instead of carrying the saloon mail) and spit in the gutter and stare back at the staring tourists and have even considered getting a camera to take pictures back at them, but that's really too much trouble. And I wouldn't want the pictures anyway. It's only "us natives" anybody wants to show to the relatives.

Now this old man, stripped to the waist and watering his lawn, was really a great deal more agreeable than his expression would lead you to believe. Turned out he just didn't like being photographed. Something like that. But once he got over that first grumpiness, he was really quite agreeable. And he knew simply everything about Virginia City, past and present. Told us the best places to go if we wanted to see the real thing. Abe Kendall's *The Way It Was* museum for the mining part; the Comstock Bonanza Mine for an underground tour; the Yellow Jacket's new shaft for the most impressive foundations; the restored Savage Mining office among the mansions; the Sharon House for the best dinners and photographs of the old city, and so on. Only on one thing, either he's forgotten what it's really like (he's much too old to be drinking now himself. Said he came here in the fall of 1864) or he was having a little private joke at our expense. He said the best place for night drinking was the old Union Brewery Saloon—and, my dear, you should have seen the place! A hole in the wall so small we nearly missed it, and all full of local yokels and dogs and cats and I don't believe anything in it had been moved or cleaned since the place was built. But he was quite right about everything else, it turned out. Especially Piper's Opera House— I'll show you that in just a minute. It is being handsomely restored by a doctor's wife who is the granddaughter of the original owner, John Piper, and it had a most amusing old melodrama, *The Drunkard*, playing in it. Two shows every afternoon, and is going to have a light opera and musical comedy, maybe even a real opera this coming winter. And the old Miners' Union Hall, it's been fixed up too, and there's what they call a "melodron" troop playing there, with tables around and drinks and chicken in the basket. Such fun. And he was quite kind about those shows, for a man who'd seen the real thing a century ago. He spoke quite good English too, considering. Said he'd had to do something about it, since he'd given up mining to be a newspaperman. His name? Henry, can you

*Walter Clark with President N. Ed Miller of the
University of Nevada, receiving honorary doctorate, June 1969.
Courtesy of Robert M. Clark*

remember his name? Oh, yes, that's right. He gave us an old
yellow clipping from a newspaper he said he used to own and
edit, and he autographed it for us. Where did I put that thing?
Of course, he could have been exaggerating about owning and
editing. Doesn't seem likely, a man who when he's over a hundred years old would be out in public half naked, just watering
somebody's grass. But the clipping was real enough, all old and
yellow and—Oh, yes. Here it is, *The Gold Hill Evening News,*
that was the paper. And see, here's the editor's name printed
and he signed it the same way, see? Alf Doten. And the paper
does have a name on it—1876. Only, right at the end he did say

the queerest thing. It was something like—we couldn't help asking how old he'd been when he first came here—who could—and he said something like "not old enough to matter," but he was now, because he'd lived with that S.O.B.'s life seven times over.

At any rate, the coming of age [his sixtieth birthday was August 3, which he thought of as a milestone] was fittingly and doubly, if somewhat redundantly, observed. Dave and Marge flew up from Albuquerque on the first (non-stop, save for fueling at Vegas, and in seven hours).... For the rest, I water, and putter with Alf (who will be done this fall I swear) and with preparation for my "revised" courses (to keep me awake) at the U this fall, and ideas for a paper I have to write which will also be a speech I have to give next October in Utah, upon the occasion of becoming the fourth honorary lifetime member of the Western Literature Association (U. of Nevada gave me an honorary Doctor of Letters this spring too. Everything is adding to this posthumous feeling that has been growing on me ever since I started Alf) and Barbara picks her sugar peas and cultivates her squash and tomatoes and flowers and knits on small things for the one Bobby and Betsy are expecting in December. Oh, every now and then I buck out and take the dog for an early morning walk up a near and not too large mountain (we're doing the circle one by one, meaning to finish with Cedar Hill and Sun Mt. Before the snow comes). (8/15/69)

⟪ CHAPTER EIGHTEEN ⟫

THE SWEET PROMISED
LAND OF NEVADA

IN JUNE OF 1969 BARBARA had an almost constant stomachache, and although suspecting an ulcer, she decided to self-medicate with antacid tablets. After two weeks she went to see a doctor, who prescribed more pills. In August, at another visit to the doctor, she was told that he suspected a gall-bladder problem rather than an ulcer. There were further exams, X-rays, and lab tests, and the doctor found cancer. In early September she was admitted to the hospital; following an exploratory operation, it was determined that the cancer was terminal—nothing to do. It was very unexpected for everyone. The family, including Barbara of course, had been worried about Walter's health, and then there was this sudden turnaround—it was a shock.

Walter was devastated. He wrote to Caples in late October:

A hard note to write and I can't make it more than a note—but I thought I should tell you before the word is final. Barbara is in St. Mary's Hospital, enduring the late stages of a terminal cancer. She has been ill since June—but doctored just medically for gall bladder trouble until the first of Sept. when she went into the hospital. They operated the seventh and found—an apparently rare condition—an advanced cancer of the gall bladder—already too far advanced and ramified to be operable. She was home until two weeks ago, when her meds got beyond me and Mgt. [Margaret] Marks—our local nurse. Fred Anderson, long our doctor and an old friend too, is taking care of her. Her mind is far from clear now—she loses track of time, fades in the middle of a sentence, and at her request I'm her only visitor. She doesn't have to keep face or pay attention with me. But she is being kept quite comfortable physically....

I'm getting along fine—so don't worry about me either. I'm still teaching—only half time this semester, fortunately, and I keep busy with house work and looking after our little dog and marketing, etc....

When you can, I'd like a word about how it's going with you too—but please, Robert, not a phone call. On paper I can get by. The loud voices shake me up too much still—as they do Barbara. (10/29/69)

She died on November 12, and the funeral was held a few days later. Walter wrote once again to Robert and his wife, Rosemary:

So, it is done. And she did it just as she meant to do it—not a tear all the way—only practical concerns, worries about the kids and me after she was gone. We held the funeral ... altogether according to her specified wishes, a high, hillside lot in the v.c. cemetery, family only, and oak casket with a covering of pine boughs, cones, and wild grasses and berries ...

Made a beginning on the way back last night, with a birthday party of Leah, Bab's fetching youngest—and tomorrow I return to the teaching. There is a big vacuum, but we're all doing well. Can't do much else after Barbara. (11/17/69)

Barbara and Walter were very compatible and had a successful thirty-six-year marriage, although it must be said that this success was largely due to the fact that Barbara adapted to her husband's tastes and was happy to take on the traditional role of housewife as dictated by the times. Intelligent and witty, she was a good companion for an intellectual. Like Walter, she enjoyed socializing both at home and in saloons; like him, she was a reader (and she loved to solve word puzzles); and like him, she came to love the old mining towns of Nevada. She was also sensible and dependable, a hard worker who supported Walter by doing all the housework, cleaning, cooking, washing, and gardening. Outside, she planted trees, shrubs, and lawn and maintained a vegetable garden. She weeded, dug little trenches to irrigate her garden, clipped and trimmed, and spread topsoil. Inside, in addition to her housekeeping, she kept the household accounts, paid the bills, and dealt with the insurance and taxes. It is clear that Walter not only lost a loving companion — the love of his life to whom he was always true — but also lost the central pillar of his daily life, who contributed considerably, both physically and emotionally, to his ability to write and teach, to be what he became.

On Christmas Eve of 1969, Walter reported to Robert on his situation:

> I make progress, minor progress to be sure, but progress nevertheless, in the household arts, and find them far more salutary at present than of my sit-still occupations. . . . After Christmas I'll get back to picking at Alf Doten again. It will probably take a week just to find out again where I am in him, since he's been gathering dust since the middle of June. But there isn't too much left to do on him, and I expect to have him off my table before summer. (Until that million words of proof-reading begins.) Then, I hope, back to some writing of my own, with only half-time teaching. I promise nothing, even to myself.

Just play it day to day, as I can, but busy is a hell of a lot better than not. The only question, so far as the writing is concerned, is whether or not enough of me will care again to move the imagination. (12/24/69)

Would enough of him care again? Barbara's death would not leave him for a long time, if it ever did. He kept himself busy with little tasks around the house, and while he continued to teach, he procrastinated on going back to work on the Doten papers. In April of the year following his wife's death, he wrote to Caples, who, worried that he'd had no word from Clark for months, had called him on the phone (disobeying his instructions):

I feel guilty—as if my own silence—a new phenome-non—had forced you out of yours. Nonetheless, it was good to hear your hello—a sound from the other cave. Miriam [Clark's sister] has relayed your telephone messages (I should have written long ago, but a great inertia possess me still, both within and without) and I am grateful both for them and for your thoughtfulness in not phoning directly. I was never at ease talking on the telephone and—irrational, but true, ever since last November the sound of that bell has scared me stiff. I'd have the thing taken out if it weren't for Babs and Bob and their families, who constitute practically the whole of my social life still. . . .

My chief diversion is taking walks with my little dog— up in the hills away from town. Her delight out among the piñons and junipers (which are multiplying and flourishing wonderfully) is an uplift in itself. Of late, I have given myself an extra preoccupation on such strolls—have, as it were, appointed myself custodian (janitor) of the outer Comstock and carry a big gunny-sack and bring it back full of beer cans, pop-bottles, and other blessings bestowed by the omnipresent God-damned tourist now that the trail bike, the dune-buggy, the four-wheel and the camper have enabled him to invade even the final privacies without raising his fat ass off the seat. My labors are inadequate (after all, I'm outnumbered about 5,000 to 1) but soothing....

No—I give too dark an impression. There are real signs of internal gain, though they are neither as clear nor as steady as my improvement in hanging up the laundry, mopping the floor and boiling unsalted chicken and frozen vegetables. I begin to teach as one man again—a whole me, with his mind on what's going on. I can again read something besides detective stories, and most of the time I even understand what I'm reading and remember it afterwards. I can look at the hills and see them, though not yet with my own eyes only....

In short, the great indifferent freeze is beginning to crack, though, as I'm making all too clear, nothing much is coming through the cracks yet. And I sin grievously in one respect. There lies the lengthy and multidimensional life and letters of old Alf Doten all over everything upstairs, very nearly completed. The main test, the journals, altogether so, with the undisturbed dust of nine months upon them. I don't really understand why I find it so hard to go back to him.... The kind of steady, unthinking but meticulously attentive plugging he now requires, would seem on the face of it, to be just the thing to make time pass. And also he's long overdue, and is the only specific, tangible debt I owe in this world. (4/18/70)

Clark was conservative about what he considered his duty and proper behavior, but in other respects he was liberal and almost always sided with students in their causes and grievances. Occasionally there was an internal conflict between his sense of proper behavior and his liberal sympathies. Although he was as disturbed as many students were about the shootings at Kent State (on May 4, 1970), he viewed some student demonstrations with skepticism.

He wrote to Caples in May that the "U. of Nevada has finally caught up with the contemporary trend in higher education. Last week hippies heckled ferociously at the annual ROTC review, and there were two fire-bombings" (5/15/70).

Colleague Robert Harvey remembers that it was about this time that a group of militant students came to Clark to ask him about an idea they had. They picked him to talk to because he lived in Virginia City and because he was known for his sympathy for students. Their proposal was that if they could get help from some folks in the Bay Area, they could take over Storey County, a tiny county with Virginia City its center of population. They told him, "We could vote in our own Sheriff and make our own laws." Clark turned to them and said, "Well, if a bunch of you guys want to come up to Virginia City, I am sure you will get a hearty welcome." It was not a change in the city he loved that he could endorse.

Caples sent Clark a birthday present (his birthday was on August 3) and Clark thanked him, revealing that he still had not totally recovered:

> Your bird sits lovely on my TV set—and I hear him soft and far away, but clearly, so that is perfect too, for it is the only kind of good music I can take yet. Odd, isn't it? I do quite well in most other matters, but can't bear serious music—and begin to suspect I may never be able to. It breaks me up. One of the reasons I dread going to other people's homes. There is always that God damned hi-fi softly playing something beautiful and intolerable.

He did report, however, that

> I have worked my way through all practical procrastination. The house is cleaned. The laundry is done. I have cooked the chicken parts for Dogette and me. The lawns are mowed, the

Walter Clark on the steps of the "little red house," ca. 1970.
Courtesy of Hugh Gallagher

trees are trimmed, the edges are clipped. The weeds are pulled.
(In fact the place looks like a Disney version of a Mother Goose
house) and I have put in a double stint as Custodian of the
Outer Comstock, despite 100 degree temperatures.... All that
remains between me and letters, about twenty of them, is Alf
Doten (the text is complete and I'm into the final notes, preface, etc.) and a stack of student MSS. (8/13/70)

During the fall of 1970, he seemed to be getting his life back on
track, teaching, working again on Doten, and more or less suc-
cessfully taking over the many chores his wife had performed for
the two of them. But just before Christmas his earlier prostate
symptoms returned, this time with the addition of a "mysterious
bleeding." He told Caples,

> I am about to take another semester off from the university by
> way of returning to St. Mary's for a third bout of whittling at
> my lower plumbing.... Anyway, I get variety—a different
> kind of operation every time. This time "an exploratory,
> to see what's going on in there, to be followed, possibly,
> by post-operational radiological therapy."

Clark said, further, that he was looking forward to the layoff,
since he had been suffering for some time with a weariness that
lead to procrastination and frequent dozing, even while sitting upright. But his conscience would not rest. He thought that the layoff
would also be good because after recovering from the operation,
he would have "the rest of the semester to correct my longest and
most serious procrastination—that about Alf Doten" (1/30/71).

When he got out of the hospital, he went to stay at the Chisms
(his sister, Miriam, and her husband, John), whose children were
gone and who had a separate apartment in their house available in
which he could recuperate. He told Caples in mid-February of 1971

that he was living the life of a "sycophantic Riley," simply enjoying the warm sunlight through the southern-exposure windows
and only exerting himself to get his own breakfast and take his
daily stroll "very slowly in p.j., slippers and a bright red dressing
gown that would make a fine robe for an African chief, if there are
any left, and accompanied by my small black dog, round the yard."
He added that he would be starting a cobalt series, five treatments
a week for the time being (his doctor joked that no one gets sick
on a weekend). Caples had sent him a recording of the sounds of
the humpback whale, and Clark told him, "Am sharing the musical wisdom of the hump-back with the Chisms. I do not understand it yet—but I have inklings. I will learn" (2/14/71).

A week later he provided an update:

Progress report: General: Still faltering in semi-mindless indo-
lence and marvelous privacy at the old Chism ranch between
the Truckee River and the SP [Southern Pacific] railroad. "Intellectual" activities have absorbed about a dozen who-dunnits
and espionage and who-chisels-who yarns, the daily papers
and weekly mags and, of late, with first stirrings of conscience,
and something resembling a distantly remembered kind of
concern, achieved by frequent naps with book on chest and
specs on nose, a new (and the first good) anthology of western
lit., a fine, lively sardonic novel of the frontier, *Little Big Man,*
and John Ciardi's new Translation of Dante's *Purgatorio....*
Intellectual *output*—nil. Window pleasure—two or three
downy snowfalls and the daily feeding of a multitude of quail
and pigeons. (2/23/71)

He slowly got back on his feet, began to socialize in Reno, and
went with his son to the state basketball tournament. On March 14
he moved back into his little red house in Virginia City, but the
move seemed to exhaust him:

I am a very old man today, thinking carefully in order to discover what I must do next and then doing it slowly and attentively—as if I'd never done it before. You know, such complicated things as making coffee or washing a dish. So I must postpone my return to Alf Doten and the Union Brewery at least one more day. Also, I am not shoveling the snow—just letting it melt. (3/15/71)

During the first week of April, however, he was able to resume his daily walks. "Dogette," he wrote Caples, "is pleased though she is also puzzled because I go slowly and turn back so soon" (4/6/71). But shortly after this, he got news from his doctor, giving him his "one way ticket for the long voyage" (4/8/71). He wrote several of his friends to tell them, including Ray and Lou West:

It was no particular jolt when the doctor told me. Tougher on him. He'd been procrastinating also for over two weeks. And I'd more than guessed it for a long time—since well before Christmas anyway. This is easy compared to a year ago September, very easy. And I'm feeling fine so far, only I tucker out too quickly. Have to putter at things—Alf Doten, who must be finished, the housework, the yard. But putter I do, and quite happily. Set out some new plants and trimmed my trees and roses of their snow drift breaks for instance. Still drinking boiler-makers too—though not quite so often up-town, and cocktail hours instead of evenings. (4/8/71)

He also wrote Caples:

Nobody knows when the boat leaves. So I am not hanging around on the wharf. I like it better up here. I owe work I haven't finished and I peck at it. I put some new plants out in the garden yesterday and have begun to clear winter grass and leaves to make room for spring grass and leaves. There was a

Drawing by Robert Caples on the back of a postcard,
posted from New Preston, Connecticut, March 15, 1971.
Caples sent many such little encouragements to Clark during
the year before his death. Courtesy of Robert M. Clark

beautiful sunrise this morning—clear, slow and very quiet—
silent—with the near hills dark and distinct of outline against
it. I am going to bed so early most of the time that I see almost
every daybreak—but most of them have been clouded this
spring—and even now the little north wind breathes. I am
waiting for the time when I can sit out on the south side of
the house and take the sun without an overcoat.

Don't worry about me. I am not hit hard by the word at
all. I knew it before he told me, long before.

Much love to you both—

Walter

And thank you very much for the Panamints [probably a photograph of a painting by Caples of the Panamint Mountains in
eastern California, west of Death Valley]. They are beautiful,
and they sit on my bureau. There is a clock beside them, but it
does no harm. I don't really see it any more. (4/8/71)

At the end of April he visited the doctor to make sure of the diagnosis and to ask how much time he had left. The answer was only a few months. Clark then resigned from the English Department, and his family had a resignation party for him, "a roast beef, Idaho baked and red wine dinner ... to mark the momentous occasion" (4/23/71). Word spread among his friends, and the Herb Wilners, the Ray Wests, and the Caples traveled to Virginia City to see him.

By mid-June he reported that he was rebelling against all medications except for Alka-Seltzer and Bufferin at bedtime. It would be a rebellion he would cling to even as his health deteriorated. One of the first things that happened was that he found it difficult to sleep except for a half hour at a time, and then he had a severe pain in his leg so that he had to walk with a cane. He confessed to Caples, "I'm getting a shameful amount of help for the immobility it causes—from Bob, Babs, Ross, Sam, Nell, Debbie—custards, broths, house cleaning, lawn mowing, painting" (6/14/71).

Regardless of his poor physical condition, he still read the proof of Caples's *Potter* for him. The book was being published privately after all. Upon sending the proofs back to his friend, Clark noted,

> Really very clean copy as things go these days. Liked the conclusion of the fable much better this time, too, though I must admit I fall far short of the Potter's faith in other and resolving worlds. But the Potter, I'd agree, must believe. Otherwise, it would be as Conrad put it in *Heart of Darkness* "altogether too dark." (6/14/71)

In his last letter to Caples in August, he thanked him for another gift:

> He is a fine owl, and I find myself listening to his soundless hooings often in the night, when I find myself often watching,

also, the strange and growing luminosity—from a street lamp through slowly moving black locust shadows—of moon and cloud above the little man in the boat. Both talk to me quietly with a most useful kind of unspecific knowledge. (8/15/71)

In the fall Clark was bedridden and in pain. He was tough and stoical up until nearly the end, refusing medication as much as he was able to. His family took care of him, mostly his son Bob, in the little red house in Virginia City. He could no longer go up to C Street to greet his friends, so many came down to talk to him. In looking back, his son has said that he thought the final weeks were, in a way, a relief to him—he no longer had to worry about Doten, no longer fret about not getting any of his own work done. He was released from his burden at last and could simply sit and enjoy sports on TV.

Then came a terrible night when, as his son recalls, "the pain was much too much for Dad's mind and body to bear, overriding any morphine dose we would have dared to give him, and he went more or less out of his head, tearing out IV's and things that were already attached." That's when he had to be taken to the hospital in the county ambulance, followed by ten days of heavy sedation.

He died on November 10, 1971, at age sixty-two. There was in this a strange confluence of dates—Barbara had died on November 12, Alf Doten had died on the 11th, and Walter Clark died on the 10th. It was also strange and ironic that just a few months earlier, for a contract renewal of the paperback rights to *Ox-Bow*, he got by far the largest payment for publication that he had ever received, over forty thousand dollars. Bob Clark, who had inherited his father's sense of duty, wrote the preface to the Doten journals and cleaned up the odds and ends that were left prior to publication.

Wallace Stegner came from Stanford and Herb Wilner from San Francisco State to join Clark's Nevada colleagues Bob Gorrell and Larry Laird to act as pallbearers at the funeral. Walter Van Tilburg Clark was buried beside his wife in the Masonic cemetery in Virginia City. Herb Wilner recalled the funeral and burial:

> It was a gray, cold, snow-and-ice day that saw his funeral in Reno. But at the cemetery in Virginia City, the sky cleared and the sun broke through. And at the precise moment, when my own feelings were beginning to show as too nakedly human, too visibly self-involved, there came, through a break in the clearing sky and over the ridge of a nearby hill, a flock of intervening birds. I looked up and watched them. I was told later they were probably starlings. I know little of the names of birds, but I knew enough at that moment—someone had taught me—to watch them. They made a beautiful swoop, and then departed, and left behind them, for me, a vast and meaningful silence.

Perhaps the best memorial to Clark may be to quote from his verses from *The City of Trembling Leaves*, "The Sweet Promised Land of Nevada" (to be sung, with gusto, to the tune of "Sweet Betsy from Pike"):

> Oh, the Lord, He had labored both earnest and long
> Five days and a half, and was still going strong,
> With the sweat on His brow, but a-singing His song,
> When he came to the land of Nevada.

> Oh, He'd laid out the world just as neat as He'd planned;
> Save a few little boners 'twas smooth as His hand.
> There was plenty left over to finish this land,
> The last land, the land of Nevada.

> Oh, He leaned on His shovel and looked at the stuff
> He had piled up there handy to make the first rough.
> "My work has been good, but it's not good enough.
> I'll do better the land of Nevada."

Chorus:
"Oh, this is the land that old Moses shall see;
Oh, this is the land of the vine and the tree;
Oh, this is the land for My children and Me,
The sweet promised land of Nevada."

The song continues, outlining the Lord's progress through twelve verses to the concluding three. He looks back at his work — the Himalayas are too high, the Congo too wet, Gobi too dry — and resolves to do better with Nevada. He is going to make the climate mild, hospitable to all his creatures, and "no land of the past / Shall flower and fruit like Nevada." "The best of it all," he declares, are the waters he plans, the lakes and rivers that will water the land. But although he has only one more day of work, he has to leave the job unfinished because the next day is Sunday, and so he plans to come back to finish on Monday. But he never does. The song concludes with these verses:

So the hills are in rows, and they're piled up too high;
They are colder than death, and they trouble the sky.
Though at night you may freeze, yet at noon you will fry
In the unfinished land of Nevada.

So the lakes are all dry and the rivers all flow
Underground and no green thing will venture to grow,
And all the sweet breezes that come there to blow,
Will tear off your hair in Nevada.

So, with rivers and lakes that forever run dry,
The Lord's only creatures that can multiply
Are the rattler, the jack and the little bar-fly,
The little bar-fly of Nevada.

Chorus:
"So this is the land that old Moses would see,
So this is the land of the vine and the tree,

So this is the land for My children and Me,
The sweet promised land of Nevada—O-o-o-o-oh,
The sweet promised land of Nevada."

"The Sweet Promised Land" testifies to Clark's humor, his joy in living, and his affection for his land. One tribute after his death quotes Clark saying that his "constant effort was to personalize the land and put the human tragedy back in its natural setting." We may regret that he didn't publish more, but we can be grateful for the contribution he did make, a contribution that included the *Ox-Bow Incident*, which Orville Prescott in the *New York Times* called "the best novel about the old West I ever read." It also included *The Track of the Cat*, which Mark Schorer in that same newspaper called "one of the great American novels of place."

Then, of course, there are the short stories, such as "Hook," "The Wind and the Snow of Winter," "The Indian Well," "The Portable Phonograph," and "The Buck in the Hills," which will likely endure for a long time to come. These novels and stories, taken together, shine like jewels produced by a writer whom many called brilliant and would seem to shine the more brilliantly because of their rarity.

But what Walter Clark was most proud of was his record of more than thirty years of devoted teaching. As we have seen, he cared as much about his students as any teacher ever has. Perhaps the most telling aspect of his career was that he was as proud of being a teacher in a small high school as he was of being a professor teaching in a university. He didn't give a damn about fame or money or status. He lived to serve others, and he did.

《 NOTES AND DOCUMENTATION 》

On the following pages, sources and notes for each chapter are listed under the following categories (when applicable): (1) Interviews, (2) Published Material by Walter Clark, (3) Unpublished Material by Walter Clark, (4) Published Material About Walter Clark or Related Topics, and (5) Notes and Sources for Quotations and Topics (listed by page number and introductory phrase). Items in sections (2), (3), and (4) are listed in order of their initial appearance in the text of the chapter. No notes are provided for the quoted letters; instead, the source for letters (almost all of them by Clark himself) and the recipient are indicated in the text, with the date of each letter given in parentheses at the end of the quotation. The dates for the letters are given to provide a further guide to the chronology of Clark's life. A series of quotations from a single letter is documented by a date at the end of the last quotation. With one exception, a very long letter from Clark to his son, single letters are not included in (3), Unpublished Material; only extensive correspondences are included.

Three items that appear frequently throughout the notes are abbreviated as follows: Library of the University of Nevada, Reno = LUNR;

Charlton Laird, ed., *Walter Van Tilburg Clark: Critiques* (Reno: U of Nevada P, 1983) = Laird; and Max Westbrook, *Walter Van Tilburg Clark* (New York: Twayne Publishers, 1969) = Westbrook.

The specific editions of Walter Clark's books referred to in the chapter listings are abbreviated as follows (since first editions of most of Clark's works are difficult to find, I have used the most available editions except in the case of *The Watchful Gods,* to be reissued this fall 2004):

NOVELS

The Ox-Bow Incident. New York: Signet Classic, Penguin Books, 1968 (original edition, 1940) = *Ox-Bow.*

The City of Trembling Leaves. Reno: U of Nevada P, 1991 (original edition, 1945) = *City.*

The Track of the Cat. Reno: U of Nevada P, 1993 (original edition, 1949) = *Cat.*

STORIES

The Watchful Gods and Other Stories. New York: Random House, 1950 = *Gods.*

CHAPTER ONE: BORN IN THE EAST

Interviews

My thanks to Robert Clark (10/23/97), Barbara Clark Salmon (11/3/98), Miriam Chism (interviewed by James Maguire, 5/17/92), David Chism (8/21/00), Walter Brown (5/26/00), Robert Gorrell (7/9/97), Rosemary Caples (8/9/00).

Published Material by Walter Clark

"Autobiographical Information," Laird, 265–74.

"The Indian Well," *Gods.*

"On Learning to Look: A Note on the Working Life of Robert Cole Caples" (referred to here in manuscript, LUNR, later published as a foreword to *Robert Cole Caples: A Restrospective Exhibition, 1927–1963* [Reno: U of Nevada P, 1964]).

Published Material About Walter Clark or Related Topics

Robert M. Clark, "Chronology," Laird, 275–86.

Notes and Sources for Quotations and Topics

1–3. Clark's father and early childhood, "Chron.," Laird, 275.

1–2. "hated the city," "horse drawn," "Chron.," Laird, 266.

3. "socialize with them," David Chism; Clark's mother, "Chron.," Laird, 275.

4. "two stories," David Chism.

5. "lots of space," "Auto.," Laird, 266; "deep interest," "Auto.," Laird, 266.

6. "The Indian Well," *Gods*, 125–48.

7. "Learned then," "Auto.," Laird, 268.

8. "On farm, too," "Auto.," Laird, 266.

9. "To be aware," "On Learning," 5; "About a hawk," Robert Gorrell; "quests in search," Westbrook, 37.

10. "a very wet," "Auto.," Laird, 266; "very adventurous," "Auto.," Laird, 266.

12. "In Reno," *City*, 3.

13. "an eagle-eyed," "Auto.," Laird, 267.

14. "even began," "Auto.," Laird, 267; "the knowledge," "Auto.," Laird, 267.

15. "Well, maybe in the next life," as quoted by Velda Morby in her column "Art in the Silver Circle," *Gazette, Journal* [Reno] 17 Feb. 1960: 9A.

16. "probably about," *City*, 61; "very clumsy," *City*, 64.

17. "the affair," *City*, 65; "The Potter," dust-jacket copy from *The Potter and His Children*.

CHAPTER TWO: TWO MAJOR INFLUENCES — ROBERT COLE CAPLES AND ROBINSON JEFFERS

Interviews

My thanks to Rosemary Caples (8/9/00), Mike Steiner (8/30/00).

Published Material by Walter Clark

"On Learning to Look: A Note on the Working Life of Robert Cole Caples" (referred to here in manuscript, LUNR).

Unpublished Material by Walter Clark

"A Study in Robinson Jeffers." Thesis, U of Vermont, 1934.

Published Material About Walter Clark or Related Topics

Robert Brophy, ed., *Robinson Jeffers: Dimensions of a Poet* (New York: Fordham UP, 1995).

James Karman, *Robinson Jeffers: Poet of California* (Brownsville, Ore.: Story Line, 1995).

Notes and Sources to Quotations and Topics

19. "shipped," "unbelievable," "On Learning," 1.

20. "The desire," "I thought," "On Learning," 1; "close the gap," "On Learning," 2; "a view of the Truckee," "On Learning," 2.

21. "A seeing," "On Learning," 2; "Oh, this isn't the first time," *City*, 591.

22. "I wander," *City*, 595; "In Death Valley," 617; "There in the middle," 645.

23–30. "I never make," *City*, 660.

24. "They sought Indian," "On Learning," 3; "There is a quiet," Jeff Kelley, "The Vision of Robert Caples" (clipping), *Gazette* (Reno): n.d., n.p.

25. "Unpleasant experience," letter to author from Mike Steiner, 8/30/00.

26. "Biggest adventure," "On Learning," 4–5.

28. "lively conversation," Miriam Chism (5/17/92); "helped out," "Auto.," Laird, 268.

31. "most profound," Westbrook, 31; "the additional pleasure," "A Study," 2.

33. "It is quite possible," Westbrook, 31.

34. "Jeffers postulates," "A Study," 27.
35. "Robinson, their first," Brophy, 2. Most of the information here regarding Jeffers's life and work comes from Brophy and Karman, as noted previously, and from Clark's thesis, "A Study," as noted previously.
37. "a soap opera," Brophy, 3; "no lines," quoted in Karman, 14.
38. "thematically turbulent," Brophy, 4; "Integrity is wholeness," Karman, 104.
39. "also I heard," "A Study," 25.
41. "My favorite," "Auto.," Laird, 269.

CHAPTER THREE: MARRIAGE, CHILDREN, AND CAZENOVIA CENTRAL SCHOOL

Interviews

My thanks to Robert Clark (10/23/97), Barbara Clark Salmon (11/3/98), David Chism (8/21/00), George Lowe (5/22/00), Carl Straub (9/2/00), John Bennett (5/25/00), Glen Slack (6/12/00), Grace Westcott Drennan (6/7/00), Barclay Webber (5/28/00), Elizabeth Finke (2/5/98), Betty Shaw Heffernan (audio tape n.d.), Berry O'Connor (11/29/00), Robert P. Moon (5/28/00), Paul Everts (9/20/00), Dorothy Collier (9/30/00), Loretta Kelner (letter to Robert Clark, 1/7/96), Rita P. Osborne (9/8/00), Sonia Sweetland (letter, 11/12/98), Joyce Norton Burney (10/16/00).

Published Material by Walter Clark

"Autobiographical Information," Laird, 265–74.

Published Material About Walter Clark or Related Topics

Robert A. Grills, *Cazenovia: The Story of an Upland Community* (Cazenovia, N.Y.: Cazenovia Preservation Foundation, 1977).
Interview of Clark by Joseph H. Adams in *The Post Standard* (Syracuse), 12 Dec. 1940: n.p.
Charlton Laird, "Literate Voice in Nevada," Laird, 3–19.

Notes and Sources for Quotations and Topics

48. "[I] found the subjects," "Auto.," Laird, 272; "A long story," (interview in newspaper clipping), 8 Oct. 1950, n.p.; "shoveling snow," Random House publication blurb for *Ox-Bow*.

49. "We weren't too well heeled," Adams; "a fine life," Adams.

51. "scared green," "my chief means," "Auto.," Laird, 268.

52. "an occupation," "Auto.," Laird, 268.

52–53. Cazenovia (history and geography), Grills.

62. "too many cigarettes," "Literate," Laird, 6.

CHAPTER FOUR: *THE OX-BOW INCIDENT* AND THE WESTERN NOVEL

Interviews

My thanks to Betty Shaw Heffernan (audio tape, n.d.), Robert Clark, 10/23/97.

Published Material by Walter Clark

The Ox-Bow Incident (New York: Signet Classic, Penguin Books, 1968 [original edition, 1940]).

"Hook," *The Watchful Gods* (New York: Random House, 1950), 3–30.

"The Buck in the Hills," *Gods*, 95–109.

"Credo," Laird, xi–xiii.

"On 'The Wind and the Snow of Winter,' " Laird, 119–25.

Published Material About Walter Clark or Related Topics

Charlton Laird, "Literate Voice in Nevada," Laird, 3–19.

Charlton Laird, "Introduction" (to Part II, "Studies of Major Published Works"), Laird, 73–78.

Mark Twain, *Life on the Mississippi* (New York: Bantam Books, 1945).

Wallace Stegner, "Making a Myth," *One Way to Spell Man: Essays with a Western Bias* (Garden City, N.Y.: Doubleday, 1982).

Conversations with Wallace Stegner on Western History and Litera-

ture, rev. ed., ed. Richard W. Etulain (Salt Lake City: U of Utah P, 1990).

Thomas J. Lyon, "Revisionist Western Classics," *Reading the West: New Essays on the Literature of the American West,* ed. Michael Kowalewski (New York: Cambridge UP, 1996).

Mark Twain, "The United States of Lyncherdom," *The Portable Mark Twain* (New York: Viking Press, 1962), 584–93.

Herbert Wilner, "Walter Clark: Complicated Simplicity," Laird, 31–52.

Wallace Stegner, "Walter Clark's Frontier," Laird, 53–70.

Ann Ronald, "Walter Van Tilburg Clark's Brave Bird, 'Hook,' " *Studies in Short Fiction* 25 (1988): 433–39.

Robert M. Clark, "On the 'Voice' of Walter Clark," *Gods,* 248–62.

Notes and Sources for Quotations and Topics

69. "I regret," "Credo," Laird, xiii; "an idea 'which was probably,' " "Literate," Laird, 15; "plot the incident," "Literate," Laird, 15.

70. "I had become," "Intro.," Laird, 74–75.

71. "The first draft" (clipping), 12 Dec. 1940, n.p.

72. "a first novel," Fred T. Marsh, "The Ox-Bow Incident and Other New Fiction," *Saturday Review of Literature,* n.d., n.p.; "There is a kind of cabinet-worker," Clifton Fadiman, "Books: Make Way for Mr. Clark," rev. of *The Ox-Bow Incident, New Yorker* 12 Oct. 1940: 84–85.

73. "In [these] pages," Stegner, "Making," 109.

74. "A curious exemplification," Twain, *Life,* 317.

75. "your ordinary citizen," as quoted by James K. Folsom in *The American Western Novel* (New Haven, Conn.: College and UP, 1966), 123; "reading their own myth," Stegner and Etulain, 165.

76. "did not view the West," Lyon, 144; "The important romantic," M. H. Abrams, *A Glossary of Literary Terms,* 4th ed. (New York: Holt, Rinehart and Winston, 1981), 114; "he attempted to go beyond," Lyon, 145.

77. "was on a kind of frontier," Lyon, 146.

78. "The struggle," Lyon, 148; "The difference," Stegner and Etulain, 194; "Why does a crowd," Twain, "Lyncherdom," 588.

79. "Repeatedly Art," Westbrook, 59; "an exaggerated evaluation," Westbrook, 57; "the lynch mob," Westbrook, 57; "they fear," Westbrook, 59.

80. "Humankind," Wilner, 31–32; Images of light and dark, John R. Milton, "The Western Attitude: Walter Van Tilburg Clark," *Critique: Studies in Modern Fiction* 2 (1959): 62.

81. "was trying," "Civilization," Stegner, "Frontier," Laird, 61, 67–68; "a story that is first of all," Laird, "Intro.," 77; "I sense," Stegner, "Frontier," 57; "Fiction, all fiction," Clark, "On the Wind," 119.

82. "The broken pillar," Ronald, 435.

83. "has nowhere," Ronald, 437; "without flame," "Hook," *Gods*, 95; "Many analogies," Ronald, 437.

84. "The peak," *Gods*, 95; "I climbed," *Gods*, 95–96; "pure Clark" and comparison to Hemingway, Westbrook, 135.

85. "God, I was happy," *Gods*, 98; "he thought," "He told me," *Gods*, 107; "There was something," *Gods*, 109.

86. Ernest Hemingway, "Big Two–Hearted River: Part I," *The Short Stories of Ernest Hemingway* (New York: Random House, 1938), 307.

87. "dominated by," "an anger," Robert Clark, "Voice," Laird, 259, 261.

CHAPTER FIVE: WRITER OF
STORIES, POEMS, AND LETTERS

Published Material by Walter Clark

"The Wind and the Snow of Winter," *Gods*, 22–50.
"On 'The Wind and the Snow of Winter,'" Laird, 119–25.

Unpublished Material by Walter Clark

"Mark Agnew's Cat" (poem), LUNR (published in part in Susan Baker, "The Poetry of Walter Clark," Laird, 131).
"Benedict Morales' Wife" (poem), LUNR (Laird, 135).

Published Material About Walter Clark or Related Topics

Susan Baker, "The Poetry of Walter Clark," Laird, 126–46.

Notes and Sources for Quotations and Topics

89. "made no communal," *Gods*, 46.

90. "dark," *Gods*, 47; "laid out," *Gods*, 41; "he could remember," *Gods*, 37.

91. "The snowy cold," *Gods*, 39, 40; "an idea," "suddenly moved," "whatever it is," Clark, "On the Wind," Laird, 120; "the exploratory story," Laird, 120–21.

92. "In the bright," Laird, 121; "it was just the spring," Laird, 122; "This man came back," 123–24.

93. "The moment I was," Laird, 124.

94. "Mad, so you'd call," Laird, 131; "the white one," Laird, 135.

95. "Crucial to both," Baker, "Poetry," Laird, 130–31.

96. "in the bright sunlight," "a little bastard poem," Clark, "On the Wind," Laird, 121–22.

97. "When I say," Laird, 120–21; "make whatever idea," Laird, 120.

CHAPTER SIX: THE *OX-BOW* MOVIE AND *THE CITY OF TREMBLING LEAVES*

Interviews

My thanks to Robert Clark (10/23/97), Barclay Webber (5/28/00), Barbara Salmon (11/3/98).

Published Material by Walter Clark

"Autobiographical Information," Laird, 265–74.

The City of Trembling Leaves (Reno: U of Nevada P, 1991 [original edition, 1945]).

Published Material About Walter Clark or Related Topics

George Bluestone, *Novels into Film: The Metamorphosis of Fiction into Cinema* (Berkeley: U of California P, 1973).

Charlton Laird, "The Gospel According to the Trembling Leaves," Laird, 147–80.

Robert M. Clark, "On the 'Voice' of Walter Clark," Laird, 248–62.

Notes and Sources for Quotations and Topics

107. "only two changes," Bluestone, 170.

108. "Where films are taken seriously," Bluestone, 170–71.

109. "writing . . . into the small hours," "Auto.," Laird, 273.

109–10. Information on the composition of *The City of Trembling Leaves* comes from Laird, "On the Gospel," 157–60, and R. Clark, "On the 'Voice,' " 252–58.

110. "To be at his best," R. Clark, 252; "work on our," R. Clark, 254.

111. "employs at least five," Westbrook, 71; "Formless," "The Gospel," Laird, 156.

112. " 'The Ox-Bow Incident,' " rev. of *City* (clipping), 31 May 1945: 19; "Idea permeates," "The Gospel," Laird, 171.

114. "I am not Tim Hazard," Laird, 159; "anti-autobiographical," Laird, 179, 180.

117. "the trees of Reno," *City*, 3; "superficially," Laird, 151.

118. "expectancy," "Clark explains," Laird, 166.

119. "he heard," *City*, 9; "Little Mary," *City*, 690.

120. "a study of a sacred youth," "a story primarily," Westbrook, 73, 74; "symbolic of that balance," *Westbrook*, 77; "a blaring and martial," *City*, 184.

121. "Then, during one lap," *City*, 184–85; "You can run," 186; "the real contest," Westbrook, 77.

122. "Tim 'felt a steady,' " *City*, 192; "go faster each lap," 192; "He could feel," 193–94; "A kind of golden," 194; "The spring sunlight," 194–95.

123. "felt as if," *City*, 197; "how Tim grew," "But the scene," Laird, "The Gospel," 177.

124. "Tim had felt," *City*, 209; "declared his preference," Westbrook, 76.

125. "I believe," "Auto.," Laird, 269–70; "There are a great many," 270.

CHAPTER SEVEN: BACK TO NEVADA
AND *THE TRACK OF THE CAT*

Interviews

My thanks to Robert M. Clark (10/23/97), Barbara Clark Salmon (11/3/98), David Chism (8/21/00).

Published Material by Walter Clark

"Autobiographical Information," Laird, 265–74.

The Track of the Cat (Reno: U of Nevada P, 1993 [original edition, 1949]).

"On the Track of the Cat," Laird, 181–88.

Published Material About Walter Clark or Related Topics

Douglas McDonald, *Virginia City and the Silver Region of the Comstock Lode* (Las Vegas: Nevada Publications, 1982).

Douglas McDonald, *Nevada: Lost Mines and Buried Treasures* (Las Vegas: Nevada Publications, 1981).

Pioneer Nevada (Reno: Harolds Club, 1951).

Notes and Sources for Quotations and Topics

126–27. Mable Dodge Luhan, R. Clark.

127. "[I was] in Taos," "Auto.," 273.

129. "named after," "we were . . . back," "Auto.," 273.

135. "In his first novel," rev. of *Cat* (clipping), *Kirkus Reviews* 4 Jan. 1949: n.p.

136. "perhaps the finest," Westbrook, 93.

137. Blackness of the painter, "On the Track," Laird, 182.

138. "parallel that is," "On the Track," Laird, 183; "are quite separate," 183.

138–39. "The relationship," "the cats come," Laird, 184.

139. "the very central," "On the Track," Laird, 185.

140. "He [Curt] is," Westbrook, 99, 100; "The idealist," "On the Track," Laird, 185; "he is beginning," 183.

142–49. Virginia City history: McDonald, *Lost Mines*; McDonald, *Virginia City*; Harolds Club, *Pioneer Nevada*.

143. " 'Bueno,' he would say," Harolds, 41

144. "Tents of dirty," McDonald, *Virginia*, 13; "It has been," McDonald, *Virginia*, 14.

145. "An example of a typical pump," McDonald, *Virginia*, 105.

147. "This was no small," McDonald, *Virginia*, 30; Carson City was near starvation, Harolds, 43.

148–49. Prostitution, McDonald, *Virginia*, 74.

149. "Although this community," 75; "many stories were invented," McDonald, *Virginia*, 75.

CHAPTER EIGHT: VIRGINIA CITY AND *THE WATCHFUL GODS AND OTHER STORIES*

Interviews

My thanks to Gordon Lane (8/18/00), Hugh Gallagher (7/6/00), Robert M. Clark (10/23/97).

Published Material by Walter Clark

"Autobiographical Information," Laird, 265–74.

The Watchful Gods and Other Stories (New York: Random House, 1950).

"On 'The Watchful Gods,' " Laird, 187–88.

"The Writer and the Professor," *Chrysalis Review* 2 (Spring 1962): 60–107.

Published Material About Walter Clark or Related Topics

Douglas McDonald, *Virginia City and the Silver Region of the Comstock Lode* (Las Vegas: Nevada Publications, 1982).

Pioneer Nevada (Reno: Harolds Club, 1951).

Robert Laxalt, "Foreword to the New Edition," *The City of Trembling Leaves* (Reno: U of Nevada P, 1991).

Kelsey Guilfoil, rev. of *The Watchful Gods, Chicago Sunday Tribune* 8 Oct. 1950: iv, 6.

Robie Macauley, rev. of *The Watchful Gods, Bulletin of Bibliography* (Sept.–Dec. 1956): 70–73.

Vernon Young, "Gods Without Heroes: The Tentative Myth of Van Tilburg Clark," *Arizona Quarterly* 7 (Summer 1951): 110–19.

Robert M. Clark and Charlton Laird, "The 'Silent' Period," Laird, 207–15.

Robert M. Gorrell, "Problems in 'The Watchful Gods' and Clark's Revisions," Laird, 189–206.

Max Westbrook, "To Escape the Tiger: The Short Stories," Laird, 105–18.

Notes and Sources for Quotations and Topics

150–52. Virginia City, McDonald, *Virginia City*; Harolds, *Pioneer*.

150. Piper's Opera House, Harolds, 87.

151. "the intense young people," Harolds, 87; "Some of the very wealthy," McDonald, 106.

151–52. Reviving the mines, McDonald, 48–52.

152. Beebe and Clegg, McDonald, 51.

156. "Virginia City and the Chollar House," Laxalt, *City*, xiv–xv.

158–59. "Walter Clark," Laxalt, xv; reading list, Laxalt, xvi.

159. "I also believe," "Auto.," Laird, 270.

162. "The final judgment," Guilfoil, iv, 6.

163. "In a sense, every story," Macauley, 70–72.

164. "A man appeared," "The Rapids," *Gods*, 53.

164–65. "D.L. Called," "D.L. will be wild," 62, 64.

165. "He don't even know," "The Anonymous," *Gods*, 92.

166. "White as a sainted," "Why Don't You Look Where You're Going?" *Gods*, 113; "What are you fussing," "The Fish Who Could Close His Eyes," *Gods*, 161; "Tad stood there," *Gods*, 175.

167. "On the inside of the bed," "The Portable Phonograph," *Gods*, 188.

168. "somewhat as a play might," Young, 114; "his concern for the allegory," "Silent," Laird, 212.

169. "he [Clark] conducted," "Learn to incorporate," "You know that symbolized," 212.

170. "Tentatively," Young, 112; "is more than a story," Gorrell, 204.

171. "I have no final conviction," Young, 116.

171–72. "Comparisons of the versions," Gorrell, 204.

172. "they have always haunted," Clark, "On 'Watchful,' " Laird, 187; "The theme I finally," 188.

173. "expressionless," "The betraying," *Gods*, 306.

174. "Certainly all," "[The] story of a twelve year," Clark, "Writer and Professor," 72, 78; "centrally concerned," Westbrook, 108–9.

CHAPTER NINE: AWAY FROM HOME — FRUSTRATION AND LONGING

Interviews

My thanks to Robert M. Clark (10/23/97).

Unpublished Material by Walter Clark

Letters from Walter Clark to his wife, Barbara, Sept. 1951 to March 1952, LUNR.

CHAPTER TEN: FROM IOWA CITY, TO OMAHA, AND TO COLUMBIA, MISSOURI

Interviews

My thanks to George Bluestone (letter, 7/2/00), Ruth Prigozy (letter, 3/26/00).

Unpublished Material by Walter Clark

Letters from Walter Clark to his wife, Barbara, March to June 1952, LUNR.

Notes and Sources for Quotations and Topics

194. "In the year I studied," letter to author, 7/2/00.

195. "he was tall," letter to author, 3/26/00.

CHAPTER ELEVEN: TWO
RESIGNATIONS, SON AND FATHER

Interviews

My thanks to Robert Gorrell (7/9/97), Gordon Lane (8/18/00), David Chism (8/21/00), Robert M. Clark (10/23/97).

Unpublished Material by Walter Clark

Resignation letter to Robert M. Gorrell, Chairman, English Department, 6/1/53, LUNR.

Published Material About Walter Clark or Related Topics

(Most of the published material that follows, concerning the controversy involving Walter E. Clark, his resignation, and his death, as well as the resignation of Walter Van Tilburg Clark, was provided by Jacque Sundstrand, Manuscripts/Archives Librarian at LUNR.)

"Lecturer Quits University Post in Protest Move," *Reno Evening Gazette* 5 June 1953: 13.

Minutes of the Board of Regents, University of Nevada, 6–7 June 1953.

James W. Hulse, *The University of Nevada: A Centennial History* (Reno: U of Nevada P, 1974).

"Walter Clark Quits Nevada Faculty," *New York Times* (clipping), 6 June 1953: n.p.

Duane Bush, Chairman of the Investigating Committee, "Report to the Nevada State Senate," 13 March 1929.

"Talbot Resolution Demanding Clark's Resignation Rejected at Meeting of the Board of Regents," *Sparks Tribune* 1 Feb. 1928: 1.

Letter from Walter E. Clark to the Board of Regents (request to retire), 9/23/38, LUNR.

Silas E. Ross, "Recollections of Life at Glendale, Nevada, Work at the University of Nevada, and Western Funeral Practice," Part I, transcript of tapes in Oral History Project, LUNR.

"Yes, Recall Them," editorial in *Fallon Standard* (clipping), 22 Feb. 1928: n.p.

Notes and Sources for Quotations and Topics

218. "The administration," *Gazette*, 13; "Regent Hardy," Minutes of the Regents, 6–7 June 1953.

219. "[He] has long been remembered," Hulse, 45.

221. "A series of offenses," Hulse, 44.

222. "He has maintained," Minutes, 31 Jan. 1929, Item 9; "The hearings," Hulse, 44; "Far-fetched," Hulse, 44.

223. "If we succeed," Hulse, 44; "some university-watchers," Hulse, 46.

224. "Chairman Ross," "Clark thanked," Minutes, Dec. 1937.

CHAPTER TWELVE: ALONE IN MISSOULA AND IN PALO ALTO

Interviews

My thanks to Walter Brown (5/26/00), Robert M. Clark (10/23/97), Richard Scowcroft (9/28/00), George Bluestone (letter, 5/2/00).

Unpublished Material by Walter Clark

Letters from Walter Clark to his wife, Barbara, Sept. 1953 to May 1954, LUNR.

CHAPTER THIRTEEN: THE MOVE TO MONTANA AND UNCOMPLETED WRITING PROJECTS

Interviews

My thanks to Geoffrey Brown (10/4/00), Robert M. Clark (10/13/97), Merrel Clubb (letter, 2/7/02), Mark Brown (10/3/00), Walter Brown (5/26/00), Jesse Brier (letter, n.d.), Jim Elder (10/29/00).

Published Material About Walter Clark or Related Topics

"Dr. W. E. Clark, Ex-President of University Dies," *Reno Evening Gazette* (clipping), 2 May 1955: n.p.

Martin Bucco, "Epilogue: The Development of Western Literary

Criticism," *A Literary History of the American West*, ed. J. Golden Taylor et al. (Fort Worth: Texas Christian UP, 1987), 1283–1316.

Wallace Stegner and Richard W. Etulain, *Conversations with Wallace Stegner on Western History and Literature*, rev. ed. (Salt Lake City: U of Utah P, 1990).

Robert M. Clark and Charlton Laird, "The Silent Period," Laird, 207–15.

Notes and Sources for Quotations and Topics

258. "A masterful stylist," Bucco, 1312; "saw some guy," Stegner and Etulain, 180.

260. "It was really," Geoffrey Brown.

262–3. Clark's silent period and his "overall writing plan," Robert Clark and Laird (Clark did the research and Laird, the writing), "The 'Silent' Period," Laird, 207–15.

263. "protagonist, Galt Mason," Clark and Laird, 209.

264. "has learned about women," 209; "Clark had not," Clark and Laird, 208; "Its prose is often," 208–9.

265. "Like *The Cat*," Clark and Laird, 210.

266. "on which he [Clark]," 211.

267. "a jumble of Christianity," 210; "a non-religious," 213; "emotional greed," 213.

268. "While *The Cat* covered," 213; "a somewhat footloose," 213; "the commonest guess," 214.

269. "learn to incorporate," 212.

269–70. "I don't . . . think," "This is the last," R. Clark letter to author, 4/22/02.

271–2. Mackay Brown, from Walter Brown.

CHAPTER FOURTEEN: ON TO MILL VALLEY AND TO TEACHING AT SAN FRANCISCO STATE

Interviews

My thanks to Jim Elder (10/29/00), Robert M. Clark (10/23/97), Irving Halperin (6/12/00), Charles Brashear (3/21/00), John Christgau (6/1/00).

Unpublished Material by Walter Clark

Letters from Walter Clark to his editor, Saxe Commins, April 1956 to November 1956.

Published Material About Walter Clark or Related Topics

Robert M. Clark, "Chronology," Laird, 275–86.

Herbert Wilner, "Walter Clark: Complicated Simplicity," Laird, 31–52.

Charles Brashear, "The Younger Brother of God," *Writing* (1979): 10, 27, 31.

Notes and Sources for Quotations and Topics

286. "Talking at luncheons," Clark, 284.

291. "I once saw Clark," Wilner, 33; "My 'conversations,' " Wilner, 35–36.

294. "We were a pack," Brashear, 10, 27.

295. "We knew he wasn't," Brashear, 27.

297. "For him, it demonstrated," Christgau; "one of the things," Brashear.

CHAPTER FIFTEEN: BACK TO NEVADA AND BECOMING ALF DOTEN

Interviews

My thanks to Professor Fred Moramarco (letter on the "Howl" case, 5/23/02), Walter Brown (5/26/00), Thurston Womach (5/21/00), Irving Halperin (6/12/00), Robert M. Clark (10/23/97), David Chism (8/17/00).

Published Material by Walter Clark

"Autobiographical Information," Laird, 265–74.

Unpublished Material by Walter Clark

Letters from Walter Clark to his wife, Barbara, July and August 1957.

Letters from Walter Clark to Saxe Commins and Robert Caples, 1957 to 1962.

Unpublished material by Barbara Clark, diary, starting 1 Jan. 1961.

Published Material About Walter Clark or Related Topics

Howl of the Censor, ed. and intro. by J. W. Ehrlich (San Carlos, Calif.: Nourse Publishing, n.d.), 53–56.

Robert M. Clark, "Chronology," Laird, 275–86.

Robert M. Clark, "Preface," *The Journals of Alfred Doten, 1849–1903,* ed. Walter Van Tilburg Clark (Reno: U of Nevada P, 1973).

Notes and Sources for Quotations and Topics

301. "They seem to me," Ehrlich, 54.

302. "Yes, when I knew," Ehrlich, 54; "It's very hard to define," 55.

303. "Aside from this test," Ehrlich, 56.

311. "interested in coming back," letter to Clark's wife, 8/10/57.

320. "California 49er," "Auto.," Laird, 274; Doten journals initial description, R. Clark, "Chron.," Laird, 285; "almost unbelievable," "Auto.," Laird, 274.

323–24. Problems with "Old Gallery," B. Clark, diary.

324. "The first book was tentatively," R. Clark, "Preface," xiii.

327–28. The story of Ishi, "Ishi: The Last Yahi," *Galen II, Archives and Special Collections.* Online. Library. UCSF. 15 July 2002. Gretchen Kell, "Ishi Apparently Wasn't the Last Yahi," *berkeley.edu/news.* Online. 5 February 1996.

CHAPTER SIXTEEN: TEACHING AND TELLING STORIES IN RENO

Interviews

My thanks to Robert M. Clark (10/23/97 and letters, 7/15/02, 7/25/02), Tom Massey (12/19/00), David Chism (8/17/00), Robert Harvey (7/7/00), Mike Steiner (letter, 8/30/00), Robert Gorrell (video, "Reminiscences of Walter Clark," n.d.).

Published Material by Walter Clark

"Alf Doten in Como," *Nevada Highways and Parks* 24 (Oct. 1964): 27–29, 34, 37.

The Journals of Alfred Doten, 1849–1903, ed. Walter Van Tilburg Clark (Reno: U of Nevada P, 1973).

Unpublished Material by Walter Clark

Letters to Robert Caples, 1962 to 1965.
Letter to Robert M. Clark, 2/14/65.
Diary entries by Barbara Clark.

Notes and Sources for Quotations and Topics

332. "a kind of blessing," R. Clark, 7/25/02; "I incline to think," Caples, card LUNR, n.d.

334. "in part he took," R. Clark, 7/15/02.

337. "now home for good," to Caples, 12/31/63.

342. "He was one of the best," Gorrell video.

343. Ma Greer, Gorrell video.

344. "No, all I wanted to do," Massey.

CHAPTER SEVENTEEN: THE DOTEN JOURNALS AND DECLINING HEALTH

Interviews

My thanks to David Chism (8/21/00), Robert M. Clark (10/23/97 and numerous e-mails during November and December 2002).

Published Material by Walter Clark

Clark's contribution to "The Western Novel—A Symposium," *South Dakota Review* 2 (Autumn 1964): 17–19.

"Introduction" to Mrs. Hugh Brown's *Lady in Boomtown* (Reno: U of Nevada P, 1984), 9–16.

Unpublished Material by Walter Clark

Diary entries by Barbara Clark.
Letters from Walter Clark to Robert Caples, 1965 to 1969.

Published Material About Walter Clark or Related Topics

Robert M. Clark, "Preface," *The Journals of Alfred Doten, 1849–1903,* ed. Walter Van Tilburg Clark (Reno: U of Nevada P, 1973), xi–xx.

Notes and Sources for Quotations and Topics

353–54. "Are you conscious," "Symposium," 17–19.

357. "it presents in graphic," as quoted in R. Clark, "Preface," xiii–xiv.

358. "New Year's Day," Doten, I, 65; "Short entries," I, 65.

359. "Snowed all day," Doten, I, 65–66.

359–60. Headnote to books 3 to 12, "his small town eastern," 89.

360. "attacked Chinn," 99.

361. "arguing the case," 100; "was a desperate villain," 103.

362. "winds up a bitter," Clark as quoted by R. Clark, "Preface," xiv.

369. "The fact is," *Boomtown,* 13.

CHAPTER EIGHTEEN: THE SWEET PROMISED LAND OF NEVADA

Interviews

My thanks to Robert Harvey (7/7/70), Robert M. Clark (10/23/97), Robert Gorrell (7/9/97).

Published Material by Walter Clark

The City of Trembling Leaves (Reno: U of Nevada P, 1991).

Unpublished Material by Walter Clark

Letters from Walter Clark to Robert Caples, 1969 to 1971.

Published Material About Walter Clark or Related Topics

Herbert Wilner, "Walter Clark: Complicated Simplicity," Laird, 31–52.

(Unsigned—probably Charlton Laird), "A Tribute to Walter Van Tilburg Clark: Saturday, October 13, 1971," ms. at LUNR.

Robert D. McFadden, "Walter Van Tilburg Clark Dies; Wrote the 'Ox-Bow Incident,'" *New York Times* 12 Nov. 1971: n.p.

Notes and Sources for Quotations and Topics

390. "It was a gray," Wilner, Laird, 51–52; "Oh, the Lord, He had labored," *City*, 662–65.

390–92. "The Sweet Promised Land" is the title of a novel published by Clark's friend, Robert Laxalt, in 1957. He may have gotten his title from the song in *The City of Trembling Leaves* (1945). The phrase may have come to Clark from a hymn, the words of which were composed by John Rippon and published in 1787. The words of the hymn, "On Jordan's Stormy Banks," stand in ironic contrast to those of Clark's song:

> I am bound for the promised land. . . .
> O the transporting, rapturous scene,
>   That rises to my sight!
> Sweet fields arrayed in living green,
>   And rivers of delight!"

392. "constant effort," "A Tribute" ms.; "the best novel," "one of the great," "Clark Dies" (clipping), *New York Times* 12 Nov. 1971: n.p.

« INDEX »